kneadlessly
simple

kneadlessly simple

Fabulous, Fuss-Free, No-Knead Breads

NANCY BAGGETT

WILEY

JOHN WILEY & SONS, INC.

Published by John Wiley & Sons, Inc., Hoboken, New Jersey
Published simultaneously in Canada

For general information on our other products and services or for technical support, please contact our Customer Care Department within the United States at (800) 762–2974, outside the United States at (317) 572–3993 or fax (317) 572–4002.

Wiley also publishes its books in a variety of electronic formats. Some content that appears in print may not be available in electronic books. For more information about Wiley products, visit our web site at www.wiley.com.

Library of Congress Cataloging-in-Publication Data

Baggett, Nancy, 1943-
Kneadlessly simple: fabulous, fuss-free, no-knead breads / Nancy Baggett.
   p.   cm.
Includes index.
   ISBN 978-0-470-39986-6 (cloth: alk. paper) 1. Bread. I. Title.
TX769.B1745   2009
641.8'15—dc22

         2008036192

Printed in the United States of America

10 9 8 7 6 5 4 3 2 1

Book design and typography by Ralph Fowler / rlfdesign

contents

acknowledgments

Many people played a part in making this book a reality. I'm grateful to every one of them.

First, a big thank-you to Justin Schwartz, my editor, and the whole Wiley team, for enthusiastically supporting this project and working diligently to ensure that it moved along smoothly and efficiently. I also greatly appreciate the efforts of publicist Gypsy Lovett, book designer Ralph Fowler, and cover designer Jeff Faust. And I'm grateful to photographer Alexandra Grablewski and food stylist Brian Preston-Campbell, who created the enticing images for the book.

Thanks also to Judith Riven, my agent, for her enthusiasm, very professional representation, and wise counsel along the way.

Many thanks to my recipe testers: My kitchen assistants Linda Kirschner and Judy Silver Weisberg helped test so many hundreds of recipes they probably dreamed about bread at night. Connie Hay also spent a number of days in my kitchen deep in dough! Home testers Sally Churgai, Erica Horting, and Dollene Targen provided valuable insights on what techniques and tips work best for the home baker and on how to make the recipes as clear and reliable as possible.

Another thank-you goes to Joe Yonan and Bonnie Benwick of the *Washington Post* Food Section, and to the staff at *Eating Well*, whose keen interest in my work on accessible no-knead bread recipes helped spawn the idea for this book.

Finally, thanks to the dozens of fine professionals whose expertise in all aspects of bread baking underpins the *Kneadlessly Simple* approach. It seems ironic that making things simple involved so much background research, but I needed to understand the chemistry and myriad practical applications of yeast baking to simplify and streamline without negatively affecting bread quality.

I am particularly indebted to gifted baker and teacher Nick Malgieri for offering some valuable suggestions for improving my manuscript. Another thank-you goes to Dr. R. Carl Hoseney for helping me understand some of the complicated chemical processes that occur during yeast baking. Here, in alphabetical order, are the other experts whose observations, theories, methods, tips, treatises, experiments, and bits of wisdom have expanded my knowledge and influenced my thinking, recipes, and method. Some of these folks I know well, others a little, others only from their work: Rose Levy Berenbaum, Emily Buelher, Bernard Clayton, Raymond Cavel, Shirley Corriher, Elizabeth David, Rosada Didier, Carol Field, Maggie Gleser, Philippe Gosselin, George Greenstein, Jeffrey Hamelman, Jim Lahey, Daniel Leader, Joe Ortiz, Beatrice Ojakangas, Craig Ponsford, Peter Reinhart, Nancy Silverton, Monica Spiller, and Daniel Wing. Besides these individuals, I must thank the dedicated people behind two wonderful Web sites, thefreshloaf.com and theartisan.net, who provide a wealth of accurate, completely free information on a whole array of yeast baking topics.

introduction

I've loved making homemade yeast bread since my mother first let me "help" prepare her cinnamon buns when I was five. I was lulled by the peaceful, calming nature of the process and amazed and proud of what wondrously good food—fresh, warm, irresistible bread—we could create from such ordinary kitchen supplies. Until I was a teenager, my mother was a stay-at-home mom, so she gave me the gift of many leisurely hours of baking by her side. My memories of those quiet times in our farmhouse kitchen are still vivid.

Once I was grown and had my own home, I carried on my mother's baking traditions, loving the feeling of tranquility and connectedness with my past, and the extraordinary sensory experience and satisfaction of serving my family bread that came straight from our oven. Ironically, after I started writing food articles and cookbooks and honed my baking skills in professional pastry school, it was harder and harder to find the stretches of personal time my mother's old-fashioned yeast recipes required—even though I was usually working in my own kitchen! I realized that for people who spent most of their waking hours away from home, it was much more difficult to squeeze yeast baking into their lives.

Convinced that those who couldn't enjoy baking their own bread were missing out, I began experimenting with the new fast-rising yeasts that were introduced to the market in the 1980s. These launched with the claim that they needed no proofing, and that breads could now be turned out in half the usual time. By accelerating the process with lots of yeast and fast, warm rises, I found that it was indeed possible to have homemade yeast bread on the table in less than two hours—I even created a book full of recipes to prove it! But, sad to say, the hurried rises yielded loaves that were more fluff than flavor, and the off-putting muss and fuss of bread baking still remained.

For nearly two decades I set aside my yearning to make yeast baking more accessible to busy home cooks, spending most of the interim producing stories and recipes on other baking and sweets topics, as well as writing several well-received cookbooks on cookies, chocolate, and, most recently, American desserts. Like so many other people who have to snatch a few minutes here and there for bread baking, I gravitated more and more to quick breads. Yeast baking didn't seem to fit the increasingly hectic pace of life.

Then, early in 2006, the editors at *Eating Well* asked me to create a yeast bread to go with a soup story. They wanted it easy as well as healthful, they said, because their readers were usually pressed for time. They, their readership, and I were all very pleased with my streamlined, no-knead recipe, although it was completely counter to a growing trend toward more complicated, multi-step artisan-style loaves.

Since the late 1980s, a passionate group of professional artisan bakers and earnest hobbyists had been switching away from the typical American "direct method" formulas (mixing commercial yeast, water, and all the flour together and letting the dough rise) to long, slow rises and more complex and time-consuming sponge and sourdough techniques popular in Europe. (Actually, these methods were also widely used in America until the twentieth century: Nineteenth-century cookbook authors routinely directed their readers to "set a sponge," the day before they made bread. And so many prospectors during the California Gold Rush baked sourdough bread that they came to be called "sourdoughs" themselves.)

As a result of the artisan movement, the quality of bread in this country was getting better and better. But it bothered me that the recipes being published almost invariably demanded multiple days and mixtures and effectively shut out all but the most dedicated home hobbyists from America's bread revolution.

I began thinking about some of the techniques the artisan bakers had newly introduced or rediscovered these past decades, with an eye toward simplifications that would make them more accessible to the legions of busy and inexperienced home cooks. Baker Jim Lahey's clever no-knead, slow-rise French bread recipe in an October 2006 *New York Times* article by Mark Bittman definitely headed in that direction. It reminded me of a minimal-knead, refrigerator-rise technique that I (and others) had experimented with in the early 1980s, but Lahey's approach was better: It included a much longer countertop rise, which encouraged fuller gluten and flavor development. For his crusty bread he also revived—with fantastic results!—the old custom of baking in a covered Dutch oven, a technique commonplace when most Americans had to cook at a fireplace or campfire, but largely forgotten (except by die-hard campers) today.

I wanted to see if all kinds of quality breads—from the currently popular crusty boules and focaccias to the soft, comfy home-style loaves of my childhood and everything in between—could be adapted to an even less demanding and more flexible no-knead, slow-rise approach. I also wanted to eliminate or minimize hand shaping. This often intimidates the inexperienced baker, plus it involves time, kitchen mess, and cleanup that discourage the busy cook. And I wanted to incorporate a recently developed yeast-retarding, cold-rise technique that arguably delivers the absolute best bread flavor. Finally, I aimed for a process so flexible that those who have to be away from the house for long periods can adjust the timing of *all* the usual yeast bread stages—mixing and first rise; second rise and shaping; and baking—to fit neatly into their own schedules.

The results of my initial experimentation led to a story and recipes that appeared in the *Washington Post* in the fall of 2007. Almost immediately, readers blitzed the *Post* food section staff and me personally with enthusiastic feedback. The story generated lots of Internet buzz, too. Even more amazing than the sheer number of e-mails I received was the wide variety of people who wrote them: novices who had been afraid to try yeast bread before; veteran bakers who liked my easier, fuss-free approach; and time-pressed cooks excited that they could finally fit yeast baking into their schedules again. I even received several e-mails containing traditional recipes, with fervent requests for advice on how to convert them to my no-knead method. (These requests led to the last chapter in this book—Chapter 8, the *Kneadlessly Simple* Recipe Makeover Guide.)

The enormous positive reaction proved not only the obvious that people love, love, love good, fresh-from-the-oven yeast bread—but that when provided with a method that *truly is simple and convenient*, they are eager to join America's bread revolution. Which brings me to *Kneadlessly Simple: Fabulous, Fuss-Free, No-Knead Breads.* As the title indicates, the recipes require *no* kneading at all! Nor do I merely dodge kneading by manipulating the dough in a mixer or food processor: It actually kneads itself during a long, slow, cool rise.

I'm excited to say that my *Kneadlessly Simple* recipes eliminate *all* the obstacles that used to deter folks from enjoying one of life's ultimate pleasures, breathtakingly fresh, wholesome home-baked bread. Anyone—*absolutely anyone*—can make all sorts of flavorful, fine-textured yeast breads easily, economically, conveniently, without fancy equipment, and, so long as the date on yeast packet indicates it's fresh, very reliably. If you can stir, measure, and read, you can make these breads! Best of all, unlike some of the baked goods produced using shortcut methods of the past, these will routinely have superior texture, aroma, and taste. In fact, unless you are lucky enough to have a world-class bakery right down the street, these may be the best breads you have ever eaten. (And they will certainly be more affordable.)

A Word of Thanks to America's Artisan Bakers

I owe a debt of gratitude to America's artisan bakers: They paved the way and contributed greatly to the knowledge base underpinning the *Kneadlessly Simple* method. Thanks to them, it's an exciting time to be eating—and making—bread in this country. From the late 1980s on, groundbreaking professional bakers like Craig Ponsford and other members of the Bread Bakers Guild of America have been dedicated to exploring and spreading the word on how to bake the best-tasting, best-quality, most interesting breads. These individuals have so raised the level of American baking that the United States now competes successfully in the *Coupe du Monde de la Boulangerie*, the world cup of baking: American teams overtook the previously dominant French to win gold medals in 1999 and 2005 and a silver medal in 2002.

Additionally, their enthusiasm and generous sharing of knowledge through workshops and "camps," lectures, and books have energized a whole cadre of sophisticated hobbyists. For home bakers who get hooked on the habit of fresh bread from their oven and want to move beyond the simple, streamlined approach offered in *Kneadlessly Simple*, the necessary information is readily at hand. Dozens of fine books and Internet bread bakers' chat rooms and Web sites provide sage discussions of *bigas, preferments, levains,* and such, and abound with photos and descriptions of loaves produced with artisanal attention to detail so aficionados around the country can now obsessively pursue the "ultimate loaf." Particularly if you are interested in learning more about the innovative technique of employing a mash to produce a sweeter-tasting, moister loaf (the method used in my whole wheat bread, page 134), check out *Peter Reinhart's Whole Grain Breads.*

My hope is that *Kneadlessly Simple* will entice casual home bakers who lack the time or inclination for such a serious commitment to join today's vibrant bread baking community. As I discovered long ago, the act of gathering together good flour, yeast, and a few other quality ingredients and turning out a simple, honest loaf is profoundly gratifying. It's an experience everyone should have. It doesn't require a fancy kitchen or huge amounts of expertise, and is amazingly easy on the budget. With *Kneadlessly Simple*, it doesn't even take much effort, because the recipes conveniently build in the time and right conditions for nature (or, more accurately, bread chemistry) to take its course and do the work for you.

Occasionally I'm asked if I ever miss making bread the old-fashioned way. I do sometimes miss the leisurely puttering and smooth, soothing feel of dough in my hands, but I'm happy to give up the kitchen mess. I'm also delighted to be able mix my ingredients in literally five minutes, and then to come back much later with the dough fully kneaded and ready for its second rise. The biggest advantage of the *Kneadlessly Simple* approach is that it provides me a trouble-free way to give my family the priceless yet inexpensive gift of memorable homemade bread as often as I like. It can enable you to do the same.

the kneadlessly
simple method

NINE EASY STEPS TO GREAT BREAD

THE *KNEADLESSLY SIMPLE* METHOD INVOLVES NINE RE-markably easy steps, all based on certain principles of yeast bread chemistry. First, I'll run through the steps. Then I'll briefly explain the chemistry, so you'll understand why some seemingly unimportant directions matter, and how (and why) the method really works.

1. Stir together the basic dry ingredients like the flour, yeast, and salt in a bowl large enough for the mixture to triple in size. (If the recipe calls for a little sugar, it goes in, too. But if there's more than 2 tablespoons per cup of flour, the excess sugar is added later.)

2. Stir a heaping cup of ice cubes into the water called for in the recipe; this reduces its temperature to around 50°F. Don't worry—you don't need to check the temperature, and the ice water won't kill the yeast (I promise!). If the recipe calls for honey, molasses, or a flavorless vegetable oil like corn or canola oil, you mix them into the ice water now. (If it calls for olive oil or butter, these are added separately, as they solidify in ice water.)

3. Stir or mix the ice water mixture into the dry ingredients just until thoroughly blended. Do this with a spoon, or, if desired, with a heavy-duty mixer.

Just remember that while the procedure does develop some gluten, it is not designed to substitute for kneading—its primary function is simply to thoroughly mix the ingredients together. Once the dough is mixed, olive oil or butter is sometimes incorporated.

4. **For the absolute best flavor (or for convenience), refrigerate the dough (covered, in its mixing bowl) for at least 3 and up to 10 hours.** The cooling period can be a little shorter or longer if necessary, and this step is optional, but it does have significant chemical benefits and is often a very convenient way to hold the dough overnight or to easily shorten or lengthen the total rise time to better fit your time awake and at home.

5. **Set the dough (covered, in its mixing bowl) out on the counter or in any cool spot and let it slowly rise for 12 to 18 hours, or in some cases 18 to 24 hours.** This step requires no attention whatsoever, but it cannot be skipped. So long as the room is cool, the rising period can extend up to 24 hours, if that's convenient, but don't shorten it much, as this is when the bubbling action of fermentation actually fully kneads the dough. (This step is the reason you can skip all the kneading.) If you don't have a cool (ideally 67° to 70°F) spot, lower the dough temperature by refrigerating it for 3 to 4 hours before beginning the countertop rise, then let it stand out for a maximum of 18 hours. In an extremely warm room, cut the rise time to 15 hours at most.

6. **Mix in (using a spoon or sturdy stand mixer) any remaining ingredients.** These include perishables such as dairy products; certain yeast-inhibiting spices and herbs; dried fruits, extra sugar, and other de-hydrating items; and, finally, enough more flour to obtain the consistency specified in the recipe. Most (but not all) *Kneadlessly Simple* recipes call for the dough to be stiffened until it's hard to stir before the second rise begins, and it's important to follow this instruction.

7. **Briefly stir the dough as directed, and, unless hand-shaping is required, invert it into the baking container for the second rise.** Many *Kneadlessly Simple* breads—including some rustically handsome boules and fancy dessert breads—are shaped entirely or mostly by their baking container. Breads such as French baguettes, Italian ciabattas, cinnamon

pinwheel loaves, and finger rolls obviously need some hand-shaping, but this step is often completed on baking parchment to minimize sticking and handling problems as well as kitchen counter cleanup. In many recipes the last stirring actually involves folding the edges of the dough into the center of its bowl using a rubber spatula; this is another small, but important, step.

8. **Complete the second rise using the rising option that best suits your schedule.** In place of a traditional 1½- to 3-hour rise, you can choose an easy "accelerated" rise and cut normal rising time almost by half. (Speeding up the second rise won't shortchange flavor because it's already there.) Or, if you need or want to put off baking until much later, simply place the shaped dough in the refrigerator and hold it as long as the recipe permits (usually 24 hours) before completing a regular rise.

9. **Bake as directed; let the loaf cool; and enjoy your bread!** Because the *Kneadlessly Simple* method produces "stirrable" doughs, they are likely to be slightly moister and require longer baking than normal to ensure the center is baked through. That's why the recipes routinely suggest a few extra minutes in the oven after loaves appear to be done. If in doubt, remember that with *Kneadlessly Simple*, breads are moist enough that they almost never dry out and actually benefit from what may seem to be overbaking.

the chemistry behind the steps

Experts almost universally agree that yeast breads benefit from a long, slow, cool or cold first rise. Developing the rich, soul-satisfying taste and aroma that make good bread one of nature's greatest foods just can't be rushed. And rushing won't save enough time to make yeast baking noticeably more convenient, anyway. On the other hand, slowing the process makes it easy to adjust the risings to the demands of daily life.

Even more important, dramatically slowing down the first rise by mixing the dry ingredients (including a rather modest amount of yeast) with ice water (yes, *ice-cold* water!) and then refrigerating the dough for a while has some remarkably positive *chemical* effects. While high temperatures can kill yeast organisms, icy temperatures just temporarily knock 'em cold (so to speak!) and put them in a sluggish state. With the yeast out of commission, some enzymes in the flour go to work breaking down damaged starch into sugars. Normally the yeast organisms would rev up activity in the presence of this banquet, but instead they remain available to significantly improve bread taste, crust color, and appearance. Other enzymes are also busy softening and smoothing the crumb and strengthening the gluten.

Known as "delayed first fermentation," this recently introduced technique is beginning to catch on with professional bakers, and, fortunately, it's an effortless way for home bakers to improve their bread, too. Peter Reinhart, who learned the basic method from a French baker and discussed it in his award-winning 2001 work, *The Bread Baker's Apprentice*, commented that it had tremendous implications for both professional and home bakers; he was absolutely right! I call for a 3- to 10-hour delayed fermentation because I've found that all the most noticeable improvements—richer dough flavor, smoother texture, and more attractive browning—occur in that period. (The time frame can be adjusted a bit to fit your typical work/sleep schedules although it does take a minimum of 3 hours for the benefits to accrue.)

The next, equally effortless step—setting the dough out in a 67° to 70°F room to slowly rise for up to 18 hours or even 24 hours—is at the heart of the *Kneadlessly Simple* process. As the dough warms and the yeast comes back to life, the long, slow fermentation produces even more flavor enhancers. If you don't have a suitably cool room, place the dough close to an air-conditioning vent or unit, or lacking that, refrigerate it for at least 3 hours first. This slows down the yeast organisms so they won't become too active from the heat and over-ferment the dough.

Fermentation also produces carbon dioxide gas bubbles that cause the mixture to expand, sometimes three- or four-fold, and have a holey, sponge-like appearance. (This, of course, is why bakers often call the bubby, airy dough mixture a "sponge.") To the naked eye, the bubbling action of the sponge may not seem significant, but, over time, it accomplishes on the molecular level exactly what kneading does faster and more obviously: It jostles and bounces around molecules called gliadin and glutenin so they hook up and form the strong, elastic gluten strands needed for good bread structure. The process, which I've dubbed "micro-kneading," isn't visible, but its effects are: Thoroughly micro-kneaded doughs are extremely elastic and springy and will stretch out so thin you can see the light through them. (Bakers call this "passing the windowpane test.")

Aside from its ease, a big advantage of micro-kneading is that certain flavorful carotenoid compounds in unbleached flour that are normally lost through oxidation during vigorous kneading are preserved. Another advantage is that the long, slow fermentation actually boosts the digestibility of bits of grain and seeds.

Bread chemists have known for several decades that doughs, especially ones moist enough to permit lots of bubbling, will eventually and very effectively knead themselves. But except for a few minimal-knead, refrigerator-rise recipes for home cooks that appeared in the 1980s, recipes don't seem to have capitalized on this phenomenon until recently. Perhaps professional bakers didn't take an interest because they already have powerful, efficient kneading equipment to do the job. But for home bakers who don't have the time, skill, desire, or equipment to knead, the value is enormous.

After the first rise, most recipes call for stirring the dough. This is done to deflate it and to incorporate any dairy or other perishable products that can't safely stand at room temperature for long periods. Sugar and dried fruit also inhibit yeast organisms by binding up water vital for their growth, so they are often added after the first rise, too. Certain herbs and spices contain chemicals that hinder yeast growth as well. (In my experience, garlic, onion, oregano, thyme, mustard, cinnamon, cloves, cardamom, and ginger have particularly strong retarding effects. So, don't toss in larger quantities than my testing has shown the yeast will tolerate!)

Once these ingredients are incorporated, it's important to add in enough flour to stiffen the dough as directed in the recipe. While superhydration facilitates the bubbling that develops the gluten in the first rise, in the second rise too much water can be a liability. It can lead to doughiness in the final product, and can weaken the gluten and add weight to the point where the loaf sinks in the center during baking.

The final step before putting the dough in its baking container is often to fold it in to the center all the way around using a rubber spatula. This particular folding action, followed by inverting the dough into its baking pan, helps organize the gluten strands properly and substitutes for "rounding," a hand-shaping technique some professional bakers use.

So now you know that the *Kneadlessly Simple* method isn't magic. Instead, it's easy because it takes clever advantage of a whole array of chemical processes that naturally happen when water, yeast, and flour co-mingle under controlled conditions. Let's make bread!

getting started

getting started with *kneadlessly simple* recipes: read this first

Each *Kneadlessly Simple* recipe provides an ingredient list and directions, but this chapter provides some additional details and background information to help you carry out the instructions correctly. It covers everything from how to measure flour and ready the ice water properly to adjusting dough consistency to deciding on a rising method, and how to judge loaf doneness. To ensure smooth sailing on your bread baking journey, read through this section before you try any recipes.

Choosing a Bowl—During the first rise, some doughs triple or even quadruple in bulk, so, following the recipe, use a large bowl (one that holds at least 4 quarts) or a very large bowl (one that holds at least 6 quarts) to avoid any chance of overflows. Stainless steel bowls are lightweight, durable, readily available, and economical, but ceramic or even plastic will do. Plastic holds odors and flavors, so be sure plastic containers are squeaky clean.

Measuring Flour—Flour is the key ingredient in bread, so accurate measurements are very important. Professional bakers always weigh their flour, and, though not essential, this is the more accurate method for the home baker, too. If you have a kitchen scale, use the flour weights that are noted in parentheses after the cup measurements in each recipe. Otherwise, using a set of cups designed for measuring dry ingredients, dip the appropriate cup into the flour sack or canister, overfilling the dry measure slightly, then sweep across its top with a long-bladed spatula or straight-edged knife to even the surface. Don't tap or shake the cup or try to compact the flour. Don't try to fluff it up either.

Even careful measuring with the right cups will not yield the same quantity of flour every time because the volume of flour is affected by many factors, including the amount of settling during production and shipping—and even whether you're scooping the flour straight from the bag or from a canister. So, it's not uncommon when filling a 1-cup dry measure by dipping and sweeping to yield 4.7 ounces one time, 5 ounces another, and 5.2 ounces the next. *Kneadlessly Simple* recipes always compensate for this variability by specifying what consistency the dough should be at key points. Be sure to add more flour or water as necessary to achieve the dough consistency indicated.

Readying Ice Water—All *Kneadlessly Simple* recipes initially call for ice water—that is, water chilled to around 50°F by adding ice cubes; this doesn't have to be exact. To obtain the correct temperature, fill a large measure designed for liquids with the amount of water specified; then add a heaping cup of ice cubes and stir vigorously for 30 seconds. Finally, measure out the exact amount of water needed (first discard the cubes) and incorporate it into the dry ingredients as directed. Recipes occasionally call for tablespoons or half-tablespoons of water and other ingredients. If you don't have a ½ tablespoon measure, note that 1½ teaspoons equals ½ tablespoon. In most cases, tap water is perfectly satisfactory, but if yours is heavily chlorinated or otherwise unpleasant-tasting, try bottled water and see if your breads improve.

Mixing by Hand or Mixer—Remember that mixing, whether by hand or electric mixer, is not done to take the place of kneading, but simply to mix together the ingredients. The first key step is thoroughly stirring together the dry ingredients so that the salt and yeast are evenly distributed. For recipes that call for all ingredients to be incorporated before the first rise, the next step is to add the liquid ingredients into the dry ones. Simply stirring vigorously with a large spoon for a minute or two is often the easiest approach. If you prefer to use a mixer, it should be a heavy-duty model fitted with the paddle beater; the dough hook normally works best after the gluten develops. (Most lightweight mixers aren't powerful enough to mix bread doughs.)

When adding ingredients after the first rise, note that the dough will be rubbery (due to the gluten development), so it will take a bit more effort to stir in the eggs, milk powder, additional flour, etc. A heavy-duty mixer fitted with its dough hook will make incorporating the second batch of ingredients easier, though this can be done by hand, too.

Correcting Dough Consistency—Often, directions call for adding enough flour to yield a stiff, or hard-to-stir (but not dry) consistency, but occasionally, a softer dough is needed. For best results, carefully follow the specific instructions for each bread. In many cases, correcting the consistency to create a stiffer dough before the second rise is especially important, as overly wet doughs can come out gummy or sink during baking. Incidentally, due to the fermentation process, it's common for a dough that was very stiff when first mixed to be moister after the first rise, requiring the addition of more flour before its second rise. Doughs containing an abundance of seeds and dried fruits, in contrast, tend to end up stiffer and drier, as these ingredients absorb a lot of excess moisture.

Spritzing (or Brushing), Slashing, and Covering the Dough—Recipes always call for brushing or spritzing doughs with oil (or perhaps butter) to prevent the surface from drying out during the long rising period. The easiest method is to use nonstick spray; be sure to use a high-quality brand containing corn oil or other neutral-flavored oil. Or, if you prefer, simply brush the dough surface evenly with a little corn oil using a pastry brush, rubber scraper, or your fingertips. When a recipe calls for slashing a loaf or cutting dough into portions, do this with a well-oiled serrated knife or, even better, with oiled kitchen shears, as these doughs are usually too rubbery and soft for a plain knife to work well. To further prevent surface drying, cover the bowl tightly with plastic wrap. As a precaution against the dough rising more than expected and sticking to the plastic, you may want to spray the plastic with nonstick cooking spray before the first rise. Recipes routinely call for coating the plastic wrap with nonstick spray before the second rise to prevent any chance of the plastic sticking to the loaf top and marring its appearance.

Estimating Rising Times and Choosing a Rising Method—The yeast are living organisms, so their growth rate depends greatly on the temperature of the dough and the room. As a result, the rising time ranges given in recipes must be considered rough guidelines only. In fact, one portion of a dough set out in a 75°F kitchen will likely rise in half the time it takes another portion of it placed in a 65°F spot. If your room is warmer than normal, simply anticipate that the yeast will grow rapidly and check the dough sooner than is indicated; if the environment is colder, expect that they will grow slowly and the dough will rise more slowly than is indicated. If you happen to live at high altitude, take that into consideration too; the lower atmospheric pressure allows bread to rise 25 to 50 percent faster than normally.

Since the *first* rise really needs to be cool and unhurried for optimum bread flavor and texture, in warm weather try to find the coolest spot in the house, for example, a table near an air-conditioning vent or unit, or in a shaded, ground floor area. It's fine to speed up or slow down the *second* rise to suit your schedule by selecting either an "accelerated" rise that provides an extra-warm environment or an "extended" refrigerator rise that provides a very chilly one.

For an accelerated rise (which can reduce second rise time by a third to a half), bring a 1-cup glass measure of tap water to a boil in a microwave oven. Let the cup stand for a minute or two to avoid any chance of being burned by an eruption of steam, then set it in one corner of the microwave. Set the dough (in its baking pan and covered) inside on the other side of the microwave, close the door, and let the yeast thrive in the comfy, draft-free environment. This rising method is particularly handy in a cold house, when a recipe indicates the dough is normally very slow-rising, or when, for whatever reason, you want your bread done as soon as possible. In a few recipes in which the dough rises particularly slowly, it's suggested that after an hour or so in the microwave, the dough should be temporarily removed and the water brought to a boil again to provide a second burst of warmth for the yeast.

Another convenience option, the extended (refrigerator) rise method lets you put off baking for up to 24 hours for many doughs and up to two days for a few. The cold temperature causes the yeast fermentation and dough rising to slow dramatically. To "restart" the rise, let the dough stand on the counter until it returns to room temperature (usually $1\frac{1}{2}$ to $2\frac{1}{2}$ hours), then proceed with a regular or accelerated rise. Note that holding a dough longer than the number of hours specified in the recipe can debilitate the yeast, resulting in a denser baked good.

All recipes suggest how high doughs should rise in their pans before baking. Follow this instruction carefully, as some doughs spring up and do much of their rising after they're in the oven, and others rise very little during baking. If you aren't sure whether a dough is raised enough, test it by pressing a finger into the surface: If the indention stays instead of gradually filling up again, the dough is sufficiently raised and ready for baking. When a loaf inadvertently rises more than it should, it's best to stir it down, return it to the pan, and let it rise again, as over-raised doughs have a tendency to sink or collapse during baking.

Selecting the Right Baking Pan or Dutch Oven—To keep things simple, this book calls for two basic loaf pan sizes: a 9×5-inch pan or an $8\frac{1}{2} \times 4\frac{1}{2}$-inch pan. But in fact, pans with similar dimensions, say $8\frac{3}{4} \times 5\frac{1}{4}$ inches or $8\frac{1}{4} \times 4\frac{3}{4}$ inches, will work just as well. The critical factor is how much each pan holds, so the finished bread fills the pan attractively but doesn't hang over the sides. The larger pan should have a volume of about 8 cups (2 quarts), and the smaller one should hold about 6 cups ($1\frac{1}{2}$ quarts). To determine the volume, simply add enough water to fill the pan to the rim, then measure out the amount of water used. Occasionally, flat 9×13-inch baking pans or 10×15-inch rimmed baking sheets are also called for. Here again, pans with similar dimensions will work fine.

Bundt-style and similar decorative pans, plain pans with a center tube, and soufflé dishes used for some of these breads come in a confusing assortment of metric and customary measurement sizes, so simply choose a pan with the volume specified by the recipe and with the shape you'd like for the finished loaf. Both for decorative metal pans and plain loaf pans, a sturdy construction and medium-colored finish will yield the best results. Flimsy pans don't hold or distribute the heat evenly and can result in burning on the bottom or sides. Very dark or black pan finishes can cause over-browning and shiny, aluminum foil–colored surfaces can lead to under-browning. Most non-stick and regular metal finishes (either is fine) are in the medium gray to brown range, which is ideal. Ovenproof glass and ceramic bake-ware are other acceptable options, though be aware that they sometimes shorten baking times or require a slightly lower oven temperature than metal pans.

For the breads baked in a covered Dutch oven, casserole, or very large ovenproof saucepan or pot, the volume of the container must be at least large enough to allow the loaf to fully expand during baking. The pot should also be straight-sided or flared at the top; as I discovered, if it narrows at the top, the loaf can't be removed in one piece! For most of the large, rustic pot boules in this book, a heavy, 3½- to 4-quart flat-bottomed pot is the optimum size. A 3-quart pot can be used if it has a domed rather than flat lid, as this allows space for the dough to rise slightly above the pot rim during baking.

A container holding more than 4 quarts will do if that's what you have, but the dough will spread out in the space, producing a flat-looking loaf. (It will still taste fine, of course!) While pricey imported enamel-coated Dutch ovens are a good choice for the pot breads, plain, seasoned cast iron or other nonreactive metal or enameled pots, such as those sold by American manufacturers (or handed down by Grandma!), are equally serviceable.

Adjusting Oven Racks and Preheating the Oven—Every recipe indicates not only the thermostat setting, but where to place the loaf in the oven. In the majority of ovens, the rack position just below the one in the center (but not the lowest one) is the best for baking the breads in the book; the bottom and interior will bake through and the top won't become overdone. For an oven with an unusual rack configuration, just try to place loaves so their bottoms are about 4 inches from the bottom heating element. Of course, both baking and browning vary from oven to oven, so if you find that breads are burning on the bottom, just place them a little further up from the heat source the next time you bake. Any time the tops of loaves are over-browning, simply cover them with a sheet of aluminum foil.

Many breads benefit from a strong initial blast of heat, so be sure to preheat the oven as directed. Each time the oven door opens, the temperature drops 25° to 50°F, which is why directions sometimes call for selecting one temperature, then immediately lowering it once the loaf is in the oven.

Testing for Doneness—Perhaps the trickiest part of making *Kneadlessly Simple* breads is telling when they are completely done. Due to the ample water required for the "micro-kneading," doughs are moister than in conventional recipes and routinely take longer to bake through. When in doubt, always err on the side of over-baking. These doughs are moist enough that they won't dry out from a few extra minutes in the oven, and the extra time will help eliminate any chance of sogginess in the middle. Plus, deeper browning of the crust also deepens flavor.

Just rapping a loaf on top or observing crust color is never sufficient for judging doneness: The most foolproof way is use an instant-read, or probe, thermometer and bake to the degree specified in the recipe. To test, insert the probe deep into the thickest part of the loaf, but for an accurate reading be careful not to touch the pan. Or, if you don't wish to invest in a thermometer, insert a skewer, cake tester, or thin knife deep into the loaf center, then withdraw it and check the crumbs on the tip. If the particles look wet or gooey, continue baking until they look dry and slightly crumbly. Then, always bake for an extra 5 to 10 minutes to be sure the center is fully done. (If the outside begins to over-brown, cover it with foil.)

Storing Breads—Due to their moistness *Kneadlessly Simple* loaves keep better than most homemade breads, but still gradually lose their freshness and appeal in a few days. Always start by putting freshly baked breads on a rack and cooling them thoroughly before packing for storage. Otherwise, moisture that condenses can be trapped and lead to deterioration and molding.

The particular storage instructions provided in each recipe depend on whether the bread needs to stay crisp or soft. Soft breads are packed airtight in a plastic bag or container, or in foil, to prevent them from drying out. To retain their crispness, crusty breads need some air circulation, so they should be placed in a paper or cloth bag, or wrapped a clean kitchen towel. Once packed as specified, loaves will keep in a cool, dry spot (not in the refrigerator) for up to three days.

While it might seem like a good idea to refrigerate breads, this actually speeds staling by causing rapid retrogradation, a process that crystallizes the starch molecules. To keep a bread longer than three days, freeze it in a heavy, airtight plastic freezer bag for up to two months. Some retrogradation will slowly occur, but it can be mostly reversed by wrapping the thawed bread loosely in foil and reheating it at 400°F for 15 to 20 minutes. Refresh individual slices or rolls by wrapping them in a tea towel and microwaving them on 50 percent power for around 15 to 20 seconds; use immediately.

ingredients

Since the emphasis in *Kneadlessly Simple* is on keeping things simple, you don't need a lot of ingredients or to go to much expense to get started baking bread. Here's a rundown of the basics:

Wheat Flour Products—Because it has greater gluten-developing potential than any other grain, wheat flour is the foundation flour in yeast baking. Much like a balloon, the stretchy protein formed during the initial stirring and subsequent "micro-kneading" traps the carbon dioxide gas released during yeast fermentation and gradually expands, in the process leavening the bread. Which is why all but the small sample of gluten-free breads in the book include at least some wheat flour and many loaves are made entirely of it.

Three wheat flours, widely available in supermarkets, are called for in the book: all-purpose unbleached white flour, white unbleached bread flour, and whole wheat flour. Both the all-purpose white flour and bread flour are produced from the starchy part (the endosperm) of the wheat kernel. These flours are much lighter in color, milder, and finer-textured than whole wheat flour because the coarse, fiber-rich "shell" of the kernel (the bran) and the oily, nutrient-rich heart (the germ) are omitted. The two differ primarily in their amount of gluten—all-purpose white flour usually has between 7.5 and 9.5 percent gluten and white bread flour has between 11.5 and 13 percent. The extra gluten in the bread flour gives it more gas-trapping power and ultimately results in airier loaves, so keep this in mind in recipes that give you a choice between all-purpose or bread flour.

Although some brands of all-purpose white flour and bread flour are bleached, seek out and use unbleached flours whenever possible. Unbleached flour retains carotenoid components that hold the natural grain flavor. Bleaching agents not only introduce unnecessary chemicals and may leave a faint aftertaste, but they also remove certain flavor components and the creamy color that help give bread its appeal. It's also worth sticking with top-quality brands of flour to ensure consistency from batch to batch, freshness, and grain carefully grown, harvested, stored, and milled using the best practices. Considering that flour is the most fundamental ingredient in bread, this is not the place to skimp or settle for second-rate.

As its name suggests, whole wheat flour is made from the whole kernel. The bran and germ provide beneficial fiber and nutrients, but also lend a slightly bitter, "wheaty" flavor and brown color, and, due to their weight, produce a more compact loaf. If you want to increase whole-grain consumption but find these characteristics distracting or unpleasant, consider trying white whole wheat flour, a whole wheat flour made from a relatively new strain of wheat that has a milder taste and lighter color (but the same nutritional benefits). The King Arthur brand is the most widely available.

Several recipes in the book not only call for whole wheat flour but also cracked wheat (broken-up wheat kernels, also called "berries") and/or additions of wheat bran and wheat germ. Because the highly perishable oily germ particles remain in whole wheat flour, cracked wheat, and germ, store these in the refrigerator, or discard after three months. White wheat flours can be kept airtight in a cool, dry spot for up to a year.

Other Flours and Grain Products—A variety of other flours and grain products, including cornmeal, corn grits (coarsely ground dried corn), and cornstarch; rolled oats; rye flour; and white and brown rice flours and cooked rice grains, contribute their distinct flavor, texture, color, and unique set of nutrients to certain *Kneadlessly Simple* breads. If you are counting on these ingredients to boost nutrition, be sure to check labels before you buy. Sometimes, the germ is removed from cornmeal or grits to increase the shelf life, so look for the words "whole-grain" or "un-degerminated" on the packaging. Whole-grain cornmeal and grits, as well as all the other whole-grain products—rolled oats, brown rice, and rye flour—stale rapidly, so store them airtight in the refrigerator. Most of these items are stocked in supermarkets, sometimes in a "whole grains" section, sometimes with the baking supplies or cereals.

Bread Yeast—Yeast is called for in modest quantities in *Kneadlessly Simple* but, like wheat flour, it's an essential ingredient. The yeast amounts needed are smaller than in old-fashioned recipes because the long, cool first rise allows ample time for the yeast organisms to become active and do their work. Adding extra yeast is not only unnecessary—it can cause overly rapid fermentation of the dough, which in turn can produce unpleasantly strong- or sour-tasting bread. Since the quantities used are small, the usual ¼-ounce commercial yeast packets contain enough for several batches of bread. Measure out the amount called for, then, to keep the remainder fresh, close the packet and place it in an airtight plastic baggie or small jar. Note the date when the packet was opened and refrigerate the container; use the yeast within 3 months. If you bake bread often, the 4-ounce jars of yeast sold in some markets will be more convenient and economical. These can be kept (refrigerated) for 6 months after opening.

All the recipes in this book have been tested with "highly active," fast-rising dry yeast (sometimes also labeled as instant or bread machine yeast). Ironically, though, this yeast isn't used to hasten rising. I call for this type because it's fuss-free and virtually foolproof when stored and handled properly: The particles are finer than those of regular active dry yeast, so it can be combined directly with the dry ingredients without preliminary proofing in warm water. (Skipping the proofing completely eliminates any chance of damaging the yeast due to overheating.) Regular active dry yeast works better when hydrated in warm water first, so is not as convenient or well suited to the *Kneadlessly Simple* cool rise approach. Old-fashioned compressed or cake yeast isn't suitable for these recipes either.

Salt—Salt is indispensable partly because bread tastes bland and dull without it. But salt slightly inhibits yeast, preventing it from growing too fast and over-fermenting the dough. Equally important, salt tightens and strengthens gluten strands, making the dough better able to trap carbon dioxide and puff up well. Every recipe calls for table salt, as it is economical and, when used *in* dough, tastes virtually indistinguishable from sea salt or other more expensive options. Just in case you prefer to use a coarse crystal salt, be aware that table salt is more compact, so 1 teaspoon roughly equals 1½ to 2 teaspoons of the coarse crystals. A few recipes that use salt as a garnish call for sea salt or other coarse salt to add visual and textural interest and flavor; here, regular table salt won't deliver satisfactory results.

Water—The role of water is vital in yeast breads: The yeast can't grow and the gliadin and glutenin molecules in flour can't join together to form gluten without it. Water, in the form of steam, also promotes crust crisping and browning by encouraging enzyme activity that breaks down surface starches into sugar-like compounds during the first 12 to 15 minutes in the oven. Steam also initially keeps the crust soft enough to allow the loaf to expand early in the baking period. (This is why it's important to follow instructions to brush a loaf with water and/or create steam in the oven just prior to beginning the baking. The steam no longer serves a useful purpose and actually hinders crisping once the first stage of baking is completed, so there's no need to replenish it later on.)

Unless your tap water is unpleasant-tasting, it is fine for making bread, although bottled spring or distilled water can be substituted; some bakers insist upon spring water. (A side-by-side comparison of a recipe made using tap and bottled water should indicate whether the latter makes a difference with your breads.) If the off taste of your water is due to heavy chlorination, letting it stand for 24 hours will allow the chlorine to dissipate.

Fats—Corn oil (or other nearly flavorless vegetable oil), olive oil, and unsalted butter are the types of fat called for in *Kneadlessly Simple* recipes. All three increase crust tenderness, promote browning, and add a pleasant smoothness, or mouthfeel, to the crumb, and in doing so help give various breads their distinctive character. The crust and crumb tenderizing properties increase as the amount of fat increases, which is why fat-laden breads such as brioche have a velvety, cake-like consistency. Olive oil and particularly butter also contribute flavor and aroma, although since all fats are flavor carriers, corn oil heightens the taste of the other ingredients, too. Remember that besides having markedly different flavors, these fats solidify at different temperatures, necessitating completely different methods of incorporation into recipes: Corn oil will stay fluid when added directly to ice water. Olive oil and butter will solidify, so must instead be separately added to dry ingredients or doughs.

Unsalted butter is the best choice for baking bread because the total salt content of the dough is easier to control and because assessing the quality and freshness of butter is easier when it lacks salt. Extra-virgin olive oil also lends a fruitier taste than "regular" olive oil, though either can be used. Due the tendency of all fats to become rancid during storage and their ability to pick up and carry flavors, for good-tasting bread, be scrupulous about using only very fresh butter and oils.

Sweeteners—Granulated and brown sugar, honey, and molasses (and in one recipe, maple syrup) have the obvious effect of adding sweetness and flavor to yeast breads, and they also promote tenderness and browning. But there are other equally important (though less obvious) consequences to adding sweeteners, and these make it risky to casually increase or decrease amounts or ignore instructions on when and how to add them. In small quantities, the granular sweeteners (white and brown sugar) encourage yeast growth by providing a readily fermentable source of food. But too much granular sugar hinders yeast organisms, because as it dissolves it draws up water they need. Increasing or decreasing liquid sweeteners also dramatically alters the dough by changing the proportion of water, which may necessitate an adjustment in the amount of flour. For best results, use clover honey, "regular" (never blackstrap) molasses, and medium amber maple syrup; these impart flavor without overpowering the other taste and aroma components of bread. Several recipes have been designed so that either honey or molasses can be used; either will work well, though honey delivers more sweetness, and the molasses more color and robust flavor.

Dairy Products—Milk products, including instant nonfat dry milk powder, buttermilk powder, and yogurt, and eggs are the dairy enrichments occasionally used in *Kneadlessly Simple*. These increase the food value of bread by increasing the protein, fat, sugar, and vitamins and minerals, of course, but are equally important for heightening and deepening flavor, increasing crumb softness and tenderness, and promoting crust browning and sheen. In fact, eggs enhance crust appearance so effectively that they are often used as a finishing wash or glaze that is brushed on loaves. Be sure to use only "drinking quality" name-brand instant nonfat milk; the particles are finer (facilitating easier incorporation into doughs) and the taste is much cleaner and more appealing than that of discount or generic brands.

Seeds, Nuts, and Dried Fruits—While these additions boost fiber and nutrients, they are even more important in lending character to certain breads by giving them a uniquely appealing appearance, taste, and texture. Sometimes dried fruits and seeds are added during the first rise so they will have plenty of time to plump and soften (or perhaps become chewy), as well as become more digestible. However, where crunchiness is desired, seeds and nuts are added later, either before or after the second rise. In general, when raisins and other dried fruits are added before the first rise, directions call for partially hydrating them by rinsing them under hot water first. This helps ensure that they won't absorb too much moisture and discourage the fermentation and gluten-developing process. This initial partial hydration is often skipped when they are added later, as their gradual plumping during the second rise helps stiffen the dough and ready it for shaping and baking.

Freshness is vital for all these additions: Seeds and nuts are rich in fat, so must be fresh to taste good. And leathery, dried-out raisins, dried cranberries, and such will be tough and tasteless and can even dry out doughs. All these items are usually most economical when purchased in bulk; health food and baking supply stores also turn over their supplies of seeds, nuts, and dried fruits rapidly, which helps to ensure their freshness. Store your purchases airtight and refrigerated.

troubleshooting *kneadlessly simple* breads

POSSIBLE PROBLEMS, CAUSES, AND REMEDIES

The *Kneadlessly Simple* method is simple and builds in many safe-guards, so that most of the problems listed below are very unlikely to occur. But just in case, here are some problems, possible causes, and suggested remedies.

No Visible Bubbling or Dough Rising and No Yeasty Aroma during the First Rise

Yeast was omitted.

> Correct the oversight by combining the yeast with ¼ cup flour, sprinkling it over the dough, then stirring vigorously to incorporate.

Yeast wasn't viable (due to improper or overly long storage or use of "expired" yeast).

> Correct the problem by adding yeast from a different, fresher package using the method above.

Dense, Heavy Loaf or Insufficient or Extremely Slow Rising

Yeast near or past its expiration date.

> Yeast organisms gradually lose potency and eventually die. Even "unexpired" but improperly stored yeast may no longer be fully active and potent, so don't take a chance on it. (Once a yeast packet has been opened, it should be placed in an airtight container, refrigerated, and used within 3 months.)

Insufficient amount of yeast was added by mistake.

> Be sure you use the right measure from your set of measuring spoons. Measure out the yeast by overfilling the appropriate

spoon (or spoons) and sweeping across the top until the quantity is level.

Excessive quantities of yeast-inhibiting ingredients were incorporated into dough.

Even relatively small quantities of certain spices, herbs, salt, and other ingredients can hinder yeast activity, so resist the impulse to change amounts of recipe seasonings.

Unexpectedly large amounts of whole grains, fat, sugar, and/or salt were incorporated.

Kneadlessly Simple recipes call for the right amount of yeast to accommodate these yeast-inhibiting ingredients, but if substitutions are made, proportions can be off and cause poor rising.

Rising took place at a very chilly room temperature and/or the dough contained colder than normal ingredients.

If the room or ingredients are unusually cold, factor this in, then simply allow extra time for the dough to rise. It needs to reach the height specified in the recipe.

Loaf was baked before the dough had enough time to rise fully.

Some doughs rise a lot in the oven, others (particularly those with a high percentage of whole grains) don't. Follow recipes on how much doughs should rise before going in the oven.

Too much sugar was added.

Excess sugar makes the dough *look* more fluid, but in fact it actually draws up water, robbing the yeast of the amount needed for vigorous growth. Use only the amount of sugar called for in the recipe.

Dough was left too long during an extended rise in the refrigerator.

Depending on the recipe, loaves should be held in the refrigerator for a maximum of 24 to 48 hours; longer storage reduces yeast potency.

Dough Overflows the Pan During Second Rise or Baking

Dough rose too long or in an overly warm room, causing over-fermentation

> If the room is overly warm, always compensate by cutting back on the rising time.

Too much yeast was added by mistake.

> The amount of yeast specified in recipes is calculated to produce the right amount of fermentation and rising. Measure carefully when adding yeast.

The pan used was too small.

> When dough is put in a pan, at least ¾ inch should remain at the top to accommodate rising. If the dough nearly fills the pan before any rising, the remaining space is insufficient to handle the normal volume increase and the excess dough may hang over the sides. Switch to a bigger pan.

Dough was too moist and soft.

> Doughs with too much liquid or insufficient flour to stiffen them can run over the rim as they rise. Be sure to stiffen doughs with more flour before the second rise if this is specified in the directions.

Loaf Sinks in the Center or Completely Collapses

Dough was over-raised before being put in the oven.

> Loaves inadvertently allowed to rise too high may not support themselves. If possible, stir down over-risen dough and let it rise the proper amount before baking.

Dough was too wet, which "diluted" the gluten and weighed down the loaf.

> Be sure to add in enough flour before the second rise, as directed in the recipe.

Loaf was removed from the oven before interior was baked through.

Carefully check for doneness with a skewer inserted in the thickest part, or, better yet, with an instant-read thermometer as directed in the recipe.

Bread Gummy, Doughy, or Wet-Looking in the Middle or on the Bottom

Loaf was under-baked.

Due to the relative moistness of *Kneadlessly Simple* loaves, they need to be more thoroughly baked than conventional recipes. Check for doneness with a skewer or, if possible, an instant-read thermometer. When the interior seems done, always bake for an extra 5 to 10 minutes to be sure. (If the top is already very brown, cover it with foil first.) An instant-read thermometer is the best insurance against under-baking.

Ingredient proportions were off due to inaccurate measuring.

Adding too much water or fat and too little flour can throw the chemistry out of balance; measure carefully. If you bake often, consider investing in kitchen scales to ensure accurate measuring.

Oven thermostat was off.

Many home ovens run too hot or too cold. If baking times are routinely long and loaves don't brown well or bake thoroughly, check temperatures with an oven thermometer.

Loaf was cut while still hot.

The pressure from the cutting can squash and compact a loaf before it has time to set up and become firm. It's hard to wait, but try to!

Loaf Crust Burns or Browns Excessively Before the Inside Is Done

Loaf was baked on the wrong oven rack.

Most loaves bake best in the lower third of the oven; in most ovens, this means the rack placement slot just below the middle one. When recipes call for baking on the *lowest* rack, choose the rack slot closest to the oven floor.

Oven thermostat was out of whack or temperature was set too high.

Breads containing a lot of dairy products, chocolate, or sweeteners tend to over-brown in a hot (over 375ºF) oven. Be sure the thermostat is operating correctly.

A very dark metal pan was used.

Dark pans absorb heat so efficiently that they sometimes over-brown baked goods, especially when loaves contain eggs, fat, sugar, and other enrichments. Switch to a lighter-colored pan.

Loaf was not covered with foil as directed in the recipe.

Enriched doughs naturally brown rapidly and many need to be covered part of the way through baking to prevent over-browning It's a good idea to occasionally check browning progress during baking, as not all ovens brown at the same rate.

Crust Looks Pale or Under-Browned

Oven thermostat was off, temperature was set too low, or preheating time was too short.

Lean doughs (those lacking fat, sugar, milk, and eggs) need a high temperature (over 375ºF) for good browning, especially during the first 15 minutes of baking.

Required wash, glaze, or spritz of water was omitted.

Some lean doughs call for an egg wash, glaze, or spritz of water to encourage crust browning. If it is omitted, they will look pale.

A very light metal baking pan was used.

Very shiny, light-colored pans are often too reflective and divert heat away from the loaf. Switch to a different pan.

Bread Lacks Flavor

Salt was omitted or too small an amount was added.

Kneadlessly Simple breads normally have plenty of flavor due to the use of a long first rise, but if salt is omitted, they can taste flat.

Loaf Tastes too Sour or Yeasty, or Has Off Flavors

Too much yeast was added.

Excessive amounts of yeast can cause over-fermentation, producing excess acid and alcohol that give breads strong aromas and flavors.

Stale ingredients were used.

Old flour, fat, nuts, or seeds, etc., will not be improved or masked by baking; start with fresh, good-quality ingredients.

Dough over-rose.

This can occur if the dough rising period is much longer than recommended; or the rising takes place in an overly warm room; or the dough is held longer than recommended in the refrigerator. All of these can lead to over-fermentation and an off taste.

Bread Is Dry and Crumbly

Overly dry additions such as stale, hard dried fruit, or dried-out cornmeal, oats, or seeds were added.

These can draw too much moisture from the dough, so always use fresh products.

Instructions to rehydrate certain ingredients were skipped.

Heed the directions to pre-soak dried fruits, seeds, etc., as they will otherwise hydrate using moisture in the dough.

Wrong flour was used.

When bread flour is called for, it is needed to provide proper structure and in some cases to prevent a crumbly texture.

Measurements were off, proportion of white wheat flour or bread flour was too low.

Wheat flours develop the gluten that keeps breads from being crumbly, so don't arbitrarily substitute other kinds of flour.

Loaf Is Misshapen

Loaf was not slashed as directed.

Not all breads require slashing, but for some it's very important: This step encourages the loaf to expand fully and the crust to split attractively, rather than in an unpredictable "blow-out" fashion.

Wrong size pan was used.

A too-small pan can cause the loaf to hang over the sides or look lopsided. A too-large pan can yield a flat or skimpy-looking loaf.

easiest ever
yeast breads

THE RECIPES IN THIS CHAPTER ARE SO EASY I COULD HAVE called them beginner breads. I didn't, though, because I don't want experienced bakers to skip them or dismiss them as unsophisticated or beneath consideration. They are neither! As the results that come from your oven will unequivocally prove, a few uncomplicated, hassle-free steps can produce breads with superb flavor and texture and plenty of eye appeal.

How is it possible to eliminate all the traditional fussing and fiddling from yeast baking without sacrificing quality? The *Kneadlessly Simple* method just builds in time for the naturally occurring chemical processes that we now know develop both flavor and gluten in yeast dough to proceed uninterrupted. In other words, this approach just lets nature take its course and do the kneading and flavor enhancing for us.

Since none of the recipes in this book require kneading, there are other things that earn the ones in this chapter the "Easiest Ever" designation:

They require no hand shaping and involve no time-consuming or tricky steps.

They call for few ingredients—usually only a couple beyond the essential flour, water, yeast, and salt.

They are especially convenient: All or most ingredients are added before the first rise.

easy white bread loaves

If you *love* fresh, homemade yeast bread, but think of it as complicated or labor-intensive to prepare, please go to your kitchen and try this recipe! You'll create light, attractive, traditional-style white bread with excellent flavor, while skipping all the traditional usual work—no yeast proofing, kneading, hand-shaping, or muss and fuss. And, like all the other recipes in *Kneadlessly Simple*, this one requires no bread machine, heavy-duty mixer, food processor, or other special equipment.

Simply stir the ingredients together in a big bowl and slip it into the refrigerator to chill for a couple hours. Then, leave it on the counter to rise all day or all night. This long, slow rise is key: It develops superior flavor and "micro-kneads" the dough so you can skip this formerly essential step. Last, simply stir the dough again; turn it out into two loaf pans; let rise, and bake.

Your reward? Two large, fine-textured loaves perfect for sandwiches, toast, or eating plain. Or, if you prefer, use half of this versatile dough for an everyday white loaf, and quickly turn the second half into a dozen large, lusciously decadent yet easy sticky buns (pages 90 to 93).

Yield: 2 medium loaves, 12 to 14 slices each

KS QUOTIENT— Super Easy: A minimum of fuss-free, easily mixed ingredients. No hand-shaping.

6½ cups (32.5 ounces) unbleached white bread flour, plus more as needed

3½ tablespoons granulated sugar

1 tablespoon table salt

1 teaspoon instant, fast-rising, or bread machine yeast

⅓ cup corn oil, canola oil, or other flavorless vegetable oil, plus extra for coating dough tops and baking pans

2¾ cups ice water, plus more if needed

FIRST RISE: In a very large bowl, thoroughly stir together the flour, sugar, salt, and yeast. In a medium bowl or measuring cup, whisk the oil into the water. Thoroughly stir the mixture into the bowl with the flour, scraping down the sides until thoroughly blended. If the mixture is too dry to incorporate all the flour, a bit at a time, stir in just enough more water to blend the ingredients; don't over-moisten, as the dough should be stiff. If necessary, stir in enough more flour to stiffen it. Brush or spray the top with oil. Cover the bowl with plastic wrap. If desired, for best flavor or for convenience, you can refrigerate the dough for 3 to 10 hours. Then let rise at cool room temperature (about 70°F) for 15 to 20 hours. If convenient, stir the dough about halfway through the rise.

SECOND RISE: Vigorously stir the dough, adding more flour if necessary to yield very stiff consistency. Using well-oiled kitchen shears or a serrated knife, cut it in half, placing the portions in 2 well-greased 8½ × 4½-inch loaf pans. Smooth and press the dough into the pans using a well-oiled rubber spatula or your fingertips. Evenly brush or spray the dough tops with oil. Make a ½-inch deep slash lengthwise down the center of each loaf. Tightly cover the pans with nonstick spray–coated plastic wrap.

LET RISE USING ANY OF THESE METHODS: For a 1½- to 2½-hour regular rise, let stand at warm room temperature; for a 1- to 2-hour accelerated rise, let stand in a turned-off microwave along with 1 cup of boiling-hot water; or for an extended rise, refrigerate, covered, for 4 to 24 hours, then set out at room temperature. Continue the rise until the dough nears the plastic. Remove the plastic and continue until the dough reaches ½ inch above the pan rims. Dust each loaf evenly with 1 tablespoon flour.

BAKING PRELIMINARIES: 15 minutes before baking time, place a rack in the lower third of the oven and preheat to 425°F.

BAKING: Reduce the oven temperature to 400°F. Bake for 35 to 45 minutes, until the tops are nicely browned. If necessary to prevent over-browning, cover the tops with foil. Bake for 15 to 25 minutes longer, until the tops are well browned and a skewer inserted in the thickest part comes out with just a few crumbs on the tip (or until the center registers 208° to 210°F on an instant-read thermometer). Then bake for 5 to 10 minutes longer to ensure the centers are baked through. Cool in the pans on a wire rack for 10 minutes, then turn out the loaves onto racks and cool thoroughly.

SERVING AND STORING: Cool thoroughly before slicing or storing. Store airtight in plastic bags or wrapped in aluminum foil. The bread will keep at room temperature for 2 to 3 days, and may be frozen, airtight, for up to 2 months.

crusty white peasant-style pot bread

Pot boules—round, peasant-style breads simply popped in a sturdy, lidded pot and baked—are about the easiest loaves possible, but among the most gratifying. They puff up well, brown beautifully, and always come out crusty, due to the moisture trapped inside the pot during the first few minutes in the oven. (In fact, the pot actually serves as a mini-oven.) As an added bonus, the loaves need no hand-shaping because the dough just conforms to the container shape as it expands.

Like the basic black dress, this basic white loaf is always appropriate and in favor. The interplay of light mild crumb, crunchy golden crust, and deep sweet yeast taste and aroma (coaxed out by long, slow rising) is downright amazing. In fact, eating this bread is a far more complex and exciting sensory experience than one might expect from the simple ingredients.

Should you ever want a change of pace from the basic loaf, it's an easy matter to add a few accents for a rather different effect. See the rosemary–black olive variation at the end of the recipe.

Yield: 1 large loaf, 12 to 14 slices

KS QUOTIENT— Super Easy: Fuss-free ingredients, added all at once. No hand-shaping.

4 cups (20 ounces) unbleached all-purpose white flour or unbleached white bread flour, plus more as needed

1 teaspoon granulated sugar

2 teaspoons table salt

¾ teaspoon instant, fast-rising, or bread machine yeast

2 cups ice water, plus more if needed

Corn oil, canola oil, or other flavorless vegetable oil or oil spray for coating dough

FIRST RISE: In a large bowl, thoroughly stir together the flour, sugar, salt, and yeast. Vigorously stir the water into the bowl, scraping down the sides and mixing until the ingredients are thoroughly blended. If the mixture is too dry to incorporate all the flour, a bit at a time, stir in just enough more water to blend the ingredients; don't over-moisten, as the dough should be very stiff. If necessary, stir in enough more flour to yield a hard-to-stir dough. Brush or spray the top with oil. Cover the bowl with plastic wrap. If desired, for best flavor or for convenience, you can refrigerate the dough for 3 to 10 hours. Then let rise at cool room temperature for 18 to

24 hours. If convenient, vigorously stir the dough once about halfway through the rise.

SECOND RISE: Using an oiled rubber spatula, gently lift and fold the dough in towards the center all the way around until mostly deflated; don't stir. Brush or spray the surface with oil. Re-cover with nonstick spray–coated plastic wrap.

LET RISE USING ANY OF THESE METHODS: For a 1½- to 2½-hour regular rise, let stand at warm room temperature; for a 1- to 2-hour accelerated rise, let stand in a turned-off microwave along with 1 cup of boiling-hot water; or for an extended rise, refrigerate, covered, for 4 to 24 hours, then set out at room temperature. Continue the rise until the dough doubles from the deflated size; remove the plastic if the dough nears it.

BAKING PRELIMINARIES: 20 minutes before baking time, put a rack in the lower third of the oven; preheat to 450°F. Heat a 3 ½- to 4-quart (or larger) heavy metal pot in the oven until sizzling hot (check with a few drops of water), then remove it, using heavy mitts. Taking care not to deflate the dough (or burn yourself), loosen it from the bowl sides with an oiled rubber spatula and gently invert it into the pot. Don't worry if it's lopsided and ragged-looking; it will even out during baking. Generously spritz or brush the top with water. Immediately top with the lid. Shake the pot back and forth to center the dough.

BAKING: Reduce the heat to 425°F. Bake on the lower rack for 55 minutes. Remove the lid. Bake for 15 to 20 minutes longer, or until the top is well browned and a skewer inserted in the thickest part comes out with just a few crumbs on the tip (or until center registers 209° to 212°F on an instant-read thermometer). When it seems done, bake for 5 minutes longer to ensure the center is baked through. Cool in the pan on a wire rack for 10 to 15 minutes. Remove the loaf to the rack and cool thoroughly.

SERVING AND STORING: Cut or tear the loaf into portions; it tastes good warm but will cut much better when cool. Cool completely before storing. To maintain the crisp crust, store draped with a clean tea towel or in a heavy paper bag. Or store airtight in a plastic bag or wrapped in foil: The crust will soften, but can be crisped by heating the loaf, uncovered, in a

400°F oven for a few minutes. The bread will keep at room temperature for 3 days, and may be frozen, airtight, for up to 2 months.

VARIATION CRUSTY ROSEMARY AND OLIVE POT BREAD—Stir 1 cup pitted, coarsely chopped black Kalamata olives (well drained) and 3 tablespoons finely chopped fresh (not dried) rosemary needles (discard the stems) into the dough along with the water. Proceed exactly as directed in the original recipe.

all-purpose
light wheat bread

3 cups (15 ounces) unbleached all-purpose white flour, plus more as needed

1 cup (5 ounces) whole wheat flour, plus 1 tablespoon for garnishing loaf top

3 tablespoons granulated sugar

Generous 1¾ teaspoons table salt

¾ teaspoon instant, fast-rising, or bread machine yeast

3 tablespoons corn oil, plus extra for coating dough top and baking pan

2 cups plus 1 tablespoon ice water, plus more if needed

A large, versatile, no-fuss loaf, this has a firm, springy interior, crusty exterior, and wonderfully light, pleasing wheat taste and aroma. It's a fine all-around bread, suitable for eating "as is," for toasting, and for making sandwiches. For a slightly "wheatier" and more nutritious bread, see the variation at right. **Yield: 1 large loaf, 12 to 15 slices**

FIRST RISE: In a large bowl, thoroughly stir together the white flour, whole wheat flour, sugar, salt, and yeast. In another bowl or measuring cup, whisk the oil into the water. Then vigorously stir the mixture into the bowl with the flour, scraping down the sides and mixing until thoroughly blended. If too dry to mix together, add just enough more water to facilitate mixing, but don't over-moisten, as the dough should be stiff. If necessary, stir in enough more white flour to stiffen it. Brush or spray the top with oil. Tightly cover the bowl with plastic wrap. If desired, for best flavor or for convenience, you can refrigerate the dough for 3 to 10 hours. Then let rise at cool room temperature for 12 to 18 hours; if convenient, vigorously stir once during the rise.

SECOND RISE: Vigorously stir the dough. If it is not stiff, stir in enough more white flour to yield a hard-to-stir dough. Using an oiled rubber spatula, gently lift and fold the dough in towards the center all the way around (this organizes the gluten for shaping the dough into a loaf). Invert it into a very well-greased 9 × 5-inch loaf pan. Using an oiled rubber spatula or fingertips, smooth out the top and press the dough out into the pan. Brush or spray the dough top with oil. Evenly sprinkle the top with 1 tablespoon whole wheat flour. Using a well-oiled serrated knife or kitchen shears, make 3 to 4 evenly spaced diagonal ½-inch-deep slashes down the loaf. Cover the pan with nonstick spray–coated plastic wrap.

LET RISE USING ANY OF THESE METHODS: For a 1½- to 2½-hour regular rise, let stand at warm room temperature; for a 1- to 1½-hour accelerated rise, let stand in a turned-off microwave along with 1 cup of boiling-hot water; or for an extended rise, refrigerate, covered, for 4 to 24 hours, then set out at room temperature. When the dough nears the plastic, remove it and continue the rise until the dough extends ⅛ inch above the pan rim or doubles from its deflated size.

BAKING PRELIMINARIES: 15 minutes before baking time, place a rack in the lower third of the oven; preheat to 375°F.

BAKING: Bake on the lower rack for 50 to 60 minutes, or until the loaf is well browned and crisp on top; as necessary cover with foil to prevent over-browning. Bake for 10 to 20 minutes more, until a skewer inserted in the thickest part comes out with just a few particles on the end (or until the center registers 208° to 210°F on an instant-read thermometer). Then bake for 5 minutes longer to make sure the center is done. Cool in the pan on a wire rack for 10 minutes. Turn the loaf onto a rack and cool thoroughly.

SERVING AND STORING: Serve warm, cool, or toasted; the bread slices best when cool. Cool thoroughly before storing in plastic or foil. Keeps at room temperature for 2 to 3 days. May be frozen, airtight, for up to 2 months.

VARIATION ALL-PURPOSE WHOLE WHEAT BREAD—Use 2 cups white flour and 2 cups whole wheat flour. If desired, add 1 tablespoon more sugar to balance the wheat flavor. Proceed exactly as directed in the original recipe.

crusty
portuguese-american
yeasted cornbread

KS QUOTIENT — Easy: A minimum of easily mixed ingredients. No hand-shaping.

1⅓ cups boiling water

1¼ cups cornmeal, preferably white stone-ground, plus 1 tablespoon for garnish

3 cups (15 ounces) unbleached white bread flour, plus more as needed

2 teaspoons table salt

¾ teaspoon instant, fast-rising, or bread machine yeast

1¼ cups ice water, plus more if needed

Corn oil, canola oil, or other flavorless vegetable oil or oil spray for loaf top

This is my version of *pao de milho*, a peasant-style yeasted cornbread popular in the Portuguese-American communities in Massachusetts and Rhode Island. The locals like to make it with a special cornmeal called white cap flint, which, unfortunately, isn't available anywhere else. I've substituted a good-quality stone-ground white cornmeal from my mid-Atlantic region with excellent results.

The large, homespun loaf has a mild, go-with-anything flavor and a delightful crusty-chewy top. It has a finer, moister crumb than most cornbreads, the result of the cornmeal being combined with boiling water and turned into a mush first. This simple, seemingly unimportant step makes a big difference in taste, too: Due to chemical changes that occur as the cornmeal begins to cook, the bread is noticeably mellow and sweet, even though no sugar is added. (For more on the chemistry behind the technique, see page 3.)

Pao de milho is doubtless a derivative of *broa*, a staple cornbread in the poorer regions of Portugal. Corn was introduced into Portugal and Spain from the New World, probably by whalers or fishermen sailing from the New England coast. The Portuguese immigrants who settled in Massachusetts and Rhode Island eventually returned the favor, introducing this very enticing yeast bread back here. Serve it with meals, along with butter, toast it, or grill it and use in all sorts of hearty meat, cheese, and roasted vegetable sandwiches. **Yield: 1 large loaf, 12 to 14 portions or slices**

FIRST RISE: In a medium bowl, gradually stir the boiling water into the cornmeal until smoothly incorporated. Let cool thoroughly. In a large bowl, thoroughly stir together the flour, salt, and yeast. Gradually but vigorously stir the ice water into the cooled cornmeal until very smoothly blended. Then vigorously stir the cornmeal mixture into the bowl with the flour, scraping down the sides until the ingredients are thoroughly blended. If too dry to mix completely, a bit at a time, stir in just enough more ice water to blend the ingredients; don't over-moisten, as the dough should be stiff. If the dough is soft, vigorously stir in enough more flour to stiffen it. Brush or spray the top with vegetable oil. Cover the bowl with plastic wrap. If desired, for best flavor or for convenience, you can refrigerate the dough for 3 to 10 hours. Then let rise at cool room temperature for 12 to 18 hours.

SECOND RISE: Vigorously stir the dough, adding more flour if needed to yield a hard-to-stir dough. Using an oiled rubber spatula, fold the dough in towards the center all the way around. Brush or spray the top with oil. Re-cover with nonstick spray–coated plastic wrap.

LET RISE USING ANY OF THESE METHODS: For a 1½- to 2½-hour regular rise, let stand at warm room temperature; for a 1- to 2-hour accelerated rise, let stand in a turned-off microwave along with 1 cup of boiling-hot water; or for an extended rise, refrigerate, covered, for 4 to 12 hours, then set out at room temperature. Continue the rise until the dough doubles from the deflated size, removing the plastic if the dough nears it.

BAKING PRELIMINARIES: 20 minutes before baking time, put a rack in the lower third of the oven; preheat to 450°F. Heat a 3 ½- to 4-quart (or larger) heavy metal pot in the oven until sizzling hot (check with a few drops of water), then remove it, using heavy mitts. Taking care not to deflate the dough, loosen it from the bowl sides with an oiled rubber spatula and gently invert it into the pot. Don't worry if it's lopsided and ragged-looking; it will even out during baking. Generously spray or brush the top with water, then sprinkle over a tablespoon of cornmeal. Immediately top with the lid. Shake the pot back and forth to center the dough.

BAKING: Reduce the heat to 425°F. Bake on the lower rack for 50 minutes Remove the lid. Reduce the heat to 400°F. Bake for 15 to 25 minutes longer, until the top is well browned and a skewer inserted in the thickest part comes out with just a few crumbs on the tip (or until the center registers 210° to 212°F on an instant-read thermometer). Then bake for 5 minutes longer to ensure the center is baked through. Cool in the pan on a wire rack for 10 to 15 minutes. Remove the loaf to the rack. Cool thoroughly.

SERVING AND STORING: This tastes good warm but will cut better when cool. Cool completely before storing. To maintain the crisp crust, store in a large bowl draped with a clean tea towel or in a heavy paper bag. Or store airtight in a plastic bag or foil: The crust will soften, but can be crisped by heating the loaf, uncovered, in a 400°F oven for a few minutes. The bread will keep at room temperature for 3 days, and may be frozen, airtight, for up to 2 months.

easy oat bread

KS QUOTIENT — Super Easy: A minimum of fuss-free, easily mixed ingredients. No hand-shaping.

Oats always seem to have a comforting, low-key flavor, and this bread does, too. The straightforward, easy recipe can be made with either honey or molasses and produces two homey, nice-to-have-on-hand loaves. (I always stash one in the freezer for later use.)

The honey version is slightly sweeter and lighter in color; the molasses version, tastes—surprise!—of molasses, though it doesn't come on strong. Attractively flecked with bits of oats, the loaves are slightly soft and make excellent toast and sandwich bread.

Yield: 2 medium loaves, about 12 slices each

5½ cups (27.5 ounces) unbleached all-purpose white flour or unbleached white bread flour, plus more as needed

1 cup old-fashioned rolled oats or quick-cooking (not instant) oats, plus 4 tablespoons for garnish

3 tablespoons granulated sugar

Scant 2¾ teaspoons table salt

1 teaspoon instant, fast-rising, or bread machine yeast

¼ cup clover honey or light (mild) molasses

¼ cup corn oil or other flavorless vegetable oil, plus extra for coating dough top and baking pans

2¼ cups plus 2 tablespoons ice water, plus more if needed

FIRST RISE: In a very large bowl, thoroughly stir together the flour, oats, sugar, salt, and yeast. In a medium bowl or measuring cup, thoroughly whisk the honey (or molasses) and oil into the water. Thoroughly stir the water mixture into the larger bowl, scraping down the sides until the ingredients are thoroughly blended. If the mixture is too dry to incorporate all the flour, a bit at a time, stir in just enough more water to blend the ingredients; don't over-moisten, as the dough should be stiff. Brush or spray the top with oil. Cover the bowl with plastic wrap. For best flavor or convenience, you can refrigerate the dough for 3 to 10 hours. Then let rise at cool room temperature for 12 to 18 hours; if convenient, vigorously stir once during the rise.

SECOND RISE: Vigorously stir the dough. If necessary, stir in enough more flour to yield a hard-to-stir consistency. Generously oil two 8½ × 4½-inch loaf pans. Sprinkle a tablespoon of oats in each; tip the pans back and forth to spread the oats over the bottom and sides. Use well oiled kitchen shears or a serrated knife to cut the dough into 2 equal portions. Put the portions in the pans. Brush or spray the tops with oil. Press and smooth the dough evenly into the pans with an oiled rubber spatula or fingertips. Sprinkle a tablespoon of oats over each loaf; press down to imbed. Make a ½-inch-deep slash lengthwise down the center of each loaf using oiled kitchen shears or a serrated knife. Tightly cover the pans with nonstick spray–coated plastic wrap.

LET RISE USING ANY OF THESE METHODS: For a 2- to 3-hour regular rise, let stand at warm room temperature; for a 45-minute to 2-hour accelerated rise, let stand in a turned-off microwave along with 1 cup of boiling-hot water; or for an extended rise, refrigerate, covered, for 4 to 24 hours, then set out at room temperature. Continue the rise until the dough nears the plastic. Remove it and continue until the dough extends ½ inch above the pan rims.

BAKING PRELIMINARIES: 15 minutes before baking time, place a rack in the lower third of the oven; preheat to 375°F.

BAKING: Bake on the lower rack for 50 to 60 minutes, until the tops are well browned. Cover the tops with foil. Then bake for 10 to 15 minutes more, until a skewer inserted in the thickest part comes out with just a few particles clinging to the bottom portion (or until the center registers 208° to 210°F on an instant-read thermometer). Bake for 5 minutes longer to be sure the centers are done. Let cool in the pans on a wire rack for 15 minutes. Turn out the loaves onto racks and cool thoroughly.

SERVING AND STORING: Cool thoroughly before slicing or storing. Best served toasted. Store airtight in plastic or aluminum foil. The bread will keep at room temperature for 3 days, and may be frozen, airtight, for up to 2 months.

everyday oatmeal
honey-raisin
bread

This homey, fairly compact loaf *looks* unremarkable but makes excellent toast, and is also nice for snacking or making a slightly unusual but pleasing peanut butter sandwich. I think of it as a good everyday bread, because it can be mixed together quickly and calls for ingredients normally on hand. I also like the fact that the loaf is not overloaded with sugar and doesn't contain a lot of fat. Plus, the oats add not only body and flavor, but also fiber and nutrients. For a slightly more nutritious bread, I often incorporate whole wheat flour into the dough; see the end of the recipe. (Note that this variation will rise a little more slowly and will be slightly denser than the original.)

Because this dough includes cinnamon, which contains a yeast-inhibiting chemical, the recipe calls for slightly more yeast than normal.

Yield: 1 large loaf, 12 to 15 slices

FIRST RISE: In a large bowl, thoroughly stir together the flour, oats, cinnamon, salt, and yeast. In another bowl or measuring cup, thoroughly whisk the honey and oil into the water. Thoroughly stir the mixture into the bowl with the flour, scraping down the sides and mixing to blend well. If the dough is stiff, stir in enough more ice water to soften it slightly; the dough should not be dry or overly stiff, as the oats draw up moisture. Brush or spray the top with oil. Cover the bowl with plastic wrap. If desired, for best flavor or for convenience, you can refrigerate the dough for 3 to 10 hours. Let rise at cool room temperature (about 70ºF) for 12 to 18 hours.

SECOND RISE: Stir the dough vigorously, adding in the raisins until evenly incorporated. Stir in enough more flour to yield a hard-to-stir consistency. Using an oiled rubber spatula, fold the dough in towards the center all the way around; this organizes the gluten for shaping the dough into a loaf. Invert the dough into a generously greased 9 × 5-inch loaf pan.

2¾ cups (13.75 ounces) unbleached white bread flour, plus more as needed

1 cup old-fashioned rolled oats or quick-cooking (not instant) oats

1¼ teaspoons ground cinnamon

1½ teaspoons table salt

1¼ teaspoons instant, fast-rising, or bread machine yeast

½ cup clover honey or other mild honey

2 tablespoons corn oil or canola oil, plus extra for coating dough top and baking pan

1½ cups plus 1 tablespoon ice water, plus more if needed

1 cup dark raisins, rinsed under warm water, then drained well and patted dry

1 teaspoon ground cinnamon mixed with 1 tablespoon granulated sugar for garnish

Brush or spray the top with oil, then using an oiled rubber spatula or fingertips, smooth out the surface and press the dough evenly into the pan. Using a well-oiled serrated knife or kitchen shears, make a ½-inch-deep slash lengthwise down the loaf. Cover the pan with nonstick spray–coated plastic wrap.

LET RISE USING ANY OF THESE METHODS: For a 1 ½- to 3-hour regular rise, let stand at warm room temperature; for a 1- to 2-hour accelerated rise, let stand in a turned-off microwave along with 1 cup of boiling-hot water; or for an extended rise, refrigerate, covered, for 4 to 24 hours, then set out at room temperature. When the dough nears the plastic, remove it and continue the rise until the dough extends ¼ inch above the pan rim. Sprinkle the cinnamon-sugar garnish over the top.

BAKING PRELIMINARIES: 15 minutes before baking time, place a rack in the lower third of the oven; preheat to 375°F.

BAKING: Bake on the lower rack for 35 to 40 minutes, or until the loaf is well browned. Cover with foil, and continue baking for another 30 to 40 minutes more. Begin testing occasionally with a skewer inserted in the thickest part, until it comes out with slightly moist particles clinging to the end (or until the center registers 208° to 210°F on an instant-read thermometer). Bake for 5 to 10 minutes longer to ensure the center is baked through. Cool on a wire rack for 15 minutes. Turn the loaf out onto a rack; cool thoroughly.

SERVING AND STORING: Serve cool, or toasted; the bread doesn't slice well until completely cooled. Cool thoroughly before storing in plastic or foil. Keeps at room temperature for 3 days. May be frozen, airtight, for up to 2 months.

VARIATION OAT–WHOLE WHEAT HONEY-RAISIN BREAD—Instead of 2¾ cups white bread flour, use 1¾ cups white bread flour (plus more if needed) and 1 cup whole wheat flour.

TIP: If you are in a hurry to get the loaf in the oven, after the cup of hot water initially placed in the microwave cools, replace it with more boiling water halfway through to keep the interior a very "yeast-friendly" 80-plus°F for the entire rising period.

great granola
breakfast bread

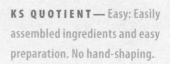

KS QUOTIENT— Easy: Easily assembled ingredients and easy preparation. No hand-shaping.

Enriched with both granola and milk, this large, slightly sweet loaf is great for breakfast on the go. It's also good for toasting and makes a fine French toast or brunch bread. The loaf has a handsome, nubby-crusty top and light crumb accented with pleasing little patches and bursts of granola flavor. It always receives compliments and is a favorite with my family and friends.

Almost any purchased or homemade granola you like will do for this recipe; I'm partial to honey-oat with almonds. Whatever your choice, if it's coarse and chunky, crush it into fine (⅛-inch) bits before using. The easiest way is to put it into a sturdy plastic bag and either squeeze and press it with your hands, or, if it's hard and crunchy, go over it with a rolling pin (or a wine bottle if that's handier!).

Makes 1 large loaf, 12 to 14 slices

3 cups (15 ounces) unbleached all-purpose white flour, plus more as needed

3 tablespoons granulated sugar, plus 1 tablespoon for garnish

1¼ teaspoons table salt

¾ teaspoon instant, fast-rising, or bread machine yeast

1¼ cups plus 2 tablespoons ice water, plus more if needed

3 tablespoons corn oil, canola oil or other flavorless vegetable oil, plus more for dough top and pan

1⅓ cups plain, raisin, honey-oat, mixed fruit and nut, or other fine-textured granola, plus 4 tablespoons for garnish

⅓ cup top-quality instant nonfat powdered milk (don't use a generic brand)

FIRST RISE: In a large bowl, thoroughly stir together the flour, sugar, salt, and yeast. In another bowl or measuring cup, whisk together the water and oil. Vigorously stir the mixture into the bowl with the flour, scraping down the sides until the ingredients are thoroughly blended. If the mixture is too dry to incorporate all the flour, a bit at a time, stir in just enough more ice water to blend the ingredients; don't over-moisten, as the dough should be stiff. Brush or spray the top with oil. Cover the bowl with plastic wrap. If desired, for best flavor or for convenience, you can refrigerate the dough for 3 to 10 hours. Then let rise at cool room temperature for 12 to 18 hours.

SECOND RISE: Vigorously stir the dough, gradually sprinkling over the 1⅓ cups granola and the milk powder; continue stirring until evenly distributed throughout the dough. Very generously oil a 9 × 5-inch loaf pan. Sprinkle with 2 tablespoons of the granola and tip the pan back and forth to distribute it over the bottom and sides. Turn out the dough into the pan. Brush or spray the loaf top with oil. Using an oiled rubber spatula or your fingertips, smooth and press the dough evenly into the pan. Sprinkle the top with the remaining 2 tablespoons granola, pressing down lightly. Cover the bowl with nonstick spray–coated plastic wrap.

LET RISE USING ANY OF THESE METHODS: For a 2- to 3-hour regular rise, let stand at warm room temperature; for a 1- to 2-hour accelerated rise, let stand in a turned-off microwave along with 1 cup of boiling-hot water; or for an extended rise, refrigerate, covered, for 4 to 48 hours, then set out at room temperature. Continue the rise until the dough nears the plastic. Remove it and continue until the dough extends ¼ inch above the pan rim.

BAKING PRELIMINARIES: 15 minutes before baking time, place a rack in the lower third of the oven; preheat to 375°F. Sprinkle the loaf with the 1 tablespoon sugar.

BAKING: Bake on the lower rack for 40 to 50 minutes, until the top is nicely browned. Cover with foil and continue baking for 25 to 30 minutes, until a skewer inserted in the thickest part comes out with just a few crumbs on the tip (or until center registers 205° to 208°F on an instant-read thermometer). When the loaf seems done, bake for 5 minutes longer to ensure the center is baked through. Cool in the pan on a wire rack for 10 to 15 minutes. Remove the loaf to the rack. Cool thoroughly.

SERVING AND STORING: The loaf slices best when cool, but tastes good warm. Cool completely before storing airtight in plastic or foil. It will keep at room temperature for 2 to 3 days, and may be frozen, airtight, for up to 2 months.

english muffin loaves

Nothing could be simpler than these highly "toastable" breakfast or brunch loaves. They are crispy on the outside, light and airy inside, and, as the name suggests, have a flavor reminiscent of English muffins. But, in contrast to English muffins, these are quite economical and easily slip in and out of the toaster slots! (For a raisin-wheat variation, see the end of the recipe.)

Yield: 2 medium loaves, about 12 slices each

FIRST RISE: In a very large bowl, thoroughly stir together the flour, sugar, salt, and yeast. In another bowl or measuring cup, whisk together the oil and ice water. Vigorously stir the ice-water mixture into the dry ingredients, scraping down the bowl sides completely and mixing until the dough is thoroughly blended. If it is too dry to mix together, gradually stir in just enough more ice water to blend the ingredients; don't over-moisten, as the dough should be fairly stiff. If necessary, stir in more flour to stiffen it. Brush or spray the dough top with oil. Tightly cover the bowl with plastic wrap. If desired, for best flavor or for convenience, you can refrigerate the dough for 3 to 10 hours. Then let rise at cool room temperature for 12 to 18 hours; if convenient, vigorously stir once during the rise.

SECOND RISE: Vigorously stir the powdered milk into the dough. Then vigorously stir in enough more flour to yield a very stiff dough. Generously grease two 8 ½ × 4½-inch loaf pans. Sprinkle them with the cornmeal, then tip the pans back and forth to coat evenly. Using well-oiled kitchen shears or a serrated knife, cut the dough in half and place the portions in the pans. Brush or spray the tops with oil, then using an oiled rubber spatula or fingertips, smooth out the surface and press the dough evenly into the pans. Tightly cover the pans with nonstick spray–coated plastic wrap.

5 cups (25 ounces) unbleached all-purpose white flour, plus more as needed

1 tablespoon granulated sugar

2 teaspoons table salt

1 teaspoon instant, fast-rising, or bread machine yeast

2½ tablespoons corn oil or other flavorless vegetable oil, plus extra for coating dough top and baking pans

2⅔ cups ice water, plus more if needed

⅓ cup top-quality instant nonfat powdered milk (don't use a generic brand)

About 2 tablespoons cornmeal for coating pans (substitute flour if unavailable)

LET RISE USING ANY OF THESE METHODS: For a 1½- to 2½-hour regular rise, let stand at warm room temperature; for a 1- to 2-hour accelerated rise, let stand in a turned-off microwave along with 1 cup of boiling-hot water; or for an extended rise, refrigerate, covered, for 4 to 24 hours, then set out at room temperature. Continue the rise until the dough nears the plastic. Remove it and continue until the dough just reaches the pan rims.

BAKING PRELIMINARIES: 15 minutes before baking time, place a rack in the lower third of the oven; preheat to 400°F. Spritz or brush the loaf tops with water.

BAKING: Reduce the oven temperature to 375°F. Bake on the lower rack for 30 to 40 minutes, or until the tops are well browned. Cover the loaves with foil and continue baking for 10 to 20 minutes, until a skewer inserted in the thickest part comes out with just a few crumbs on the tip (or until the centers register 208° to 210°F on an instant-read thermometer). Then bake for 5 to 10 minutes longer to ensure the centers are baked through. Cool in the pans on a wire rack for 10 to 15 minutes. Remove the loaves to the rack. Cool thoroughly.

SERVING AND STORING: Cool thoroughly before slicing or storing. Serve toasted. Store in plastic or aluminum foil. The bread will keep at room temperature for 3 days, and may be frozen, airtight, for up to 2 months.

VARIATION RAISIN-WHEAT ENGLISH MUFFIN BREAD—Use 4 cups white flour and 1 cup whole wheat flour. Increase the sugar to 3½ tablespoons. Add ¾ cup dark raisins when the powdered milk is incorporated.

crusty seeded
pale ale
pot boule

KS QUOTIENT — Super Easy: Fuss-free ingredients, all except garnish added at once. No hand-shaping.

Due to the hops and malt in the ale, this homespun, seed-encrusted pot boule has a hearty flavor, faint bitterness, and the same light yeasty aroma that always seems to hover in brewpubs. The interior is somewhat holey, with a pretty pale, well, ale color. If you use sesame seeds (my preference though a multi-seed blend is nice, too) for garnishing the loaf, they will turn golden and give the bread a slight nuttiness and crunch. The pleasantly springy crumb makes it suitable for toast and sandwiches. Or, cut it into generous slabs and serve along with a hearty soup or stew.

As is true of many of the peasant-style pot breads in the book, this one is simply popped into a pot, topped with a lid, and baked. *New York Times* columnist Mark Bittman created a stir when he re-introduced the idea of pot breads in a story featuring baker Jim Lahey and his French-style loaf baked in a Dutch oven. But baking bread in a heavy pot is not new in America; it was commonplace before kitchens came outfitted with ranges and ovens. (Dutch oven baking has long been popular with campfire cooks.)

In her 1833 work, *The American Frugal Housewife*, Lydia Maria Child mentions buttering a "bake-kettle," which the homemaker was instructed to fill with bread and then hang over the fire to bake. Large, cast metal pots with legs, variously called posnets, creepers, or spiders (presumably because they resembled big, creepy spiders), were standard hearth equipment when cooks still had to bake over fireplace coals.

Yield: 1 large loaf, 12 to 14 portions or slices

4½ cups (22.5 ounces) unbleached all-purpose white flour or unbleached white bread flour, plus more as needed

3 tablespoons granulated sugar

Scant 2 teaspoons table salt

¾ teaspoon instant, fast-rising, or bread machine yeast

1 bottle (12 ounces) well-chilled pale ale or beer

⅔ cup ice water, plus more if needed

Vegetable oil or oil spray for coating dough top

3 tablespoons sesame seeds or poppy seeds, or 1 tablespoon each sesame, poppy, and flax seeds blended together, for garnish

FIRST RISE: In a large bowl, thoroughly stir together the flour, sugar, salt, and yeast. Vigorously stir in the ale and ice water, scraping down the bowl sides completely and mixing until the bubbling subsides and the dough is thoroughly blended. If it is too dry to mix together, gradually stir in just enough more ice water to blend the ingredients; don't over-moisten, as the dough should be stiff. If necessary, stir in enough more flour to yield a hard-to-stir dough. Brush or spray the top with oil. Tightly cover the bowl with plastic wrap. If desired, for best flavor or for convenience, you can refrigerate the dough for 3 to 10 hours. Then let rise at cool room temperature for 12 to 18 hours; if convenient, vigorously stir once during the rise.

SECOND RISE: Using an oiled rubber spatula, lift and fold the dough in towards the center all the way around until mostly deflated; don't stir. Brush or spray the dough surface with oil. Re-cover the bowl with nonstick spray–coated plastic wrap.

LET RISE USING ANY OF THESE METHODS: For a 1½- to 2½-hour regular rise, let stand at warm room temperature; for a 45-minute to 2-hour accelerated rise, let stand in a turned-off microwave along with 1 cup of boiling-hot water; or for an extended rise, refrigerate, covered, for 4 to 24 hours, then set out at room temperature. Continue the rise until the dough doubles from the deflated size, removing the plastic if the dough nears it.

BAKING PRELIMINARIES: 20 minutes before baking time, put a rack in the lower third of the oven; preheat to 450°F. Heat a 3½- to 4-quart (or larger) heavy metal pot or Dutch oven or a deep, 4-quart, heavy ovenproof saucepan in the oven until sizzling hot (check with a few drops of water), then remove it, using heavy mitts. Taking care not to deflate the dough, loosen it from the bowl sides with an oiled rubber spatula and gently invert it into the pot. Don't worry if it's lopsided and ragged-looking; it will even out during baking. Very generously spritz or brush the top with water, then sprinkle over the seeds. Immediately top with the lid. Shake the pot back and forth to center the dough.

BAKING: Reduce the heat to 425°F. Bake on the lower rack for 55 minutes. Remove the lid. Reduce the heat to 425°F. Bake for 10 to 15 minutes longer, or until the top is well browned and a skewer inserted in the thickest part comes out with just a few crumbs on the tip (or until the center registers 208° to 210°F on an instant-read thermometer).Then bake for 5 minutes longer to ensure the center is baked through. Cool in the pan on a wire rack for 10 to 15 minutes. Remove the loaf to the rack. Cool thoroughly.

SERVING AND STORING: Cut or tear the loaf into portions; it tastes good warm but still better cool. Cool completely before storing. To maintain the crisp crust, store in a large bowl draped with a clean tea towel or in a heavy paper bag. Or store airtight in a plastic bag or foil: The crust will soften, but can be crisped by heating the loaf, uncovered, in a 400°F oven for a few minutes. The bread will keep at room temperature for 3 days, and may be frozen, airtight, for up to 2 months.

easy four-grain
pot boule

3¼ cups (16.25 ounces) unbleached all-purpose white flour or unbleached bread flour, plus more as needed

½ cup yellow or white cornmeal, plus 1 tablespoon for garnish

½ cup old-fashioned rolled oats or quick cooking (not instant) oats

¼ cup light or dark rye flour (if unavailable, substitute 2 tablespoons each more cornmeal and oats)

1 tablespoon granulated sugar

Generous 2 teaspoons table salt

¾ teaspoon instant, fast-rising, or bread machine yeast

2 cups ice water, plus more if needed

Corn oil, canola oil, or other flavorless vegetable oil or oil spray for coating dough

In the process of using up some packages and tidying my baking supplies, I tossed a little cornmeal, rolled oats, and rye flour into a white bread dough and discovered I'd created a combination worth repeating. The serendipitous blend lends this homey, crisp-crusted pot bread a light color and subtle, indefinable, grain taste that whispers rather than shouts its mixed grain heritage. It's a loaf that goes with most anything and often gets compliments. It's one of my favorites.

Makes 1 large loaf, 12 to 14 portions or slices

FIRST RISE: In a large bowl, thoroughly stir together the flour, cornmeal, oats, rye flour, sugar, salt, and yeast. Thoroughly stir the water into the bowl, scraping down the sides until the ingredients are thoroughly blended. If the mixture is too dry to incorporate all the flour, a bit at a time, stir in just enough more ice water to blend the ingredients; don't over-moisten, as the dough should be fairly stiff. If necessary, stir in enough more flour to stiffen it slightly. Brush or spray the top with oil. Cover the bowl with plastic wrap. If desired, for best flavor or for convenience, you can refrigerate the dough for 3 to 10 hours. Then let rise at cool room temperature for 12 to 18 hours; if convenient, vigorously stir once partway through the rise.

SECOND RISE: Using an oiled rubber spatula, gently lift and fold the dough in towards the center all the way around until mostly deflated; don't stir. Brush or spray with oil. Re-cover with plastic wrap.

LET RISE USING ANY OF THESE METHODS: For a 1½- to 2½-hour regular rise, let stand at warm room temperature; for a 1- to 2-hour accelerated rise, let stand in a turned-off microwave along with 1 cup of boiling-hot water; or for an extended rise, refrigerate, covered, for 4 to 24 hours, then set out at room temperature. Continue the rise until the dough doubles from the deflated size, removing the plastic if the dough nears it.

BAKING PRELIMINARIES: 20 minutes before baking time, put a rack in the lower third of the oven; preheat to 450°F. Heat a 3½- to 4-quart (or larger) heavy metal pot in the oven until sizzling hot (check with a few drops of water), then remove it using heavy mitts. Taking care not to deflate the dough, loosen it from the bowl sides with an oiled rubber spatula and gently invert it into the pot. Don't worry if it's lopsided and ragged-looking; it will even out during baking. Generously spritz or brush the top with water, then sprinkle over a tablespoon of cornmeal. Using a well-oiled serrated knife or kitchen shears, cut a ½-inch-deep, 4-inch diameter circle in the loaf center. Immediately top with the lid. Shake the pot back and forth to center the dough.

BAKING: Reduce the heat to 425°F. Bake on the lower rack for 50 minutes. Remove the lid. Reduce the heat to 400°F. Bake for 15 to 20 minutes longer, until the top is well browned and a skewer inserted in the thickest part comes out with just a few crumbs on the tip (or until center registers 210° to 212°F on an instant-read thermometer). Then bake for 5 minutes longer to ensure the center is baked through. Cool in the pan on a wire rack for 10 to 15 minutes. Remove the loaf to the rack. Cool thoroughly.

SERVING AND STORING: Cut or tear the loaf into portions; it tastes good warm but will cut better when cool. Cool completely before storing. To maintain the crisp crust, store in a large bowl draped with a clean tea towel or in a heavy paper bag. Or store airtight in a plastic bag or foil: The crust will soften, but can be crisped by heating the loaf, uncovered, in a 400°F oven for a few minutes. The bread will keep at room temperature for 3 days, and may be frozen, airtight, for up to 2 months.

hearty caraway beer bread

3 cups (15 ounces) unbleached all-purpose white flour, plus more as needed

1 cup (5 ounces) rye flour or whole wheat flour

1 tablespoon caraway seeds, plus ½ tablespoon for garnish

1 tablespoon unsweetened cocoa powder, preferably Dutch-process, sifted after measuring, optional

Scant 2 teaspoons table salt

¾ teaspoon instant, fast-rising, or bread machine yeast

⅔ cup minus 1 tablespoon ice water, plus more if needed

2½ tablespoons molasses

1 tablespoon corn oil, canola oil, or other flavorless vegetable oil, plus more for coating dough top

1 bottle (12 ounces) beer, well chilled

Excellent served along with many cheeses, smoked meats, and hearty stews, this full-bodied yet light-textured loaf tastes much like traditional caraway-seeded rye breads. However, since rye flour is often hard to find, whole wheat may be used in its place; most people won't notice the substitution. They are not likely to notice the beer in the recipe either. It simply adds a little extra yeasty-malty aroma and flavor.

Note that you can ready this bread in a large loaf pan or, for a round loaf, in a 9- to 10-inch ovenproof pot or casserole. The oblong loaf is easier to cut for sandwiches; the round has a more homespun look. Since the cocoa powder is added mainly to darken the bread color, it can be omitted, if desired. **Yield: 1 large round or rectangular loaf, 12 to 14 slices**

FIRST RISE: In a large bowl, thoroughly stir together the white flour, rye (or whole wheat) flour, 1 tablespoon caraway seeds, cocoa powder (if using), salt, and yeast. In another bowl or measuring cup, thoroughly whisk the water with the molasses and oil. Add the mixture and the beer to the bowl with the flour, vigorously stirring and scraping down the sides until the ingredients are thoroughly blended and the foaming subsides. If the mixture is too dry to incorporate all the flour, a bit at a time, stir in just enough more ice water to blend the ingredients; don't over-moisten, as the dough should be fairly stiff. If necessary, stir in enough more white flour to stiffen it slightly. Brush or spray the top with oil. Cover the bowl with plastic wrap. If desired, for best flavor or for convenience, you can refrigerate the dough for 3 to 10 hours. Then let rise at cool room temperature for 12 to 18 hours; if convenient, vigorously stir the dough about halfway through.

SECOND RISE: Vigorously stir the dough. If necessary, stir in enough more white flour to yield a very stiff consistency. Using an oiled rubber spatula, fold the dough in towards the center all the way around to bowl; this organizes the gluten for shaping the dough into a loaf. Invert the dough into an oiled 9 × 5-inch loaf pan or a 9- or 10-inch diameter (or similar) heavy ovenproof pot or flat-bottomed casserole. Brush or spray the top with oil. Smooth and press the dough into the pan using a well-oiled rubber spatula or your fingertips. Sprinkle the top with the remaining ½ tablespoon of caraway seeds. Press down to imbed. Cover the pan with nonstick spray–coated plastic wrap.

LET RISE USING ANY OF THESE METHODS: For a 1½- to 2½-hour regular rise, let stand at warm room temperature; for a 1- to 2-hour accelerated rise, let stand in a turned-off microwave along with 1 cup of boiling-hot water; or for an extended rise, refrigerate, covered, for 4 to 24 hours, then set out at room temperature. Continue the rise until the dough nears the plastic. Remove it and continue until the dough doubles from the deflated size or extends just above the pan rim.

BAKING PRELIMINARIES: 20 minutes before baking time, put a rack in the lower third of the oven; preheat to 400ºF. Using well-oiled kitchen shears or a serrated knife, cut a large × in the center top of the round loaf or a 5-inch long ¼-inch-deep slash down the center of the rectangular loaf.

BAKING: Reduce the heat to 375ºF. Bake on the lower rack for 45 to 50 minutes, or until the top is well browned. Cover the top with foil. Bake for 20 to 25 minutes longer, until a skewer inserted in the thickest part comes out with just a few crumbs on the tip (or until the center registers 204º to 207ºF on an instant-read thermometer). When the loaf seems done, bake for 5 minutes longer to ensure the center is baked through. Cool in the pan on a wire rack for 10 to 15 minutes. Remove the loaf to the rack. Cool thoroughly.

SERVING AND STORING: The loaf slices best when cool. Cool completely before storing airtight in plastic or foil. The bread will keep at room temperature for 2 to 3 days, and may be frozen, airtight, for up to 2 months.

double chocolate–honey bread

3¼ cups (16.25 ounces) unbleached all-purpose white flour, plus more as needed

⅓ cup unsweetened cocoa powder, preferably Dutch-process, sifted after measuring

2½ tablespoons granulated sugar, plus 1 tablespoon for garnish

Generous 1¼ teaspoons table salt

¾ teaspoon instant, fast-rising, or bread machine yeast

½ cup clover honey or other mild honey

¼ cup corn oil, canola oil, or other flavorless vegetable oil, plus extra for coating dough top and baking pan

1¾ cups ice water, plus more if needed

1 cup (6 ounces) semisweet chocolate morsels

Glossy Chocolate Drizzle (page 192) for garnish, optional

Studded with chocolate morsels and boldly flavored with cocoa powder, this bread is dark, moist, and full of chocolate-honey goodness. It also has an irresistible crunchy sugar crust. It's great as a snack with coffee, tea, or milk and makes a pleasing light dessert, especially if topped with the Glossy Chocolate Drizzle (page 192). For a more sophisticated taste, try either the lightly spiced or orange-hazelnut versions at right.

Yield: 1 large loaf, 12 to 15 slices

FIRST RISE: In a large bowl, thoroughly stir together the flour, cocoa, 2½ tablespoons sugar, salt, and yeast. In another bowl or measuring cup, whisk the honey and oil into the water. Thoroughly stir the mixture and chocolate morsels into the bowl with the flour, scraping down the sides and mixing until well blended. If too dry to mix together, add just enough more water to facilitate mixing, but don't over-moisten, as the dough should be stiff. If necessary, stir in enough more flour to stiffen it. Brush or spray the top with oil. Cover the bowl tightly with plastic wrap. If desired, for best flavor or for convenience, you can refrigerate the dough for 3 to 10 hours. Then let rise at cool room temperature for 12 to 18 hours.

SECOND RISE: Vigorously stir the dough. Using an oiled rubber spatula, fold the dough in towards the center all the way around (this organizes the gluten for shaping the dough into a loaf). Invert it out into a very well-greased 9 × 5-inch loaf pan. Evenly brush or spray the top with oil. Smooth out the dough and evenly press into the pan with an oiled rubber spatula or fingertips. Cover the pan with nonstick spray–coated plastic wrap.

LET RISE USING ANY OF THESE METHODS: For a 1- to 2-hour regular rise, let stand at warm room temperature; for a ½- to 1½-hour accelerated rise, let stand in a turned-off microwave along with 1 cup of boiling-hot water; or for an extended rise, refrigerate, covered, for 4 to 48 hours, then set out at room temperature. When the dough nears the plastic, remove it and continue the rise until the dough reaches the pan rim or doubles from its deflated size.

BAKING PRELIMINARIES: 15 minutes before baking time, place a rack in the lower third of the oven; preheat to 350°F.

BAKING: Sprinkle the loaf top evenly with the remaining 1 tablespoon sugar. Bake on the lower rack for 40 minutes, or until the loaf is well browned. Cover the top with foil and continue baking for 25 to 30 minutes, occasionally testing with a skewer inserted in the thickest part. When it comes out with just slightly moist particles clinging to the bottom portion (or until the center registers 204° to 206°F on an instant-read thermometer), bake for 5 minutes more to ensure the center is done. Let cool in the pan on a wire rack for 15 minutes. Loosen the loaf with a knife, then place on the rack. Cool thoroughly. Garnish the cooled loaf with Glossy Chocolate Drizzle, if desired.

SERVING AND STORING: Serve warm, or cool, or toasted; the bread slices best when cool. Cool thoroughly before storing in plastic or foil. Keeps at room temperature for 3 days. May be frozen, airtight, for up to 2 months.

VARIATION NUTMEG CHOCOLATE BREAD—Prepare as directed, except add ¾ teaspoon ground nutmeg along with the salt and increase the yeast to 1 teaspoon (the nutmeg inhibits yeast growth a bit).

VARIATION ORANGE-HAZELNUT CHOCOLATE BREAD—Prepare as directed, except add 1½ teaspoons finely grated orange zest along with the water mixture and ½ cup hulled, chopped, and lightly toasted hazelnuts along with the chocolate morsels.

simple enriched
white rolls

2½ cups (12.5 ounces) unbleached
all-purpose white flour, plus ½ cup
(2.5 ounces), plus more as needed

5 tablespoons granulated sugar,
divided

1⅛ teaspoons table salt

½ teaspoon instant, fast-rising, or
bread machine yeast

1½ cups ice water, plus more if
needed

¼ cup unsalted butter, melted and
cooled slightly, plus 1½ tablespoons
more for brushing over rolls

⅓ cup top-quality instant nonfat
dry milk powder (don't use a
generic brand)

These rolls are tender, rich, and aromatic, due to an ample addition of
butter and a very long first rise that develops a fine yeast flavor and fragrance. They taste like the classic home-style butter rolls my mother
sometimes baked, but I've eliminated the hand-shaping, which makes
these much easier to prepare. I simply plop portions of dough into muffin
tins, butter the tops, then set them aside to rise. Yes, sidestepping the traditional shaping means that the rolls come out looking like plain muffins,
but since the dough is moister and is manipulated less, they are even more
succulent and tender than hand-shaped ones.

To bake all the rolls at once, you'll need 18 standard-size muffin tin
cups (about 2¾ inches across at the top), or 12 jumbo muffin tin cups
(3½ to 3¾ inches across at the top). If you don't have enough muffin
cups, use what's on hand to bake an initial batch of rolls. Keep the unused
dough refrigerated for up to 24 hours, then stir well. Place in the tins and
rise and bake as for the first batch.

Yield: 12 large or 18 medium muffin-shaped rolls

FIRST RISE: In a large bowl, thoroughly stir together 2½ cups flour, 3 tablespoons of the sugar, the salt, and yeast. Stir in the water, scraping down
the sides just until the ingredients are thoroughly blended. The mixture
should be the consistency of very thick pancake batter; if necessary, stir in
just enough more water, a bit at a time, to thin it, or more flour to thicken
it slightly. Cover the bowl with plastic wrap. If desired, for best flavor or
for convenience, you can refrigerate the dough for 3 to 10 hours. Then let
rise at cool room temperature for 15 to 20 hours.

SECOND RISE: Vigorously stir ¼ cup butter, the milk powder, and remaining 2 tablespoons of sugar into the dough until very well blended. Stirring
vigorously and scraping down the bowl as needed, gradually add ½ cup

flour or enough more flour to yield a dough slightly thicker than thick pancake batter.

Generously grease or spray 12 giant-size muffin cups or 18 regular-size muffin cups with nonstick spray. For large muffin cups, use a well-greased ¼-cup measure and scoop up *scant cupfuls* of dough; for small muffin cups, use a ⅛-cup measure (or coffee scoop) and scoop up *generous cupfuls* of dough. Put the portions in the cups, then divide any leftover dough evenly among them. Drizzle 1½ tablespoons butter over the roll tops, dividing it among them. With fingertips, spread out the butter and smooth each top until the dough surface looks completely smooth. Tent the muffin tins with nonstick spray–coated foil.

LET RISE USING ANY OF THESE METHODS: For a 1½- to 2½-hour regular rise, let stand at warm room temperature; for a 1- to 2-hour accelerated rise, let stand in a turned-off microwave along with 1 cup of boiling-hot water; or for an extended rise, refrigerate, covered, for 4 to 48 hours, then set out at room temperature. Continue the rise until the dough nears the foil. Remove it and continue until the dough doubles from its deflated size. Sift a little flour over the roll tops for garnish.

BAKING PRELIMINARIES: 15 minutes before baking time, place a rack in the lower third of the oven; preheat to 375°F.

BAKING: Bake on the lower rack for 18 to 23 minutes, until the tops are nicely browned. Tent the pans with foil and continue baking for 5 to 10 minutes more, until a skewer inserted in the thickest part of a center roll comes out with just a few particles clinging to the bottom (or until the center registers 205° to 208°F on an instant-read thermometer), to be sure the centers are done. Cool in the pan on wire racks for 10 minutes. Sift a little more flour over the rolls if desired. Transfer the rolls to a bread basket for serving.

SERVING AND STORING: Best served warm. Reheat, wrapped in foil in a 350°F oven for 5 to 10 minutes, or wrapped in paper towels in a microwave oven on medium power for 15 seconds per roll. Store airtight in plastic at room temperature for 2 to 3 days, or freeze, airtight, for up to 2 months. Thaw before reheating.

american favorites

WHEN PEOPLE THINK OF AMERICAN BREADS, THEY usually think "comfort food," and with good reason. There could hardly be more comforting fare than well-made loaves of puffy, fragrant, home-style white bread, or cinnamon-raisin pinwheel bread, or ooey-gooey sticky buns. But some of America's best-loved breads have a different character: San Francisco sourdough is as crusty as any of Europe's rustic loaves and gets a kick from a pungent starter. Another popular savory loaf is cheese bread; the one in this chapter is zippy with sharp cheese and green chiles.

Of course, due to the artisan bread movement in this country, interesting new breads more in the style of those in Europe are coming on the scene here all the time: The Sonoma-Style Multigrain Crunch Bread is an adaptation of a terrific crackly-crusted boule from northern California's Artisan Bakers. My Crunchy Yeasted Cornbread with Coarse Salt and my updated Easy Buttermilk Pot Bread with Coarse Salt are also simple crispy-topped peasant-style boules.

county fair
white bread

Unlike the fluffy-stuff loaves lining supermarket shelves, this traditional enriched white bread has substance and texture and a buttery, yeasty smell. A bit more voluptuous, softer, and more fine-grained than the Easy White Bread Loaves on page 29, this is reminiscent of the loaves that often won the white bread category at the local county fairs when I was a child. True, it's not the sort of loaf that cutting-edge shops are selling these days, but when you want comfort food, or maybe a taste of home, this is it.

This same dough can easily be turned into Pull-Apart Butter-Top Rolls (page 63) and Cinnamon Pinwheel Raisin Bread (page 66).

Yield: 1 large loaf, 12 to 14 slices

3 cups (15 ounces) unbleached white bread flour, plus ⅔ cup (3.33 ounces) or as needed

2½ tablespoons granulated sugar

1½ teaspoons table salt

¾ teaspoon instant, fast-rising, or bread machine yeast

1¾ cups ice water, plus more if needed

3 tablespoons unsalted butter, melted and slightly cooled, plus extra for coating dough top and baking pan

¼ cup good-quality instant nonfat dry milk (don't use a generic brand)

1 large egg, at room temperature and beaten with a fork

FIRST RISE: In a large bowl, thoroughly stir together 3 cups of the flour, the sugar, salt, and yeast. Thoroughly stir the water into the bowl, scraping down the sides and mixing just until the ingredients are thoroughly blended. If the mixture is too dry to incorporate all the flour, a bit at a time, stir in enough more water to blend the ingredients and produce a fairly soft dough. Brush the top with butter. Cover the bowl with plastic wrap. If desired, for best flavor or for convenience, you can refrigerate the dough for 3 to 10 hours. Then, let rise at cool room temperature for 16 to 20 hours; if convenient, vigorously stir the dough about halfway through the rise.

SECOND RISE: In a medium bowl, stir together the butter, milk powder, and 2 tablespoons of the beaten egg until thoroughly blended; reserve the remaining egg for glazing the loaf top. Vigorously stir (or beat on low speed with a heavy-duty mixer with a dough hook) the butter mixture into the dough until smoothly and evenly incorporated; this may take several minutes. Gradually mix in ⅔ cup or enough more flour to yield a very hard-to-stir dough. Using a well-oiled rubber spatula, fold the dough in towards the center, working all the way around the bowl; this helps organize the gluten for shaping into a loaf.

Invert the dough into a well-greased 9 × 5-inch loaf pan. Smooth out the top and press evenly into the pan using a well-buttered rubber spatula or fingertips. Evenly brush the loaf top with the reserved beaten egg; don't allow the egg to pool around the pan edges, as it will cause sticking. Using well-buttered kitchen shears or a serrated knife, make a ½-inch-deep slash lengthwise down the center of the loaf. Cover the pan with nonstick spray–coated plastic wrap.

LET RISE USING ANY OF THESE METHODS: For a 1½- to 2½-hour regular rise, let stand at warm room temperature; for a 1- to 2-hour accelerated rise, let stand in a turned-off microwave along with 1 cup of boiling-hot water; or for an extended rise, refrigerate for 4 to 48 hours, then set out at room temperature. Continue the rise until the dough nears the plastic. Remove it and continue until the dough extends slightly above the pan rim.

BAKING PRELIMINARIES: 15 minutes before baking time, place a rack in the lower third of the oven; preheat to 375°F.

BAKING: Bake on the lower rack for 40 to 50 minutes, or until the top is nicely browned. Cover the top with foil and continue baking for 10 to 15 minutes longer, until a skewer inserted in the thickest part comes out with just a few particles clinging to the bottom (or until the center registers 208° to 210°F on an instant-read thermometer). Then bake for 5 to 10 minutes more to be sure the center is done. Cool in the pan on a wire rack for 10 minutes. Turn out the loaf onto the rack; cool thoroughly.

SERVING AND STORING: Cool thoroughly before slicing or storing. Store airtight in plastic or aluminum foil. The bread will keep at room temperature for 2 to 3 days, and may be frozen, airtight, for up to 2 months.

pull-apart
butter-top rolls

KS QUOTIENT—Fairly Easy: Easily assembled ingredients; two-stage mixing. Simple hand-shaping required.

The mild aroma, mellow taste, and melting texture of these home-style rolls remind me of ones that were the pride of the gray-haired ladies who baked for the frequent fund-raising church suppers my family attended during my childhood. Neatly aproned and hair-netted, they would stand in the back of the parish kitchen deftly turning out dozens of sheet pans of rolls, which were whisked straight from the ovens and devoured by eager tables of diners. For me (and probably for many other patrons) the highlight was not the featured ham or oysters or turkey, but those amazing all-you-could-eat butter rolls!

These rolls are made using the same dough as the County Fair White Bread (page 61). The very easy shortcut shaping method is one I borrowed from the church supper roll bakers, who used it because they had to produce huge quantities very quickly. It involves merely forming portions of dough into long logs and then cutting them crosswise into plump rectangles, so it's handy for inexperienced or very busy cooks as well. The rolls always expand and join together again during rising and baking, but, as their name suggests, they neatly pull apart when served.

Prepare the County Fair White Bread recipe up to the point it would normally be put into a loaf pan for the second rise; be sure to add the butter, milk powder, and egg as directed before proceeding with the following steps. (Note that the 1 tablespoon of egg reserved to glaze the loaf is not needed for the rolls.)

1 recipe County Fair White Bread dough (page 61), ready for the second rise

Unbleached white bread flour or all-purpose white flour for dusting

2 tablespoons unsalted butter, melted and slightly cooled

Yield: 24 finger rolls

SECOND RISE: Coat a 9 × 13-inch baking dish or pan with nonstick spray. Coat a large sheet of baking parchment with nonstick spray, then dust with flour. Coat a very large cutting board with nonstick spray, then generously dust with flour.

Working in the bowl, generously dust the dough with flour, turning it until lightly coated all over. Smooth and press the flour into the dough until it is less sticky and easier to handle. Using well-oiled kitchen shears, divide the dough into thirds, placing each portion cut-side down and well separated on the parchment.

Working on the cutting board, press and pat one portion out into about a 5 × 10-inch rectangle, dusting with flour as needed to prevent stickiness. If the dough is resistant and springs back, let it rest for a few minutes, then continue. Tightly roll up the rectangle from the 10-inch side, forming a log. Pinch the seam tightly closed along the length of the log. Dust with more flour, then turn seam-side down. Stretch the log out from the middle until evenly thick and about 12 inches long, then flatten the log until it's about 2½ inches wide.

Using well-oil kitchen shears or a large serrated knife, cut the log crosswise into 8 equal slices. Pat the row of rolls back into the log shape, then use a wide spatula to transfer them to the baking pan, placing the row lengthwise in the pan. Pull the rolls apart slightly so they fill the 13-inch length. Repeat the shaping and cutting process, laying the second and third log of rolls so they completely cover the pan; the rows will come together and fill it as they rise and bake. Brush the roll tops with half the butter. Tent the pan with nonstick spray–coated foil.

LET RISE USING ANY OF THESE METHODS: For a 1½- to 2½-hour regular rise, let stand at warm room temperature; for a 1- to 2-hour accelerated rise, let stand in a turned-off microwave along with 1 cup of boiling-hot water; or for an extended rise, refrigerate for 4 to 48 hours, then set out at room temperature. Continue the rise until the rolls double from their original size, removing the foil if the dough nears it.

BAKING PRELIMINARIES: 15 minutes before baking time, place a rack in the lower third of the oven; preheat to 350°F.

BAKING: Bake on the lower rack for 20 to 25 minutes, until the roll tops are nicely browned. Then cover with foil and bake for 3 to 5 minutes more or until a skewer inserted in the thickest part comes out with just a few particles clinging to the bottom (or until a center roll registers 204° to 206°F on an instant-read thermometer), to be sure the center is done. Brush the rolls with the remaining butter. Cool on a wire rack for 10 minutes. Lift the rolls from the pan and serve immediately.

SERVING AND STORING: Best served warm; reheat wrapped in foil in a pre-heated 350°F oven if desired. Cool thoroughly before storing. Store airtight in plastic or aluminum foil. The rolls will keep at room temperature for 2 to 3 days, and may be frozen, airtight, for up to 2 months.

cinnamon pinwheel raisin bread

1 recipe County Fair White Bread dough (page 61), ready for the second rise

¾ to 1 cup dark raisins, rinsed under hot water, drained well, and patted dry

Corn oil or other flavorless vegetable oil or oil spray for coating dough top and baking pan

Unbleached white bread flour or all-purpose white flour for dusting

1 large egg, at room temperature and beaten with a fork

Generous ⅓ cup granulated sugar combined with 1 tablespoon ground cinnamon, divided

1 tablespoon cool and firm unsalted butter, cut into fine bits

Cinnamon raisin is one of America's most popular breads, and no wonder. The touch of sweetness is always welcome, and the aroma and taste of the classic cinnamon-raisin combo is completely irresistible. This large, light, fine-textured loaf is excellent for toast, but is also tasty eaten plain for a snack.

The starting point for this loaf is a batch of the County Fair White Bread dough (page 61). Prepare it exactly as directed in the original recipe up to the point it is to go into a loaf pan to rise. Don't forget to add the butter, milk powder, and egg as instructed *before* proceeding with the directions below.

Yield: 1 large loaf, 12 to 15 slices

SECOND RISE: Once all the second rise ingredients have been added to the dough as directed on page 61, vigorously stir in the raisins until fully and evenly incorporated. Instead of turning out the dough into a baking pan as directed in the original recipe, set it in the refrigerator to rest for 10 minutes.

Coat a 16-inch-long sheet of baking parchment with nonstick spray. Generously dust the parchment with flour. Turn out the dough onto the center of the parchment. Evenly dust with flour, then shape it into a rough rectangle with flour-dusted fingertips. Dusting with more flour as needed to prevent sticking, press out the dough into a 9 × 14-inch evenly thick rectangle. Brush some of the beaten egg evenly over the dough to within ⅛ inch of the edge all around. (Reserve the remaining egg for garnishing the loaf.) Sprinkle all but ½ tablespoon of the cinnamon-sugar mixture evenly over the dough to within ¼ inch of the edge all around; reserve the ½ tablespoon cinnamon-sugar for garnish. Sprinkle the bits of butter over the sugar.

Tightly roll up the dough from a 9-inch-wide side to form a pinwheel log, using flour-dusted hands and lifting up the parchment to assist the rolling as you work. Pinch the seam together tightly all along the length of the log, then lay seam-side down. Firmly tuck the ends of the log underneath. Transfer the loaf, seam-side down, to a well-greased 9 × 5-inch baking pan. Brush or spray the top with oil. Cover the pan with nonstick spray–coated plastic wrap.

LET RISE USING ANY OF THESE METHODS: For a 1½- to 2½-hour regular rise, let stand at warm room temperature; for a 1- to 2-hour accelerated rise, let stand in a turned-off microwave along with 1 cup of boiling-hot water; or for an extended rise, refrigerate for 4 to 48 hours, then set out at room temperature. Continue the rise until the dough nears the plastic. Remove it and continue until the dough rises ½ inch above the pan rim.

BAKING PRELIMINARIES: 15 minutes before baking time, place a rack in the lower third of the oven; preheat to 350°F. Evenly brush the dough top with the reserved beaten egg. Wipe away any egg that pools around the pan edges, as it will cause the dough to stick to the pan. Evenly sprinkle the remaining ½ tablespoon of cinnamon-sugar over top.

BAKING: Bake on the lower rack for 25 to 30 minutes, or until the loaf is nicely browned. Cover with foil and continue baking for 25 to 35 minutes longer, occasionally testing until a skewer inserted in the thickest part comes out with just a few particles on the end (or until the center registers 207° to 209°F on an instant-read thermometer). Then, bake for 10 to 15 minutes more to make sure the center is done. Cool in the pan on a wire rack for 10 minutes. Turn the loaf onto the rack; cool thoroughly.

SERVING AND STORING: Serve warm, or cool, or toasted; the bread slices best when cool. Cool thoroughly before storing in plastic or foil. Keeps at room temperature for 2 to 3 days. May be frozen, airtight, for up to 2 months.

san francisco–style sourdough bread

3½ cups (17.5 ounces) unbleached white bread flour or unbleached all-purpose white flour, plus more as needed

1¾ teaspoons table salt

¼ to ¾ teaspoon instant, fast-rising, or bread machine yeast (use the larger amount if substituting yogurt and vinegar for sourdough starter)

1 tablespoon corn oil, canola oil, or other flavorless vegetable oil, plus more for coating dough top and pan

⅔ cup wild yeast sourdough starter or Easy Cultured "Sourdough" Starter (page 71) (or substitute ½ cup chilled plain "active culture" yogurt and 2½ tablespoons apple cider vinegar)

1½ cups ice water, plus more if needed

This golden, crackly-crusted round is reminiscent of the bread so many tourists take a fancy to and tote home from San Francisco: The texture is noticeably, pleasingly chewy, the aroma pungently enticing, and, as the name suggests, the loaf strikes a deliciously sour note. Like the classic loaf that the Boudin Bakery has been turning out since 1849, it is a straightforward, unenriched bread, incorporating no eggs, sugar, or flavor enhancers other than salt and a suitably sour starter.

As purists will immediately note, my recipe does veer off the traditional path in incorporating a little commercial baking yeast. (Some sourdough devotees consider this a capital offense.) I haven't found that it affects the desired sour flavor, and it's a sensible, convenient fail-safe that guarantees success even if your starter doesn't happen to be lively enough to fully lift the bread on its own. (In fact, the practice of boosting starters by adding some commercial yeast to dough before baking it is fairly common in Germany, and even the esteemed French expert on bread, the late Raymond Calvel, noted that a small amount of a commercial strain could be used in a proper sourdough, or pain au levain, without affecting its taste.)

Unlike most of the sourdough bread recipes circulating today, this one calls for baking the bread in a heavy lidded pot. Yes, it better approximates the method of the original California prospectors cooking over open fires, but it also comes much, much closer to producing the crackly, well-colored loaves turned out by the steam-jetted commercial bakery ovens of today. Due to its leanness, classic sourdough bread requires a very moist environment during the first stage of baking for good browning and crisping, and a heavy pot automatically traps the necessary steam inside.

As purists will rightly point out, for an absolutely authentic, City-by-the-Bay boule, you need the local wild yeast starter. However, I've found that using any purchased or homemade tangy sourdough starter in this recipe will yield loaves that roughly approximate the typical San Francisco versions. Additionally, I've experimented with a simplified, much more predictable shortcut cultured starter inoculated with a small amount of commercial "instant" baking yeast (see page 71 for the recipe). Though it tastes tamer than starter produced by its wild cousins, once it matures (this takes 10 days or so), it delivers enough tang for a satisfying sourdough-style loaf. Whatever the starter, read page 71 on getting it ready to bake bread.

Another even more convenient, "cheater's" alternative (which yields a delicious—though less sour-tasting—bread) is to replace the starter with some plain yogurt (be sure it includes "active cultures") mixed with cider vinegar. This combo instantly introduces a little of the same lactic and acetic acids that account for the zip of typical yeast starters, though the bread is, of course, not a real sourdough. **Yield: 1 large loaf, 12 to 14 slices**

A TANGY TASTE OF HISTORY: The California sourdough culture, of course, dates back to the Gold Rush, when so many prospectors leavened their crude camp breads and biscuits with a tangy yeast starter that they came to be called "sourdoughs" themselves. The miners relied on the primitive leavening mostly because, unlike other leavening agents, it was easily renewed and maintained in the rugged frontier conditions.

FIRST RISE: In a large bowl, thoroughly stir together the flour, salt, and yeast. In another bowl or measuring cup, whisk the oil and starter (or yogurt and vinegar) into the water. Vigorously stir the mixture into the bowl with the flour, scraping down the sides and mixing just until the ingredients are thoroughly blended. If the mixture is too dry to incorporate all the flour, a bit at a time, stir in just enough more ice water to blend the ingredients; don't over-moisten, as the dough should be very stiff. If necessary, stir in enough more flour to stiffen it. Brush or spray the top with oil. Cover the bowl with plastic wrap. If desired, for best flavor or for convenience, you can refrigerate the dough for 3 to 10 hours. Then let rise at cool room temperature for 18 to 24 hours. If convenient, vigorously stir the dough once partway through the rise.

SECOND RISE: Vigorously stir the dough, adding more flour as needed to yield a very stiff and hard to stir dough. Then, using a well-oiled rubber spatula, fold the dough in towards the center, working your way all the way around the bowl; this helps organizes the gluten for shaping a loaf. Let the dough rest for 10 minutes. Invert the dough so the underside is up. Sprinkle evenly with 3 to 4 tablespoons of flour. Working in the bowl, shape the dough into a ball; roll it in the flour until coated all over; then work in the flour until it holds its shape. Lightly dusting with flour as needed, form the dough into an evenly shaped high-domed 6-inch diameter round by firmly tucking the edges under all the way around; work gently, as the dough is tender and prone to tearing.

Gently transfer the loaf to an oiled 3½- to 4-quart Dutch oven or similar heavy ovenproof pot. Dust the loaf top with more flour, smoothing out evenly. Using a well-oiled serrated knife, make 3 or 4 parallel shallow slashes across the loaf top. Then, working on a diagonal, slash 3 or 4 more lines diagonally across the first set to create a diamond pattern. Brush or spray the dough with oil. Cover the pot with its lid.

Let rise until the dough doubles from its deflated size using any of these methods: Stand at warm room temperature for a 1½- to 2½-hour regular rise; or in a turned-off microwave along with a cup of boiling-hot water for a 1- to 2½-hour accelerated rise. Or, for an extended rise, refrigerate for 4 to 24 hours, then set out at room temperature. Continue the rise until the dough doubles in size.

BAKING PRELIMINARIES: 15 minutes before baking time, put a rack in the lower third of the oven; preheat to 450°F. Generously sprinkle or spray the loaf with water.

BAKING: Reduce the heat to 425°F. Bake on the lower rack, covered, for 55 to 60 minutes, or until the loaf is lightly browned and crusty. Uncover and continue baking for 10 to 15 minutes more, until a skewer inserted in the thickest part comes out with just a few particles on the end (or until the center registers 207° to 209°F on an instant-read thermometer). Then bake for 5 minutes longer to ensure the center is done. Cool on a wire rack for 10 minutes. Turn the loaf onto the rack; cool thoroughly.

SERVING AND STORING: Cut or tear the loaf into portions; it tastes good warm, but will cut much better when cool. Cool completely before storing. To maintain the crisp crust, store draped with a clean tea towel or in a heavy paper bag. Or, to prevent the loaf from drying out, store airtight in a plastic bag or wrapped in foil: The crust will soften, but can be crisped by heating the loaf, uncovered, in a 400°F oven for a few minutes. The bread will keep at room temperature for 3 days, and may be frozen, airtight, for up to 2 months.

VARIATION WHOLE WHEAT SOURDOUGH BREAD—Proceed exactly as for San Francisco–Style Sourdough Bread, except reduce the white bread flour to 2½ cups (12.5 ounces) and add 1 cup (5 ounces) whole wheat flour.

easy cultured
"sourdough" starter

(WITH COMMERCIAL YEAST)

KS QUOTIENT— Easy: Minimal ingredients. Super-reliable.

½ cup (2.5 ounces) unbleached all-purpose white flour, plus more for daily and maintenance "feedings"

⅛ teaspoon instant, fast-rising, or bread machine yeast

About ⅓ cup room temperature bottled spring water or other chlorine-free water, plus more for daily and maintenance "feedings"

The easiest way to get started with a wild yeast sourdough starter is to beg or borrow a little from somebody who has already a good one bubbling away. For those lacking a necessary personal contact, the King Arthur Flour Company in Vermont is a reliable source for a vigorous, tangy starter that needs only a couple of feedings of water and flour to be ready for use. I've found that it makes an excellent San Francisco–style sourdough loaf, even though the company doesn't claim its starter has a West Coast pedigree! If you feel you must have an actual San Francisco starter, check out www.sourdoughbreads.com or other Internet vendors whose sourdough contains the *Candida milleri yeast* and *Lactobacillus sanfrancisco* bacteria.

If you choose to make your own starter, there are two basic ways to go: The purist's approach followed by professional bakers involves setting out a flour-water mixture and hoping that it has the right strains of wild yeast and lactic acid bacteria. The easier, virtually foolproof (some would say cheater's) approach involves seeding your water-flour mixture with a little commercial instant yeast, which is a "domesticated" cousin of the wild organisms. Since creating a wild yeast, or "spontaneous" starter, is a hit-or-miss proposition, and producing what is technically referred to as a "cultured" starter is quite easy and reliable, it seems appropriate to go the second route in *Kneadlessly Simple*.

There's no trick to this recipe other than to use bottled spring water or any other pleasant-tasting water, good-quality unbleached all-purpose flour, and a very clean glass bowl, crock, or other container that doesn't react with acid. The mixing, feeding, and maintenance directions below are fairly specific, but in truth they don't have to be followed exactly for success.

It usually takes 10 days from the initial mixing for the cultured starter to yield a noticeably sour loaf. I've made the San Francisco–style boule (page 68) with a young (5-day-old) homemade starter, and though the bread was delicious, it wasn't really sour. For a very tangy loaf, give the starter a full 14 days.

TO START THE STARTER: In a medium glass bowl or large, wide-mouth jar, thoroughly stir together the flour and yeast. Stir in ⅓ cup water or enough water to yield a gravy-like consistency. Loosely drape a clean tea towel over the top. If possible, stir the mixture with a clean spoon once in a while; aeration causes more rapid development. You'll probably see bubbling whenever you stir. Let the mixture stand overnight at room temperature.

TO FEED THE STARTER: For the next 3 or 4 days, stir in another ⅓ cup of flour and ¼ to ⅓ cup more spring water daily, stirring once in a while if possible. If the mixture seems to be getting thicker, add the larger amount of water at the feeding. If it's becoming thin, add the smaller amount of water to maintain a gravy-like consistency. The mixture will gradually become more sour tasting and smelling, and may have the aroma of alcohol, too. This means it's maturing.

On the fourth or fifth day pour off and discard about a third of the mixture before feeding the starter with the usual amount of flour and water. Then continue to feed the same way as before, every day for 4 or 5 more days, allowing the quantity of starter to build up again. At this point there will be plenty to bake with and a sufficient maintenance amount left over to store.

TO LIVEN AND REFRESH THE STARTER FOR BAKING: Pour off a third of the mixture, then stir in 1 cup flour and ½ to ⅔ cup water. Let the starter stand for at least 4 hours until very bubbly before using it. Then stir it down and measure out the amount you need.

TO MAINTAIN THE STARTER: Replenish the remaining starter by stirring in the usual ½ cup flour and ¼ cup water or enough to maintain a pancake batter consistency. It's a good idea at this point to transfer the mixture to a large, clean container. Loosely cover it; don't use a tight lid. Once it is bubbly again, transfer it to the refrigerator.

After about a week, stir; then pour off about a third of the mixture; then feed the remainder by stirring in the usual ⅓ cup flour and ¼ cup water.

Return it to the refrigerator for another week, and repeat this maintenance feeding weekly.

TO REVIVE A REFRIGERATED STARTER: If left unfed for a long time, the refrigerated starter can become very sour and separate into layers. (You may also find that your sourdough loaves actually come out too sour.) Pour off most of the liquid on top, then give it a feeding (adding extra water if necessary), stir well, and set it out at room temperature. If it doesn't bubble at all, also add a tiny pinch of commercial yeast. Repeat the feedings each day for several days, pouring off some of the buildup, until it is bubbly and less sour again. The revived starter can go back in the refrigerator and kept indefinitely on its weekly maintenance feeding schedule. Pour off some of the old amount every time you feed so the quantity doesn't become too large. It's very rare for a starter to spoil even over years, but if it smells very unpleasant or moldy or has an orange color, it's time to discard it and start fresh.

sonoma-style
multigrain crunch
bread

KS QUOTIENT— Fairly Easy: Fairly long ingredient list, but easily mixed. Some hand-shaping.

4½ cups (22.5 ounces) unbleached white bread flour, plus more as needed

1½ cups (7.5 ounces) whole wheat flour

½ cup old-fashioned or quick-cooking (not instant) rolled oats

3 tablespoons yellow cornmeal, polenta, or corn grits

3 tablespoons bulgur wheat or cracked wheat, optional

2 tablespoons wheat bran

Scant 1 tablespoon table salt

1¼ teaspoons instant, fast-rising, or bread machine yeast

3 tablespoons millet seeds

3 tablespoons flax seeds

3 tablespoons sesame seeds

3 tablespoon poppy seeds

2⅔ cups ice water, plus more if needed

(continued on page 75)

This loaf was adapted (and greatly simplified) from a terrific bread recipe shared with me by Craig Ponsford, one of America's world-class bakers and founder of Artisan Bakers of Sonoma, California. Craig brought some of his beautiful multigrain loaves to a baking conference in nearby Napa, and, even though I'm not a great fan of multigrain breads, I was bowled over by the unique flavor and texture and handsome look of his version. The secret is the particular combination of nine different whole and ground grains and seeds, which adds a wonderful graininess and crunch, yet doesn't hurt the teeth and completely avoids that earnest "it's good for you, so eat it," character of some multigrain breads.

The longish list of ingredient makes the recipe a bit time-consuming to assemble, though once everything is on hand, it comes together quickly. The reward for the effort is two generous, seed-studded boules with delightfully crisp crusts. (After cooling the loaves thoroughly, stash one loaf in the freezer for great bread with no effort whatsoever.)

Yield: 2 large round loaves

FIRST RISE: In a very large bowl, thoroughly mix together the bread flour, whole wheat flour, oats, cornmeal, bulgur, wheat bran, salt, and yeast until blended. In a small bowl, combine the millet, flax, sesame, and poppy seeds. Reserve 4 tablespoons of the seed mixture for garnish, then stir the remainder into the flour mixture. In another bowl or measuring cup, whisk together the water, honey, and oil until well blended. Vigorously stir the mixture into the bowl with the flour, scraping down the bowl and mixing until very well blended. If the dough is dry and hard to blend, stir in enough more ice water to yield a moist, yet slightly stiff dough. (The seeds will absorb moisture, stiffening the dough further.) Cover the bowl tightly with nonstick spray–coated foil. If desired, for best flavor or for convenience, you can refrigerate the dough for 3 to 10 hours. Then let rise at cool room temperature for 12 to 18 hours.

SECOND RISE: Vigorously stir the dough for 1 minute; it should be very stiff. If not, thoroughly stir in enough more bread flour to make it hard to stir. Generously oil two 9-inch deep-dish pie plates, or similar-sized deep-sized ovenproof skillets, or Dutch ovens. Sprinkle 1 tablespoon of the remaining seeds in each plate. Using an oiled serrated knife or kitchen shears, cut the dough in half, then put each half in a plate. Evenly sprinkle each portion with 2 to 3 tablespoons of flour. Working in the plate, shape each portion into a ball and smooth the flour into the surface all over. Lightly dusting with flour as needed, shape each portion into a high-domed 6-inch round, smoothing and tucking the edges underneath all the way around. Generously and evenly brush each loaf with the Cornstarch Glaze (or liquid egg substitute). Immediately sprinkle the remaining seeds over the loaves. Tent them with nonstick spray–coated foil.

LET RISE USING ANY OF THESE METHODS: For a 1½- to 2½-hour regular rise, let stand at warm room temperature; for a 1- to 2-hour accelerated rise, let stand in a turned-off microwave along with 1 cup of boiling-hot water; or for an extended rise, refrigerate for 4 to 24 hours, then set out at room temperature. Continue the rise until the dough doubles from its deflated size.

BAKING PRELIMINARIES: 15 minutes before baking time, place a rack in the lower third of the oven; preheat to 450°F. Place a broiler pan on the oven floor.

BAKING: Reduce the temperature to 425°F. Immediately add a cup of water to the broiler pan—be careful of splattering and steam. Bake, uncovered, on the lower rack for 30 minutes, until the loaves are browned and firm. Remove the loaves from their pie plates, and transfer them to a baking sheet. Cover the tops with foil (leave the sides uncovered) and continue baking for 20 to 25 minutes, occasionally testing with a skewer inserted in the thickest part until it comes out with just slightly moist particles clinging to the bottom portion (or until the center registers 208° to 210°F on an instant-read thermometer). Then bake for 5 to 10 minutes more to be sure the centers are done. Let cool on wire racks for 10 minutes. Transfer the loaves to wire racks; let cool completely.

3 tablespoons clover honey or other mild honey

1½ tablespoons corn oil, canola oil, or other flavorless oil, plus extra for coating dough tops

2 tablespoons Cornstarch Glaze (page 189), or 2 tablespoons liquid egg substitute, for finishing the loaves

SERVING AND STORING: The loaves slice best when cool, but the bread is good served warm, at room temperature, or toasted. Cool completely before storing. To maintain the crisp crust, store draped with a clean kitchen towel; or to prevent the loaf from drying out, store airtight in plastic or foil. (Loaves can be re-crisped in a preheated 375ºF oven for a few minutes, if desired.) Store at room temperature for 2 to 3 days; freeze, airtight, for up to 2 months, then thaw, unwrapped, at room temperature. When thawed, re-crisp the crust in a 375ºF oven for a few minutes.

crusty yeasted
cornbread with
coarse salt

This very corny, sweet-smelling 2-pound round loaf is crusty and golden on the outside, and owing to the corn grits, slightly crunchy-chewy on the inside. It is in the style of artisan loaves, but takes none of the special skill. It is great served with a pot of chili, hearty soup, or stew. It is best when very fresh, as the crunch gradually diminishes in time.

Yield: 1 large loaf, 12 to 14 portions or slices

FIRST RISE: In a medium bowl, stir together the corn grits and boiling water until lump-free. Let stand until cooled. In a large bowl, thoroughly stir together the flour, cornmeal, sugar, table salt, and yeast. Whisk the ice water and oil into the corn grits mixture, then vigorously stir the mixture into the bowl with the flour, scraping down the sides and mixing until thoroughly blended. If too dry to mix together, add just enough more water to facilitate mixing, but don't over-moisten, as the dough should be fairly stiff. If necessary, add in enough more flour to stiffen it slightly. Brush the top with oil. Tightly cover the bowl with plastic wrap. If desired, for best flavor or for convenience, you can refrigerate the dough for 3 to 10 hours. Then let rise at cool room temperature for 12 to 18 hours; vigorously stir once partway through the rise, if convenient.

SECOND RISE: Using an oiled rubber spatula, lift and fold the dough in towards the center all the way around but don't deflate it completely; don't stir. Oil a 9- to 9½-inch deep-sided pie plate. Sprinkle 2 tablespoons of the cornmeal in the plate, then tip back and forth to spread the cornmeal on the bottom and sides. Loosen the dough from the bowl sides with an oiled rubber spatula and gently invert it into the plate. Sprinkle the dough with more cornmeal. Pat and press it into the dough with your fingertips. Then firmly tuck the sides of the loaf underneath all the way around to form a smooth, round, high domed loaf, about 7 inches in diameter.

KS QUOTIENT— Easy: Fuss-free ingredients, added before the first rise. Some hand-shaping required.

⅓ cup corn grits (or substitute very coarse uncooked polenta)

⅓ cup boiling water

2¾ cups (13.75 ounces) unbleached white bread flour, plus more as needed

1 cup cornmeal, preferably yellow, plus about 6 tablespoons for dusting the dough and pie plate

2 tablespoons granulated sugar

Scant 1¼ teaspoons table salt

¾ teaspoon instant, fast-rising, or bread machine yeast

1⅔ cups ice water, plus more if needed

1½ tablespoons corn oil or other flavorless vegetable oil, plus more for brushing dough top and pie plate

¼ to ½ teaspoon coarse salt for garnish

Using well-oiled kitchen shears or a serrated knife, cut 5 or 6 2-inch curved shallow slashes radiating from the center of the dome to create a pinwheel effect. Tent with nonstick spray–coated foil.

LET RISE USING ANY OF THESE METHODS: For a 1½- to 2½-hour regular rise, let stand at warm room temperature; for a 1- to 2-hour accelerated rise, let stand in a turned-off microwave along with 1 cup of boiling-hot water; or for an extended rise, refrigerate for 4 to 24 hours, then set out at room temperature. Continue the rise until the dough doubles from its deflated size, removing the foil if the dough reaches it.

BAKING PRELIMINARIES: 20 minutes before baking time, put a rack in the lower third of the oven; preheat to 450°F. Set a broiler pan on the oven floor. Generously sprinkle the loaf top with water. Immediately sprinkle the top with the coarse salt.

BAKING: Put 1 cup ice water in the broiler pan; watch out for steam. Reduce the heat to 425°F. Bake, uncovered, on the lower rack for 25 to 30 minutes, until the top is nicely browned and the loaf is firm. Transfer the loaf from the pie plate to a baking sheet. Cover the top loosely with a square of foil; the sides of the loaf should remain uncovered. Bake for 30 to 35 minutes more, until a skewer inserted in the thickest part comes out with just a few particles clinging to the bottom portion (or until the center registers 208° to 210°F on an instant-read thermometer). Then bake for 5 to 10 minutes more to be sure the center is done. Cool in the pan on a wire rack for 15 minutes. Remove the loaf to the rack; let cool completely.

SERVING AND STORING: Serve the bread warm, or cooled, cut into wedges or crosswise into slices. To maintain the crisp crust, store wrapped in a clean tea towel or heavy paper bag. If desired, re-warm, uncovered, on a baking sheet in a 400°F oven for a few minutes. The bread will keep at room temperature for 2 days, and may be frozen, airtight, for up to 1 month.

easy buttermilk
pot bread with coarse salt

KS QUOTIENT— Easy: Fuss-free ingredients; two-stage mixing. No hand-shaping.

Puffy, and crusty, and faintly tangy, this big, craggy-topped loaf is such good eating it may become a standard in your repertoire. Since the dough is baked in a lidded Dutch oven, it usually springs up a lot and is light and airy. The acid in the buttermilk also makes the crumb moist and tender. Sprinkling the top with coarse salt is a contemporary touch that I think adds to the appeal, but feel free to omit it if you prefer a more old-fashioned loaf.

Buttermilk breads have been popular with American home bakers for decades, not only because these loaves are tasty and fuss-free, but also because in the past they used up leftover buttermilk. When families still churned their own butter, buttermilk was the butter-flecked liquid remaining after the fat separated out from the cream and formed butter.

Yield: 1 large loaf, 12 to 14 wedges or slices

4 cups (20 ounces) unbleached white bread flour or unbleached all-purpose white flour, plus ½ cup (2.5 ounces), plus more as needed

2 tablespoons granulated sugar

Scant 1¾ teaspoons table salt (increase to 2 teaspoons if coarse salt garnish is omitted)

¾ teaspoon instant, fast-rising, or bread machine yeast

Corn oil, canola oil, or other flavorless vegetable oil for coating dough

1¾ cups plus 2 tablespoons ice water, plus more if needed

⅓ cup dried buttermilk powder

2 tablespoons unsalted butter, melted and cooled slightly

¾ teaspoon coarse crystal salt for garnish, optional

FIRST RISE: In a large bowl, thoroughly stir together 4 cups of the flour, the sugar, salt, and yeast. Thoroughly stir the water into the bowl, scraping down the sides until the ingredients are thoroughly blended. If the mixture is too dry to incorporate all the flour, a bit at a time, stir in just enough more ice water to blend the ingredients; don't over-moisten, as the dough should be slightly stiff. If it is very soft, stir in enough flour to firm it slightly. Brush or spray the top with oil. Cover the bowl with plastic wrap. If desired, for best flavor or for convenience, you can refrigerate the dough for 3 to 10 hours. Then let rise at cool room temperature for 12 to 18 hours.

SECOND RISE: Vigorously stir the buttermilk powder and butter into the dough until evenly and thoroughly incorporated. (Or use a dough hook and heavy-duty mixer on low speed, if desired.) Then, thoroughly incorporate the remaining ½ cup flour, plus enough more to make the dough very stiff. Scrape down the bowl sides thoroughly. Using an oiled rubber spatula, lift and fold the dough in towards the center all the way around.

Evenly brush or spray the dough top with oil. Cover the bowl with nonstick spray–coated plastic wrap.

LET RISE USING ANY OF THESE METHODS: For a 1½- to 2½-hour regular rise, let stand at warm room temperature; for a 1- to 2-hour accelerated rise, let stand in a turned-off microwave along with 1 cup of boiling-hot water; or for an extended rise, refrigerate for 4 to 24 hours, then set out at room temperature. Continue the rise until the dough doubles from its original size, removing the plastic if the dough nears it.

BAKING PRELIMINARIES: 20 minutes before baking time, put a rack in the lower third of the oven; preheat to 450°F. Heat a 4-quart Dutch oven or similar heavy metal pot in the oven until sizzling hot (check with a few drops of water), then remove it, using heavy mitts. Taking care not to deflate the dough (or burn yourself), loosen it from the bowl sides with an oiled rubber spatula and gently invert it into the pot. Don't worry if it's lopsided and ragged-looking; it will even out during baking. Lightly spritz or brush the dough top with water. Then evenly sprinkle over the coarse salt. Slash a large, ¼-inch-deep × in the dough top with well-oiled kitchen shears. Immediately top the pot with the lid. Shake the pot back and forth to center the dough.

BAKING: Lower the heat to 425°F. Bake on the lower rack for 50 to 55 minutes or until puffed and firm on top. If the loaf is nicely browned, continue baking with the lid on; if the loaf looks pale, remove the lid. Bake for 10 to 15 minutes longer, until the top is well browned and crusty and a skewer inserted in the thickest part comes out with just a few crumbs on the tip (or until center registers 205° to 207°F on an instant-read thermometer). Then, bake for 5 to 10 minutes longer to ensure the center is baked through. Cool in the pan on a wire rack for 10 to 15 minutes. Remove the loaf to the rack. Cool thoroughly.

SERVING AND STORING: Cut the loaf into wedges or crosswise slices; it tastes good warm, but will cut much better when cool. Cool completely before storing. To maintain the crisp crust, store draped with a clean tea towel or in a heavy paper bag. Or store airtight in a plastic bag or wrapped in foil: The crust will soften, but can be crisped by heating the loaf, uncovered, in a 400°F oven for a few minutes. The bread will keep at room temperature for 3 days, and may be frozen, airtight, for up to 2 months.

cheddar and chiles bread

The Hispanic influence on American culture over the past decades has been pervasive and shows up not only in the popularity of Mexican and Tex-Mex fare, but also in the widespread availability of ingredients like assorted chiles. Once found only in ethnic communities and markets, green chiles turn up in everything from soups and quiches to corn casseroles and both quick and yeast breads. (If you aren't familiar with green chiles, note that they are just slightly piquant; they are not the same as jalapeños.)

This is a delightfuly savory bread, particularly if a top-quality white cheddar is used. The loaf is shot through with cheese and bits of green chiles, and the crust is golden brown. It is great with chili, hearty, full-bodied soups, and bean dishes; it also makes an unusual but very appealing sandwich bread.

For a different look and milder taste, prepare the equally easy cheddar and pimiento variation provided at the end of the recipe.

Yield: 1 large loaf, 12 to 14 slices each

3½ cups (17.5 ounces) unbleached white bread flour, plus more as needed

1 tablespoon granulated sugar

1½ teaspoons table salt

1 teaspoon instant, fast-rising, or bread machine yeast

2 tablespoons corn oil, canola oil, or other flavorless vegetable oil, plus extra for coating dough top and baking pan

1⅔ cups ice water, plus more if needed

8 ounces (3 lightly packed cups) coarsely grated very sharp cheddar cheese, preferably white cheddar

½ cup very well-drained and patted dry chopped canned green chiles

FIRST RISE: In a large bowl, thoroughly stir together the flour, sugar, salt, and yeast. In another bowl or measuring cup, whisk the oil into the water. Thoroughly stir the mixture into the bowl with the flour, scraping down the sides until the ingredients are thoroughly blended. If the mixture is too dry to incorporate all the flour, a bit at a time, stir in just enough more ice water to blend the ingredients; don't over-moisten, as the dough should be stiff. If necessary, stir in enough more flour to stiffen it. Brush or spray the top with oil. Cover the bowl with plastic wrap. If desired, for best flavor or for convenience, you can refrigerate the dough for 3 to 10 hours. Then let rise at cool room temperature for 15 to 20 hours. If convenient, stir the dough once partway through the rise.

SECOND RISE: Vigorously stir the dough, gradually sprinkling over and incorporating the cheese and chiles. Fold them in very thoroughly to ensure they are evenly distributed . If necessary, thoroughly stir in enough more flour to yield a very stiff dough. Using a well-oiled rubber spatula, fold the dough in towards the center, working all the way around the bowl. Invert the dough into a well-greased 9 × 5-inch loaf pan. Evenly brush or spray the dough top with oil. Using well-oiled kitchen shears or a serrated knife, make a ¼-inch-deep slash lengthwise down the center of the loaf. Cover the pan with nonstick spray–coated plastic wrap.

LET RISE USING ANY OF THESE METHODS: For a 1½- to 2½-hour regular rise, let stand at warm room temperature; for a 1- to 2-hour accelerated rise, let stand in a turned-off microwave along with 1 cup of boiling-hot water; or for an extended rise, refrigerate for 4 to 24 hours, then set out at room temperature. Continue the rise until the dough nears the plastic. Remove it and continue until the dough reaches ½ inch above the pan rim.

BAKING PRELIMINARIES: 15 minutes before baking time, place a rack in the lower third of the oven; preheat to 425°F.

BAKING: Reduce the heat to 400°F. Bake for 30 to 40 minutes, until the top is nicely browned; cover the top with foil as needed. Continue baking for 20 to 30 minutes longer, or until a skewer inserted in the thickest part comes out with just a few particles clinging to the bottom (or until the center registers 204° to 206°F on an instant-read thermometer). Then bake for 5 minutes more to be sure the center is done. Cool in the pan on a wire rack for 10 minutes. Turn out the loaf onto the rack; cool thoroughly.

SERVING AND STORING: Cool thoroughly before slicing or storing. Store airtight in plastic or aluminum foil. The bread will keep at room temperature for 2 to 3 days, and may be frozen, airtight, for up to 2 months.

VARIATION CHEDDAR AND PIMIENTO BREAD—Omit the green chiles and substitute an equal amount of well-drained and patted dry chopped jarred pimientos. Otherwise proceed exactly as directed.

Easy Buttermilk Pot Bread with Coarse Salt (page 79)

Opposite: **Cheddar and Chiles Bread** (page 81)
Above: **Cherry and Chocolate Coffee Ring with Kirsch** (page 179)

Above: **Cinnamon Pinwheel Raisin Bread** (page 66)
Opposite: **Easy Cinnamon Sticky Buns** (page 90)

Opposite: **Crunchy-Munchy Pumpkin, Sunflower, and Flax Seed Boule** (page 146)
Above: **Crusty White Peasant-Style Pot Bread, Rosemary and Olive variation** (page 31)

Above: **Double Chocolate—Honey Bread** (page 54)
Opposite: **Easy Oat Bread** (page 39)

Opposite: **Rosemary Foccacia with Coarse Salt** (page 110)
Above: **Going with the Grain Bread Kit** (page 184)

Above: **Great Granola Breakfast Bread** (page 43)
Opposite: **Tomato Sauce and Mozzarella Pizza** (page 116)

Opposite: **Crusty Portuguese-American Yeasted Cornbread** (page 36)
Above: **Pull-Apart Butter-Top Rolls** (page 63)

Simple Streusel Coffeecake (page 166)

farmhouse potato bread with dill and chives

Dill, chives, and yogurt are all wonderful companions for potatoes, and they are absolute dynamite in this homey, savory bread. The herbal aroma given off during baking is so tantalizing that I find myself pacing around the oven, repeatedly checking to see if the loaf is done. It's difficult to slice while hot and tastes better once it's cooled, but I usually saw off an end and scarf it down anyway.

The exterior of the loaf is nicely crispy; its interior is tender-moist and stays that way, due to the touch of yogurt. (Some older versions of this bread call for cottage cheese instead, but it has to be pureed first and doesn't taste nearly as good.) This bread seems tailor-made for serving along with roast chicken, baked fish, or steaming bowls of tomato soup.

Yield: 1 large loaf, 12 to 14 slices

FIRST RISE: In a large bowl, thoroughly stir together 2 cups of the flour, the sugar, salt, and yeast. In another bowl or measuring cup, whisk the oil into the water. Thoroughly stir the mixture into the bowl with the flour, scraping down the sides and mixing to form a smooth, well-blended dough; it should be slightly moist and fairly easy to stir. Brush the top with oil. Cover the bowl tightly with plastic wrap. If desired, for best flavor or for convenience, you can refrigerate the dough for 3 to 10 hours. Then let rise at cool room temperature for 12 to 18 hours.

SECOND RISE: In a medium bowl, stir together the mashed potatoes, yogurt, dill, chives, and 1 teaspoon of the dill seeds (if using) until the potato is free of lumps. Vigorously stir the mixture into the dough until completely blended. (If desired, use a dough hook and heavy-duty mixer on low speed.) Scraping down the sides as you work, thoroughly mix in the remaining 1 cup of flour, plus enough more flour to yield a hard-to-stir dough.

2 cups (10 ounces) unbleached white bread flour, plus 1 cup (5 ounces), plus more as needed

1½ tablespoons granulated sugar

1½ teaspoons table salt

¾ teaspoon instant, fast-rising, or bread machine yeast

2 tablespoons corn oil, canola oil, or other flavorless vegetable oil, plus extra for coating dough top and baking pan

1 cup plus 2 tablespoons ice water, plus more if needed

⅓ cup leftover mashed potatoes, preferably at room temperature

⅓ cup plain low-fat or nonfat yogurt, drained of any liquid, preferably at room temperature

¼ cup finely chopped fresh dillweed

¼ cup finely chopped fresh chives

1 teaspoon dill seeds, plus ½ teaspoon for garnish, optional

Using an oiled rubber spatula, lift and fold the dough in towards the center all the way around the bowl. Invert into a 9 × 5-inch loaf pan. Brush or spray the top with oil. Smooth out the dough top with the spatula or oiled fingertips. If using dill seeds, sprinkle ½ teaspoon over the loaf top, pressing down to imbed. Cover the pan with nonstick spray–coated plastic wrap.

LET RISE USING ANY OF THESE METHODS: For a 2- to 2½-hour regular rise, let stand at warm room temperature; for a 1- to 1½-hour accelerated rise, let stand in a turned-off microwave along with 1 cup of boiling-hot water; or for an extended rise, refrigerate for 4 to 24 hours, then set out at room temperature. When the dough nears the plastic, remove it and continue the rise until the dough just reaches the pan rim.

BAKING PRELIMINARIES: 15 minutes before baking time, place a rack in the lower third of the oven; preheat to 375°F. Using well-oiled kitchen shears, cut a ¼-inch-deep slash lengthwise down the loaf center.

BAKING: Bake on the lower rack for 50 to 55 minutes, or until the loaf is golden brown. Cover the top with foil to prevent over-browning and continue baking for 15 to 20 minutes longer, until a skewer inserted in the thickest part comes out with just a few particles clinging to the bottom (or until the center registers 208° to 210 °F on an instant-read thermometer). Bake for 5 minutes longer to be sure the center is done. Cool in the pan on a wire rack for 10 minutes. Turn out onto the rack; cool thoroughly.

SERVING AND STORING: Serve warm, or cool, or toasted; the bread slices best when cool. Cool thoroughly before storing in plastic or foil. Keeps at room temperature for 2 to 3 days. May be frozen, airtight, for up to 2 months.

VARIATION FARMHOUSE POTATO BREAD—Increase the sugar to 3 tablespoons. Omit the dillweed, chives, and dill seeds from the recipe but otherwise proceed exactly as directed.

TIP: Don't use dried dillweed or chives, as they will contribute nothing but flecks of color. If you lack fresh herbs, make the plain potato bread variation below. And don't use extra herbs, as they can retard rising.

anadama
bread

Anadama breads have been around since at least the mid-nineteenth century, and most often appear in old-fashioned New England cookbooks. This is not surprising, since cornmeal and molasses often teamed up in dishes in the region in Colonial times; Indian pudding, Boston brown bread, and anadama bread are just several of the many heritage recipes still being prepared that take great advantage of this twosome.

The combination is particularly pleasant in anadama bread. Both the touch of molasses and the cornmeal add gentle fragrance and flavor. And because the cornmeal absorbs a lot of moisture and becomes mush-like when boiling water is poured over it, it helps keep the loaf very moist. A comfort food of the highest order, this bread goes well with white chowders, mild soups, and other gently seasoned dishes. I also like it for toast.

Yield: 1 large loaf, about 12 to 15 slices each

½ cup boiling water

½ cup stone-ground yellow cornmeal

3 tablespoons light or dark molasses

2¾ cups (13.75 ounces) unbleached all-purpose white flour, plus ½ cup (2.5 ounces), plus more as needed

Generous 1½ teaspoons table salt

¾ teaspoon instant, fast-rising, or bread machine yeast

1 cup plus 2 tablespoons ice water, plus more if needed

Corn oil, canola oil, or other flavorless vegetable oil or oil spray for loaf top

1 large egg, at room temperature and beaten with a fork

2 tablespoons unsalted butter, melted and cooled slightly

FIRST RISE: In a medium bowl, gradually stir the boiling water into the cornmeal until smoothly incorporated. Let cool to warm, then stir in the molasses until evenly incorporated. In a large bowl, thoroughly stir together 2¾ cups of the flour, the salt, and yeast. Vigorously stir the ice water into the cooled cornmeal until very smoothly blended. Then vigorously stir the cornmeal mixture into the bowl with the flour, scraping down the sides until the ingredients are thoroughly blended. If too dry to mix completely, a bit at a time, stir in just enough more ice water to blend the ingredients; don't over-moisten, as the dough should be fairly stiff. Brush or spray the top with vegetable oil. Cover the bowl with plastic wrap. If desired, for best flavor or for convenience, you can refrigerate the dough for 3 to 10 hours. Then let rise at cool room temperature for 12 to 18 hours.

SECOND RISE: Vigorously stir the beaten egg, butter, and remaining ½ cup of flour into the dough. (If desired, use a dough hook and heavy-duty mixer on low speed.) Then vigorously stir in enough more flour to yield a hard-to-stir dough. Using an oiled rubber spatula, lift and fold the dough in towards the center all the way around; this organizes the gluten for forming a loaf. Invert the dough into a generously greased 9 × 5-inch loaf pan. Brush or spray the top with oil. Using the spatula, smooth out the surface and press the dough evenly into the pan. Cover the pan with non-stick spray–coated plastic.

LET RISE USING ANY OF THESE METHODS: For a 1½- to 2½-hour regular rise, let stand at warm room temperature; for a 1- to 2-hour accelerated rise, let stand in a turned-off microwave along with 1 cup of boiling-hot water; or for an extended rise, refrigerate for 4 to 24 hours, then set out at room temperature. Continue the rise until the dough nears the plastic. Remove it and continue until the dough extends ½ inch above the pan rim.

BAKING PRELIMINARIES: 15 minutes before baking time, place a rack in the lower third of the oven; preheat to 375°F.

BAKING: Bake for 50 to 60 minutes, covering the top with foil for the last few minutes if necessary to prevent over-browning. Continue baking for 10 to 15 minutes more or until a skewer inserted in the thickest part comes out with just a few particles on the end (or until the center registers 207° to 209°F on an instant-read thermometer). Bake for 5 minutes longer to be sure the center is done. Cool in the pan on a wire rack for 10 minutes. Turn out onto the rack; cool thoroughly.

SERVING AND STORING: Serve warm, or cool, or toasted; the bread slices best when cool. Cool thoroughly before storing in plastic or foil. Keeps at room temperature for up to 3 days. May be frozen, airtight, for up to 2 months.

cronshi's
challah

KS QUOTIENT— Easy: Fuss-free ingredients; two-stage mixing. Hand-shaping required.

My friend Cronshi makes challah regularly, and says she has used the traditional version of this recipe more than 100 times. When she heard about my *Kneadlessly Simple* method she asked me to rework her recipe to reduce her time spent baking each week. Now, except for the shaping and braiding, her bread takes only a few minutes of effort here and there. She likes to made four-strand loaves, and even if you've never braided bread before, this dough is so easy to handle you can do it, too. (I have also included instructions for a three-strand braid, in case you're more comfortable starting with that instead.)

This is a nice, middle-of-the-road challah with a pleasant but not overpowering egg and honey taste and a handsome golden crust. *Challah* originally referred to a sacred bread offering that was given to the priests, but has come to mean an enriched one special enough to serve on the Sabbath. Challah originated in eastern Europe, but is now a staple in many Jewish-American homes. **Yield: 2 large braided loaves**

5⅓ cups (26.66 ounces) unbleached all-purpose white flour, plus 1⅓ cups (6.66 ounces), plus more as needed

2¼ teaspoons table salt

1¼ teaspoons instant, fast-rising, or bread machine yeast

⅓ cup clover honey or other mild honey

¼ cup corn oil, canola oil, or other flavorless vegetable oil, plus extra for coating dough top and baking pan

2¼ cups ice water, plus more if needed

2 large eggs plus 1 large egg yolk, at room temperature and beaten with a fork

1 egg beaten with 2 teaspoons water for egg wash garnish

2 to 3 tablespoons poppy seeds or sesame seeds for garnish, optional

FIRST RISE: In a very large bowl, thoroughly stir together 5⅓ cups of the flour, the salt, and yeast. In another bowl or measuring cup, thoroughly whisk the honey and oil into the water. Then vigorously stir the mixture into the bowl with the flour, scraping down the sides and mixing until thoroughly blended. If too dry to blend together, add just enough more water to facilitate mixing, but don't over-moisten, as the dough should be stiff. If necessary, stir in enough more flour to stiffen it. Brush or spray the top with oil. Cover the bowl with plastic wrap. If desired, for best flavor or for convenience, you can refrigerate the dough for 3 to 10 hours. Then let rise at cool room temperature for 12 to 18 hours.

SECOND RISE: A little at a time, vigorously stir the beaten egg-yolk mixture into the dough. (Or use a dough hook and heavy-duty stand mixer on low speed.) Then vigorously stir in the remaining 1⅓ cups of flour, plus enough more flour to yield a hard-to-stir consistency. Let rest for 10 minutes. Spray two 15-inch-long sheets of baking parchment with non-stick spray, then dust each generously with flour. With well-oiled kitchen shears, cut the dough in half; each half will form a loaf. Then divide one of the halves into 3 or 4 equal pieces, placing them separated on a well-floured work surface. One at a time, dust the pieces all over with flour, smoothing it in until the dough is easy to handle. Working on a clean, flour-dusted work surface and using your palms, roll the 3 or 4 pieces into 12-inch-long strands, dusting with flour as needed to prevent sticking. Taper the strands so they are 2½ to 3 inches thick in the middle and about 1 inch thick at the ends. Lay the strands side by side on the parchment. Form a braid as follows:

For a 3-strand braid: Starting in the center of the strands and working to one end, lift the left strand over the center one, so the left one is in the center position. Lift the right strand over the center one, so the right one is in the center position. Repeat the process, lifting the leftmost strand, then the rightmost, until the end is reached. Then, start in the center again and braid the second half out to the end. Tuck and press the ends underneath.

For a 4-strand braid: Starting from the center and working outward, lift the far left strand over the next one to its right, then under the next one to its right, then over the far right strand. Working from the strand now at the far left, lift it over the one to its right, then under the next one, then over the far right strand. Repeat the pattern, always working from the left to the right until the end is reached. Then, start in the center of the strands again and braid the second half out to the end, working from left to right as before. Tuck and press the ends underneath.

Transfer the braid to a well-oiled baking sheet. Spray or brush the dough top with oil. Tent the pan with nonstick spray–coated foil. Repeat the preparations for the second 3- or 4-strand loaf.

LET RISE USING ANY OF THESE METHODS: For a 1½- to 2½-hour regular rise, let stand at warm room temperature; for a 1- to 1½-hour accelerated rise, let stand in a turned-off microwave along with 1 cup of boiling-hot water; or for an extended rise, refrigerate for 4 to 48 hours, then set out at room temperature. Let rise until the loaves double from their original size, removing the foil as the dough reaches it.

BAKING PRELIMINARIES: 15 minutes before baking time, place a rack in the lower third of the oven; preheat to 375°F. Brush each loaf evenly with the egg wash; be sure to reach the nooks and crannies of the braid, wiping up any egg from the baking sheet. Immediately evenly sprinkle the loaves with poppy (or sesame) seeds, if desired.

BAKING: Bake on the lower rack for 25 to 35 minutes, or until the tops are well browned. Then cover with foil and continue baking for 25 to 30 minutes longer, until a skewer inserted in the thickest part comes out with just a few particles on the end (or until the center registers 201° to 203°F on an instant-read thermometer). Then bake for 5 to 10 minutes more to make sure the centers are done. Cool on the pan on a wire rack for 10 minutes. Set the loaves on the rack; cool thoroughly.

SERVING AND STORING: Serve warm, or cool, or toasted; the bread slices best when cool. Cool thoroughly before storing in plastic or foil. Keeps at room temperature for 3 days. May be frozen, airtight, for up to 2 months.

easy cinnamon sticky buns

½ batch Easy White Bread dough (page 29), stirred and ready for the second rise

¾ cup plus 2 tablespoons packed light brown sugar

⅔ cup (3.33 ounces) unbleached white bread flour or all-purpose white flour, plus more as needed

1 tablespoon ground cinnamon

½ cup (1 stick) cool, firm unsalted butter, cut into ⅓-inch pieces, plus ⅓ cup more, melted, for muffin cups

½ cup dark raisins, rinsed under hot water, thoroughly drained, and patted dry, or ½ cup chopped walnuts, optional

18 tablespoons (1 cup plus 2 tablespoons) dark corn syrup

Most sticky buns are formed by rolling dough around a cinnamon-sugar mixture and fashioning pinwheel rolls, but these deliver the same luscious taste while skipping the fussy shaping. The dough is simply studded with little pockets and swirls of a buttery, cinnamon-sugar streusel and bathed in a gooey brown sugar sauce that forms on the bottom during baking. The buns are simultaneously shaped and baked in jumbo-size muffin cups (ones with a volume of about 1 cup each), then served inverted. So, the "tops" stay soft and the succulent sauce flows down the bun sides—yum-my!

These are best eaten right out of the oven, so the refrigerator rise option, which lets you hold the buns for up to two days until ready for them, is particularly convenient. About 2½ to 3 hours before baking, allow them to warm up and finish rising on the counter, then pop them into the oven, bake, sample, and swoon!

The following buns are made from a half batch of the Easy White Bread Loaves recipe (page 29). Use the other half to prepare a loaf of bread as directed in the original recipe. **Yield: 12 large buns**

SECOND RISE: Have on hand half a batch of Easy White Bread dough, ready for the second rise. Prepare the sticky bun streusel by briefly processing together the brown sugar, ⅔ cup flour, and cinnamon in a food processor. Add the butter pieces. Pulse the processor on and off until the mixture looks like coarse crumbs. (Alternatively, combine the dry ingredients in a bowl and cut in the butter using forks or a pastry blender.)

Vigorously stir ½ cup of crumb mixture and the raisins or nuts (if using) into the dough until fairly evenly distributed; it's all right if some patches of crumbs remain. Evenly coat 12 jumbo-size muffin cups with melted butter. Put 1 teaspoon melted butter, 1½ tablespoons corn syrup, then 1 tablespoon of the crumb mixture in each cup. Cut the dough in half with well-oiled kitchen shears, then divide each half equally among 6 cups; dust the dough with a little flour for ease of handling, if desired. Sprinkle the remaining crumb mixture over the dough portions, dividing it equally among them. Press down firmly on each with well-greased fingertips to imbed the crumbs. Drizzle any remaining butter over the tops. Tent the muffin tins with nonstick spray–coated foil.

LET RISE USING ANY OF THESE METHODS: For a 1½- to 2½-hour regular rise, let stand at warm room temperature; for a 45-minute to 1½-hour accelerated rise, let stand in a turned-off microwave along with 1 cup of boiling-hot water; or for an extended rise, refrigerate for 4 to 48 hours, then set out at room temperature. When the dough nears the foil, remove it and continue the rise until the dough doubles from the original size or extends about two-thirds of the way up the cup sides.

BAKING PRELIMINARIES: 15 minutes before baking time, place a rack in the lower third of the oven; preheat to 350°F. Set the muffin tins on a large rimmed baking sheet (to catch any boil-overs of the sauce).

BAKING: Bake on the lower rack until nicely browned on top, 20 to 25 minutes, or until a skewer inserted in the thickest part comes out with only a few particles at the bottom (or the centers register 200° to 202°F on an instant-read thermometer). Remove to a wire rack and immediately run a knife around the buns to loosen. Place a heat-proof cutting board flat against the muffin tin, then invert the tin and shake to remove the buns; the bottoms will become the tops. Transfer the buns to a serving plate. Scrape any sauce clinging to the cups out onto the buns; serve immediately.

SERVING AND STORING: These are best served hot and fresh. They will keep at cool room temperature for up to 2 days. Freeze, airtight, for longer storage. Reheat, wrapped in foil, in a low oven (or under a plastic cover at low power in the microwave for about 20 seconds) before serving.

good and easy
pecan sticky buns
(OR SAUCY MAPLE-BUTTER STICKY BUNS)

KS QUOTIENT— Easy: Fuss-free ingredients, added all at once. No hand-shaping required.

½ batch Easy White Bread dough (page 29), stirred and ready for the second rise

½ cup dark raisins, rinsed under hot water, thoroughly drained, and patted dry, optional

6 tablespoons (¾ stick) unsalted butter, melted and slightly cooled

1½ cups chopped pecans

1 recipe Caramel Sticky Bun Sauce (page 194) or Maple-Butter Sticky Bun Sauce (page 195), at room temperature

Unbleached white bread flour or all-purpose white flour if needed for dusting

Though remarkably easy, these, as the Keebler elf might say, are uncommonly good. You may never want to bother with the fussier traditional versions of this all-American favorite again.

Unlike most sticky buns, these require no hand-shaping, so they are perfect for people lacking the time or expertise to fiddle with that task. The dough—half a batch of the Easy White Bread recipe—is quickly divided up and shaped as it bakes in muffin pans. The sticky bun sauce can be readied well ahead (as can the dough), making the preparations before the second rise very simple. For convenience, the second rise can take place in the refrigerator, so you can hold the rolls up to 48 hours before baking.

The following buns require only a half-batch of the dough recipe; use the other half to ready a loaf of bread as directed in the original recipe. For the dozen buns, you'll need two 6-cup muffin tins with "jumbo," or "Texas-size" cups—that is, cups measuring 3½ to 3¾ inches across and with a volume of about 1 cup each. **Yield: 12 large sticky buns**

SECOND RISE: Have on hand half a batch of Easy White Bread dough, ready for the second rise. Vigorously stir the raisins into the dough until evenly distributed, if using.

Brush the 12 muffin cups generously with butter, then add a scant ½ tablespoon butter to each cup. Sprinkle ½ tablespoon nuts in each cup, followed by 1 tablespoon sticky bun sauce. Divide the dough in half, dusting with a little flour if needed for easier handling. Using well-oiled kitchen shears and fingertips, cut each half into 6 equal portions, placing them in the muffin cups as you work. Drizzle the dough tops with another ½ tablespoon sauce, then sprinkle each with ½ tablespoon more nuts. Sprinkle any remaining nuts over the dough tops. Drizzle the cups with the remaining butter. Press down firmly on each top to imbed the nuts.

Tent the muffin tins with nonstick spray–coated foil. Set the remaining sauce aside to brush the dough during baking.

LET RISE USING ANY OF THESE METHODS: For a 1½- to 2½-hour regular rise, let stand at warm room temperature; for a 45-minute to 1½-hour accelerated rise, let stand in a turned-off microwave along with 1 cup of boiling-hot water; or for an extended rise, refrigerate for 4 to 48 hours, then set out at room temperature. When the dough nears the foil, remove it and continue the rise until the dough doubles in bulk or extends two-thirds of the way up the cup sides.

BAKING PRELIMINARIES: 15 minutes before baking time, place a rack in the lower third of the oven; preheat to 375°F. Set the muffin tins on a large rimmed baking sheet (to catch any boil-overs of the sauce).

BAKING: Bake on the lower rack until nicely browned on top, 18 to 22 minutes, or until a skewer inserted in the thickest part comes out with only a few particles at the bottom end (or the centers register to 200° to 203 °F on an instant-read thermometer). Brush each top with the remaining sticky bun sauce, dividing it equally among them. Return to the oven and bake until the sauce begins to bubble, about 3 minutes longer. Remove the pans to a wire rack for 5 minutes. Immediately run a knife around the buns to loosen. Place a heat-proof cutting board flat against the muffin tin, then invert the tin and shake to remove the buns; the bottoms will become the tops. Transfer to a serving plate. Scrape any sauce and nuts clinging to the cups out onto the buns; serve immediately.

SERVING AND STORING: These are best served warm. They will keep at cool room temperature for up to 2 days. Freeze, airtight, for longer storage. Reheat, wrapped in foil, in a low oven (or under a microwave-safe cover on low power in the microwave) before serving.

old-world classics

A NUMBER OF TODAY'S FAVORITE ARTISAN-STYLE BREADS— from the French fougasse and baguette to the Italian flatbread trio: ciabatta, focaccia, and pizza—are in this chapter. Considering the enormous appeal of all of these, it's amazing how few ingredients they require. The secret is in the slow rising, which deepens the yeasty flavor and aroma. It's also in the details like dough consistency, shaping, and oven temperature, which yield the characteristic crackly, chewy, or crunchy-crisp texture desired.

Of course, not all European breads are of the crusty sort. For example, *pain d'epice* and *pain aux noix* (spice bread and walnut bread) and brioche are all soft-textured French breads, suitable for spreading with cream cheese or butter. And both Swedish limpa (a rye loaf with a subtle, intriguing taste) and Scottish oatmeal bread are superior toasting and snacking breads.

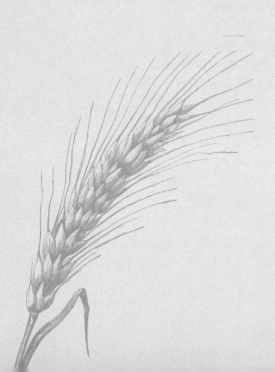

pain ordinaire

(EVERYDAY FRENCH BAGUETTES OR BÂTARDS)

KS QUOTIENT— Fairly Easy: Fuss-free ingredients, added all at once. Hand-shaping required.

It seems ironic that the most magnificent of French breads, the baguette, is called *pain ordinaire*, meaning ordinary, or everyday, bread. True, the ingredients are few in number and completely ordinary, but good baguettes are a thing of beauty, combining a shatteringly, breathtakingly crisp crust; soft, moist, yeasty interior; and a simple, balanced shape brilliantly designed for breaking, not sawing, a loaf into portions.

The *Kneadlessly Simple* method is well-suited to making fine-tasting baguettes because the long, slow, retarded rise coaxes out as much flavor as possible from the flour and yeast, which are, of course, all you've got to work with besides the salt. (Some bakers feel that using sea salt and spring water can add a flavor dimension, but in my blind tastings, almost nobody—including me—noticed any difference.) The "micro kneading" that naturally occurs during the lengthy rise also ensures thorough gluten development, an essential for the good loaf structure. And, the more fully hydrated *Kneadlessly Simple* dough keeps the interior of the loaves soft longer than is normal for French bread—for up to three or four days!

The only "gotcha" is the shaping, which is really just a matter of practice. Plus, the loaves will taste wonderful and seem impressive even if they don't look quite as perfect as those from a French bakery. Moreover, you've also got a convenient fallback position: If your baguettes come out looking a little stubby, just say you were aiming for the slightly shorter loaves called *bâtards!* (Or that longer loaves wouldn't fit in your oven!)

This recipe requires a two-loaf baguette tray, but not to worry—if you don't have one on hand it's easy to fashion homemade trays from heavy-duty aluminum foil; see the sidebar for instructions. This dough can also be used to make another attractively shaped loaf called a *fougasse* (see page 100 for instructions). **Yield: Two 14-inch baguettes (or 10-inch *bâtards*)**

3¼ cups (16.25 ounces) unbleached all-purpose white flour or white bread flour, plus more as needed

1½ teaspoons table salt

¾ teaspoon instant, fast-rising, or bread machine yeast

1½ cups ice water, plus more if needed

Corn oil, canola oil, or other flavorless vegetable oil for coating dough and pan

Tear off two 20-inch-long sheets from a large (18-inch-wide) roll of heavy-duty foil. Lay one sheet on top of the other, shiny sides facing. (The dull side promotes browning better than the shiny side.) Working from an 18-inch side, fold the two layers in half, producing a long, sturdy 10-inch-wide strip. Still working from the 18-inch side, fold the strip in half, then pinch and press together along the fold line to produce a sturdy 2-inch-high center pleat. Next, working just below the pleat, open the two foil layers out away from the pleat on each side and bend them to create two parallel, connected U-shaped troughs. Lay the tray on a large rimmed baking sheet.

FIRST RISE: In a large bowl, thoroughly stir together the flour, salt, and yeast. Vigorously stir the water into the bowl, scraping down the sides and mixing until the ingredients are thoroughly blended. If the mixture is too dry to incorporate all the flour, a bit at a time, stir in just enough more water to blend the ingredients. The dough should be very stiff; if necessary, add in enough more flour to stiffen it. Brush or spray the top with oil. Tightly cover the bowl with plastic wrap. If desired, for best flavor or for convenience, you can refrigerate the dough for 3 to 10 hours. Then let rise at cool room temperature for 20 to 24 hours. If convenient, vigorously stir the dough partway through the rise.

SECOND RISE: If the dough is sticky, working in the bowl, lift and turn it while dusting with and smoothing in more flour until stiffened and easy to handle; don't worry if it is not completely deflated. Divide the dough in half (preferably with oiled kitchen shears), placing each portion on a flour-dusted work surface. Let rest for 10 minutes.

Dusting with flour as needed to facilitate handling, shape one portion into a rough log, then press out the dough into a 7 × 11-inch evenly thick rectangle. Working from a 7-inch side, lift up and fold the rectangle into thirds as if folding a business letter. Again press out into a rectangle; then working from an 11-inch side, roll up tightly into a log. Carefully press and pinch the seam tightly closed all along the length of the log. Dusting with flour as needed, roll the log back and forth on the surface, stretching and smoothing it out from the center until evenly thick and about 13½ to 14½ inches long. (For a bâtard, roll and stretch out until about 10 inches.) Transfer to an oiled metal baguette tray (or to a well-oiled, homemade foil tray set on a baking sheet—see sidebar). Repeat the shaping with the second portion. Using a single-edged razor blade if possible, or well-oiled serrated knife or kitchen shears, make four or five 3-inch-long, ¼-inch-deep, evenly spaced slashes on a slight diagonally along each loaf. Brush or spray the tops with oil. Tent the pan (or homemade tray) with nonstick spray–coated foil.

LET RISE USING EITHER OF THESE METHODS: The extended rise will produce the absolute best flavor: for a 45- to 75-minute regular rise, let stand at warm room temperature; for an extended rise, refrigerate for 4 to 24 hours, then set out at room temperature. Continue the rise until the dough doubles from the deflated size, removing the foil if the dough nears it.

BAKING PRELIMINARIES: 20 minutes before baking time, put a rack in the lower third of the oven; preheat to 500°F. Place a broiler pan on the oven bottom. Have ready a large rimless or low-rimmed baking sheet lined with baking parchment.

BAKING: Reduce the temperature to 475°F. Immediately add a cup of ice water to the broiler pan, being careful of splattering and steam. Generously spritz or brush the loaves with water. Bake on the lower rack for 8 to 10 minutes, or until the loaves are just firm enough to hold their shape. Roll them out onto the parchment-lined baking sheet, and continue baking for 20 to 25 minutes, turning once or twice for all-over browning, until the loaves are well browned and their crusts very crisp. Test with a skewer inserted in the thickest part until it comes out with just slightly moist particles clinging to the bottom portion (or until the center registers 210° to 212°F on an instant-read thermometer). Then bake for 5 minutes more to be sure the centers are done. Transfer to a wire rack; let cool thoroughly.

SERVING AND STORING: Tear or cut the loaves into portions; the bread tastes good warm but the texture will be better when it cools. Cool completely before storing. To maintain the crisp crust, store draped with a clean tea towel or in a heavy paper bag. Or store wrapped in foil: The crust will soften, but can be crisped by heating the loaf, uncovered, in a 400°F oven for a few minutes. The baguettes keep at room temperature for up to 3 days, and may be frozen, airtight, for up to 1 month.

fougasse

(OR BLACK OLIVE FOUGASSE)

½ cup well-drained, chopped
(pitted) Niçoise olives, optional

1 batch *Pain Ordinaire* dough (page
97), ready for its second rise

Unbleached all-purpose white flour
or bread flour for dusting

White or yellow cornmeal for
dusting

Fougasse, which means "ladder," was originally a hearth bread and is related to focaccia. A tradition in Provence, fougasses are often flavored with black olives, anchovy paste, pork cracklings, or Gruyère cheese. Slightly sweet versions are also readied for holidays.

Like focaccia, fougasses are fairly thin, flat, and crisp, but, as their name suggests, their appearance is entirely different: The most prominent feature is usually deep slashes, or "ladders," that cut through and open up decorative slits in the dough; the effect is somewhat like that of the cutwork patterns in some fine table and bed linens. Besides adding visual drama, the ladders yield especially crusty loaves by increasing the surface area directly exposed to the heat.

One of the most artful and popular fougasse loaf shapes, which I love and call for here, is the "tree of life" form: One elongated slot is slashed down the center of a gently rounded pine tree shape (think rounded triangle or teardrop) and four or so perpendicular side openings fan out from the center slit on each side to suggest its branches. Don't worry, it's easier than it sounds; even an inexpert rendering looks enticing.

Traditional Provençal bakers also create much more elaborate shapes of intertwined double or even triple trees, as well as assorted round and other (usually symmetrical) fantasy forms. Sometimes fougasses include several dozen "ladders," and are almost too pretty to eat.

To make fougasses, prepare the *Pain Ordinaire* dough (page 97) and complete the first rise as directed. Then use the following recipe to prepare a "plain" or black olive version. The olives are a nice addition but hardly necessary: The "plain" fougasses have a remarkable chewiness that complements the already enticing French bread flavor.

Yield: four 9- to 10-inch-long fougasses

SECOND RISE: If adding olives, pat them dry on paper towels, then evenly fold into the dough. If it is sticky, working in the bowl, lift and turn it while dusting with and smoothing in more flour until stiffened and easy to handle. Spray four 10-inch-long sheets of baking parchment with nonstick spray. Generously dust them with flour.

Divide the dough in quarters (oiled kitchen shears work best), placing each portion on a sheet. Let rest for 10 minutes. Dusting the dough with flour as needed, pat and press one portion out into an 8- to 9-inch-long tree of life (rounded triangle) shape. Using well-oiled kitchen shears or a pizza wheel, cut a 5- to 6-inch-long center slash that goes completely through the dough and opens up a gash down its length, but stops about an inch short of the point and bottom edge. Cut three or four 1- to 1½-inch-long slashes that fan out and form slots on each side of the center one; be sure that the slashes don't cut into one another or through the edge of the dough. With flour-dusted fingertips, stretch and pull the dough out from the top, bottom, and sides so the cuts open up as much as possible; otherwise they may close up as the dough rises. Tent the fougasses with nonstick spray–coated foil.

LET RISE USING EITHER OF THESE METHODS: For a 30- to 60-minute regular rise, let stand at warm room temperature; for an extended rise, refrigerate for 4 to 24 hours, then let stand, covered, until warmed up. For loaves that have a well-defined shape, large holes, and more chew, let rise for the minimum time; for loaves with a softer, plumper look and lighter crumb, let rise longer.

BAKING PRELIMINARIES: 20 minutes before baking time, put a rack in the lowest position in the oven; preheat to 500°F. Place a broiler pan on the oven bottom. Place a very large rimmed baking sheet upside down on the lowest rack. Generously spritz or brush the loaves with water, then generously dust them with cornmeal.

BAKING: Reduce the temperature to 475°F. Immediately add a cup of ice water to the broiler pan, being careful of splattering and steam. Remove the heated upside-down baking sheet and arrange two fougasses (with parchment) on it. Return the baking sheet to the lowest rack and bake for 12 to 16 minutes, or until the loaves are well browned and their crusts very crisp. Test with a skewer inserted in the thickest part until it comes out with just slightly moist particles clinging to the bottom portion (or until the center registers 205° to 207°F on an instant-read thermometer). Then bake for about 3 minutes more, just to be sure the centers are done. Transfer to a wire rack and let cool. Repeat the baking with the remaining two fougasses.

SERVING AND STORING: Tear or cut the fougasses into portions; eat warm or cool. Cool completely before storing. To maintain the crisp crust, store draped with a clean tea towel or in a heavy paper bag. Or store wrapped in foil: The crusts will soften, but can be crisped by heating the loaf, uncovered, in a 400°F oven for 5 minutes. The fougasses keep at room temperature for up to 3 days, and may be frozen, airtight, for up to 1 month.

brioche

KS QUOTIENT— Fairly Easy: Two-stage mixing. No hand-shaping.

Brioche is one of the richest and most finely textured yeast doughs; individual slices almost look as soft and golden as pound cake, though they are almost never more than faintly sweet. Brioche is lovely eaten both as is and in fancy French toast, and is sometimes called for in very elegant bread puddings. (I personally can't bear to use brioche for this purpose; it seems too contrary to the traditional notion of bread puddings as economizers designed to salvage pieces of unwanted everyday bread.)

The most elaborate brioche is *brioche á tête*, or "brioche with a head," which is baked in a special fluted pan and has a perky topknot rising in the center. Because the *Kneadlessly Simple* dough tends to be soft, and since I recall my fellow pastry school students and I producing many lopsided and sunken topknots while learning to work with brioche dough, I have opted for an easier, but equally delicious, "headless" version here. Bake it in a large loaf pan, or for a beautiful, foolproof decorative look, in a kugelhopf, Bundt, or similar fluted tube pan. (For a very sophisticated coffee cake, fold in chocolate shards and top the brioche with chocolate ganache glaze as directed in the variation at the end of the recipe.)

This recipe calls for beating in a lot of butter and eggs before the second rise, so, while this can be done by hand, it's easiest to use a heavy-duty stand mixer fitted with a paddle. **Yield: 1 brioche, 14 to 16 slices**

2½ cups (12.5 ounces) unbleached all-purpose white flour, plus ¾ cup (3.75 ounces), plus more as needed

5½ tablespoons granulated sugar, divided

1¼ teaspoons table salt

1 teaspoon instant, fast-rising, or bread machine yeast

1¼ cups plus 2 tablespoons ice water, plus more if needed

10 tablespoons unsalted butter, soft but not melted, cut into ½-inch pieces, plus more for brushing dough top and brioche pan

⅓ cup good-quality instant nonfat dry milk powder (don't use a generic brand)

2 large eggs plus 1 egg yolk, at room temperature, plus 1 egg for egg wash (if using loaf pan)

FIRST RISE: In a large bowl, thoroughly stir together 2½ cups of the flour, 3 tablespoons sugar, the salt, and yeast. Vigorously stir in the ice water, scraping down the bowl and mixing until the dough is thoroughly blended. If the mixture is too dry to blend together, stir in just enough more ice water to facilitate mixing and yield a slightly firm dough. If the mixture is soft, stir in enough more flour to make it barely firm. Evenly brush the top lightly with butter. Cover the bowl with plastic wrap. If desired, for best flavor or for convenience, you can refrigerate the dough for 3 to 10 hours. Then let rise at cool room temperature for 12 to 18 hours.

TIP: The accelerated rise is not offered for this bread, as the extra warmth might cause the butter in the dough to soften too much.

SECOND RISE: In a medium bowl, whisk together the remaining 2½ tablespoons sugar and the milk powder, then thoroughly whisk in the 2 eggs plus egg yolk until well blended. Gradually add the egg mixture, then ¾ cup of the flour into the dough and mix vigorously to incorporate; use a paddle and heavy-duty mixer on low if available. Add the butter a tablespoon or two at a time, mixing after each addition until smoothly incorporated. If dough still seems very moist and soft, mix in a few tablespoons more flour until slightly thicker than thick pancake batter. Turn out into a well-greased 8- to 10-cup Bundt or kugelhopf pan, or a 9 × 5-inch loaf pan. Cover with nonstick spray–coated plastic wrap and refrigerate for 1 hour to firm up the butter.

LET RISE USING EITHER OF THESE METHODS: For a 2½- to 3½-hour regular rise, let stand at cool room temperature; or for an extended rise, refrigerate for 4 to 48 hours, then set out at room temperature. Let rise until the dough reaches the pan rim if using an 8-cup tube pan or loaf pan or to 1 inch below the rim if using a 10-cup pan. Remove the plastic wrap as the dough nears it.

BAKING PRELIMINARIES: 15 minutes before baking time, place a rack in the lower third of the oven; preheat to 350°F.

BAKING: If baking in the loaf pan, mix the remaining egg for the egg wash with 2 teaspoons water. Evenly brush over the dough top. Omit the glaze if the brioche will be baked in a fluted pan and served inverted. Bake on the lower rack for 35 to 45 minutes, covering the surface with foil partway through to prevent over-browning if necessary. Continue baking for 15 to 25 minutes more, until a skewer inserted in the thickest part comes out with just a few particles clinging to the bottom (or until the center registers 201° to 203°F on an instant-read thermometer); the baking time will be longer in the loaf pan. When the brioche seems done, bake for 5 minutes longer to ensure the center is baked through. Cool in the pan on a wire rack for 10 minutes. Run a knife around the brioche to loosen it from the pan and transfer to the rack; let cool completely.

SERVING AND STORING: The loaf tastes and slices best fresh and at room temperature. Cool completely before storing airtight in plastic or foil. The bread will keep at room temperature for up 3 days, and may be frozen, airtight, for up to 2 months.

VARIATION **BRIOCHE WITH CHOCOLATE SHARDS**—Shave or chop 8 to 10 ounces of fine-quality bittersweet or semisweet chocolate into shards. Thoroughly fold into the dough right after the butter and extra flour have been incorporated (before the second rise). Proceed as for the original. Top the finished brioche with Chocolate Ganache Glaze while still warm (page 193), if desired.

french
walnut bread

(PAIN AUX NOIX)

2 cups (10 ounces) whole wheat flour, plus extra as needed

2 cups (10 ounces) unbleached all-purpose white flour or white bread flour

1 teaspoon granulated sugar

2 teaspoons table salt

¾ teaspoon instant, fast-rising, or bread machine yeast

2 cups ice water, plus more if needed

Walnut oil or flavorless vegetable oil for coating dough top and baking pot

1½ cups fresh, fine-quality walnut halves

This earthy, nutty-tasting bread is a French favorite, especially in the Dordogne region. It is wonderful topped with a creamy cheese or fine butter. Some pain aux noix recipes are hand-shaped and fairly elaborate; others are fairly simple, like this one. The only remotely fussy step is toasting the walnuts, which I don't skip because it really intensifies and mellows their flavor. I don't skimp on their quality either—they must be very fresh and nutty-sweet.

My 3 ½-quart French enameled cast iron Dutch oven works well for baking this bread, but any similar 3- to 4-quart heavy pot will do. (If you don't have a Dutch oven, see page 32 for other options.)

Yield: 1 large loaf, 12 to 14 portions or slices

FIRST RISE: In a large bowl, thoroughly stir together the whole wheat and white flour, sugar, salt, and yeast. Vigorously stir in the water, scraping down the bowl and mixing until the dough is well blended and smooth. If the mixture is too dry to incorporate all the flour, a bit at a time, stir in just enough more water to blend the ingredients; don't over-moisten, as the dough should be very stiff. Brush or spray the top with oil. Tightly cover the bowl with plastic wrap. If desired, for best flavor or for convenience, you can refrigerate the dough for 3 to 10 hours. Then let rise at cool room temperature for 12 to 18 hours.

Meanwhile, reserve 4 perfect walnut halves for garnish. Spread the remainder on a baking sheet and lightly toast, stirring several times, in a preheated 325°F oven for 10 to 15 minutes, or until fragrant and just lightly browned. Let cool. Chop finely (in a food processor, if desired).

SECOND RISE: Vigorously stir the cooled walnuts into the dough. If it is not stiff, stir in enough more whole wheat flour to make it hard to stir. Using an oiled rubber spatula, lift and fold the dough in towards the center, working all the way around the bowl. Invert it into a well-oiled, then flour-dusted, 3-quart (or larger) heavy metal pot (or use a flat-bottomed round casserole with a lid). Brush or spray the top with oil, then smooth out the surface with an oiled rubber spatula or fingertips. Cut ½-inch-deep slashes to form an × in the center top; well-oiled kitchen shears work best. Put the 4 untoasted walnut halves in the angles of the × for garnish; press down very firmly to imbed them. Cover the pot with its lid.

LET RISE USING ANY OF THESE METHODS: For a 1½- to 2½-hour regular rise, let stand at warm room temperature; for a 1- to 2-hour accelerated rise, let stand in a turned-off microwave along with 1 cup of boiling-hot water; or for an extended rise, refrigerate for 4 to 24 hours, then set out at room temperature. Continue until the dough doubles from its deflated size.

BAKING PRELIMINARIES: 15 minutes before baking time, place a rack in the lower third of the oven; preheat to 400°F. Lightly dust the dough top with whole wheat flour.

BAKING: Bake on the lower rack, covered, for 45 minutes. Remove the lid and continue baking for 20 to 30 minutes, or until the top is well browned and a skewer inserted in the thickest part comes out with just a few particles clinging to the bottom (or until the center registers 207° to 210°F on an instant-read thermometer). Then bake for 5 minutes more to ensure the center is done. Cool in the pan on a wire rack for 10 minutes. Remove the loaf to the rack, running a knife around the edges to loosen it, if necessary.

SERVING AND STORING: The loaf tastes and slices best at room temperature. Cool completely before storing airtight in plastic or foil. The bread will keep at room temperature for up to 3 days, and may be frozen, airtight, for up to 2 months.

yeasted
pain d'epice

KS QUOTIENT— Easy: Fairly lengthy ingredient list, but easy one-stage mixing. No hand-shaping.

½ cup each dark raisins and golden raisins

2¼ cups (11.25 ounces) unbleached white bread flour or unbleached all-purpose white flour, plus more as needed

1 cup (5 ounces) medium rye flour or whole wheat flour

2 teaspoons anise seeds

1½ teaspoons instant, fast-rising, or bread machine yeast

1¼ teaspoon table salt

¼ teaspoon ground ginger

¼ teaspoon ground cinnamon

¼ teaspoon ground cloves

¼ teaspoon ground allspice

½ cup clover honey or other mild honey

1½ teaspoons finely grated orange zest

(continued on page 109)

This aromatic, flavorful, fruit-and-spice loaf is a French favorite, particularly in the farthest eastern region of Alsace. The French name notwithstanding, it is reminiscent of some traditional German honey cakes and gingerbreads called *Lebkuchen*—no great surprise considering that this territory lies across the Rhine river from Germany and has been under German rule on and off over the centuries.

Like many old-fashioned *Lebkuchen*, this recipe relies solely (and successfully) on honey for it sweetness and moistness. And, though it's enriched with dried fruits and spices, it contains no butter or eggs. These latter two were probably omitted because early church fasting rules prohibited rich fare during the pre-Christmas season of Advent, as well as during Lent.

The anise seeds, crystallized ginger, orange zest, and careful blend of ground spices give this admittedly plain-looking loaf a compelling, complex flavor that keeps calling you back. It's a fine change of pace from cinnamon-raisin toast—and quite spectacular spread with cream cheese or almond butter. Although popular during the holidays, it is not overly sweet. It isn't normally iced in France, but the Powdered Sugar–Lemon Drizzle (page 191) is a nice way to dress it up.

Yield: 1 large loaf, 12 to 14 slices

FIRST RISE: Soak the raisins in hot water for 10 minutes, then drain well and let cool thoroughly. In a large bowl, thoroughly stir together the white and rye flours, anise seeds, yeast, salt, ginger, cinnamon, cloves, and allspice. In another bowl or measuring cup, thoroughly whisk the honey and orange zest into the water. Vigorously stir the mixture along with the crystallized ginger and raisins into the bowl with the flours, scraping down the bowl sides and mixing just until the dough is thoroughly blended. If the dough is too dry to mix together, gradually add in just enough more ice water to facilitate mixing, as the dough should be stiff. If necessary, add in more white flour to stiffen it. Brush or spray the top with oil. Tightly cover the bowl with plastic wrap. If desired, for best flavor or for convenience, you can refrigerate the dough for 3 to 10 hours. Then let rise at cool room temperature for 8 to 12 hours.

SECOND RISE: Vigorously stir the dough, adding enough more flour to yield a very stiff consistency. Turn it out into a well-oiled 9 × 5-inch loaf pan. Brush or spray the top with oil. Smooth out and press the dough evenly into the pan with oiled fingertips or a rubber spatula. Cover with nonstick spray–coated plastic wrap.

LET RISE USING ANY OF THESE METHODS: For a 1½- to 2½-hour regular rise, let stand at warm room temperature; for a 1- to 2-hour accelerated rise, let stand in a turned-off microwave along with 1 cup of boiling-hot water; or for an extended rise, refrigerate for 4 to 24 hours, then set out at room temperature. Remove the plastic wrap when the dough nears it, then continue the rise until dough extends ½ inch above the pan rim.

BAKING PRELIMINARIES: 15 minutes before baking time, put a rack in the lower third of the oven; preheat to 350°F. Evenly brush the top with the honey wash.

BAKING: Bake on the lower rack for 50 to 60 minutes, or until the loaf is well browned, covering with foil as needed. Continue baking for 15 to 20 minutes more, until a skewer inserted in the thickest part comes out with just a few particles on the end (or until the center registers 200° to 202°F on an instant-read thermometer). Bake for 5 to 10 minutes longer to ensure the center is done. Cool in the pan on a wire rack for 10 minutes. Turn the loaf onto the rack; cool thoroughly.

If desired, decoratively top the loaf with the Powdered Sugar–Lemon Drizzle, allowing it drip attractively down the sides. Let the loaf stand a few minutes until the icing sets before serving.

SERVING AND STORING: The loaf slices best when thoroughly cooled and tastes best after being allowed to ripen for a few hours. Store airtight wrapped in plastic. The bread will keep at room temperature for up to 3 days, and may be frozen, airtight, for up to 2 months.

1½ cups ice water, plus more if needed

¼ cup diced (⅛-inch pieces) crystallized ginger

Flavorless oil for coating dough top

2 teaspoons clover honey or other mild honey, blended with 2 teaspoons water for wash

rosemary focaccia with coarse salt

2¾ cups (13.75 ounces) unbleached all-purpose white flour, plus more as needed

2 tablespoons fresh rosemary needles (remove the stems), chopped fairly fine

¾ teaspoon table salt

1 teaspoon instant, fast-rising, or bread machine yeast

1⅓ cups plus ½ teaspoon ice water, plus more as needed

2 tablespoons olive oil, divided, plus more as needed

¾ teaspoon sea salt or other coarse crystal salt

The name *focaccia* comes from the Latin *focus*, meaning "hearth," and this amazingly crusty flatbread was prepared long before modern-day ovens came on the scene. Especially in Italy, some versions are still baked on flat stones or tiles placed on coals, but for those without a hearth, a sheet pan set near the bottom of a hot, hot oven will do very well.

Puffy with hundreds of air pockets, crispy-chewy, and amazingly fragrant, focaccia makes the absolute most of simple ingredients like a little olive oil, coarse salt, and fresh rosemary. Don't even consider using the dried herb: Not only would its coarse, stick-like texture be intrusive, but during rehydration, it would draw too much moisture from the dough and discourage the formation of the gas bubbles essential for its enticing texture. This focaccia is so addictive, my husband and I often devour half a pan even before it has had time to cool. (I tell myself it's okay because we're eating mostly air!) **Yield: 12 to 15 servings**

FIRST RISE: In a large bowl, thoroughly stir together the flour, rosemary, table salt, and yeast. Vigorously stir in the water, scraping down the bowl and mixing until the dough is thoroughly blended. Vigorously stir in 1 tablespoon of the olive oil. If the mixture is too dry to blend together, stir in just enough more ice water to facilitate mixing, but don't over-moisten, as the dough should be slightly stiff. If too wet, stir in enough more flour to firm it slightly. Evenly brush the top lightly with oil. Cover the bowl with plastic wrap. If desired, for best flavor or for convenience, you can refrigerate the dough for 3 to 10 hours. Then let rise at cool room temperature for 12 to 18 hours. If convenient, vigorously stir the dough partway through the rise.

SECOND RISE: Brush a 15 × 10 × 1-inch (or similar) baking pan with olive oil, then line the pan with baking parchment. Brush the parchment with olive oil. Using a well-oiled rubber spatula, turn the dough out onto the pan; try not to deflate it any more than necessary. Drizzle the dough with 1 tablespoon of olive oil. With well-oiled hands, lightly pat and press out the dough until it is evenly thick and extends to within 1 inch of the edges all around. Tent the pan with nonstick spray–coated plastic wrap.

LET RISE USING EITHER OF THESE METHODS: For a 2 ½- to 3½-hour regular rise, let stand at warm room temperature; or for an extended rise, refrigerate for 4 to 24 hours, then set out at room temperature. Continue the rise until the dough has almost doubled from the deflated size. (If the pan has a 1-inch rim, the dough should be ¼ inch below it.) Just before baking, with oiled fingertips, make deep indentations, or dimples, all over the dough. Sprinkle evenly with coarse salt.

BAKING PRELIMINARIES: 20 minutes before baking time, place a rack in lowest position in the oven; preheat to 500°F. Place the broiler pan on the oven floor.

BAKING: Reduce the temperature to 475°F. Add a cup of ice water to the broiler pan, being careful of splattering and steam. Bake on the lowest rack for 20 to 30 minutes, until golden brown, turning the pan from front to back for even browning about halfway through. Bake for 5 to 10 minutes more (or until the center registers 209° to 212°F on an instant-read thermometer) to be sure the center is done. Cool in the pan on a wire rack for 10 minutes. Using wide spatulas, lift the bread from the pan onto the rack to cool, or onto a cutting board to cut into servings.

SERVING AND STORING: Focaccia is best when fresh. Cut into rectangles and serve warm or at room temperature. Drizzle with additional olive oil or provide more as a dipping sauce, if desired. To maintain crispness, keep, draped with a tea towel, at cool room temperature for 2 to 3 days. It may be frozen, airtight, for up to 2 months, but should be crisped in a preheated 400°F oven before serving.

VARIATION FENNEL SEED AND OREGANO (OR THYME) FOCACCIA WITH SALT— Prepare the dough exactly as for the rosemary version except omit the rosemary. When garnishing with the sea salt just before baking, also sprinkle the dough evenly with ½ teaspoon fennel seeds and ½ teaspoon dried oregano leaves or dried thyme leaves.

TIP: If you don't have fresh rosemary, try the fennel seed and oregano or thyme focaccia variation below. Don't add any more dried oregano or thyme than called for, because these herbs both have yeast-inhibiting chemicals that, in quantity, can discourage rising.

ciabatta

3 cups (15 ounces) unbleached
all-purpose white flour, plus
more as needed

Scant 1½ teaspoons table salt

¾ teaspoon instant, fast-rising, or
bread machine yeast

1½ cups ice water, plus more if
needed

1 tablespoon olive oil, plus extra
for brushing loaf top

Ciabatta means "slipper," and, if you put your imagination to work, these airy, open-crumbed loaves do vaguely resemble big, floppy slippers or soft shoes. If you don't use your imagination, they may simply look like blobs in the shape of Mr. Peanut (minus his top hat!). A tidy shape is not all that important, though, because the defining characteristic of the loaf is a noticeably holey, puffy interior, which requires a slightly softer than normal dough.

Basically, you form the breads by dumping the dough portions onto flour-dusted sheets of baking parchment, patting each into an oblong, then gently pushing them in at the "waist" to create a vaguely slipper- or shoe-like form.

The loaves are wonderfully crusty on the outside and soft on the inside, and, so long as the dough isn't over-floured or over-manipulated, full of holes. If these are absent, console yourself that you're really only missing out on extra air!

Yield: 2 ciabatta loaves

FIRST RISE: In a large bowl, thoroughly stir together the flour, salt, and yeast. Vigorously stir in the water, scraping down the bowl and mixing until the dough is thoroughly blended. Vigorously stir in the olive oil. If the mixture is too stiff to incorporate all the flour, stir in just a little more ice water, but don't over-moisten, as it should be slightly stiff. If too wet, stir in enough more flour to firm it slightly. Evenly brush the top lightly with more olive oil. Cover the bowl with plastic wrap. If desired, for best flavor or for convenience, you can refrigerate the dough for 3 to 10 hours. Then let rise at cool room temperature for 12 to 15 hours.

SECOND RISE: Spray two 9 × 12-inch sheets of baking parchment with nonstick spray, then dust each with ¼ cup flour, mounding it just slightly in the center. Line a very large rimless baking sheet (or the back of a rimmed sheet) with a new sheet of baking parchment; dust the parchment with flour.

Using a well-oiled rubber spatula, gently loosen the dough from the bowl sides all the way around, trying not to deflate it any more than necessary. Using well-oiled kitchen shears and working so as to deflate the dough as little as possible, cut it in half, then turn out each portion onto the prepared parchment sheets. Dust the dough tops with flour. With well-oiled fingertips, very gently push and pat each portion out into an oblong, or "slipper," about $9 \times 5\frac{1}{2}$ inches; don't worry about being exact. Then push in the sides so the middle of each "slipper" is narrower than its heel and toe. Gently run a flour-dusted wide-bladed spatula under the slippers to loosen them from the parchment. One at a time, lift up the loaves and invert them, spaced as far apart as possible, onto the parchment-lined baking sheet; the crinkled, floured look is traditional, so don't brush off all the excess flour. Readjust the dough to re-form the slipper shapes, if necessary. Press deep indentations, or dimples, in the slippers all over with flour-dusted fingertips. Tent the baking sheet with nonstick spray—coated foil.

LET RISE USING EITHER OF THESE METHODS: For a $1\frac{1}{2}$- to $2\frac{1}{2}$-hour regular rise, let stand at warm room temperature; or for an extended rise, refrigerate for 4 to 24 hours, then set out at room temperature. Continue the rise until the dough has doubled from the deflated size, removing the foil as the dough nears it.

BAKING PRELIMINARIES: 20 minutes before baking time, place a rack in lowest position in the oven; preheat to 500°F. Set a broiler pan on the oven floor.

BAKING: Add a cup of ice water to the broiler pan, being careful of splattering and steam. Reduce the temperature to 475°F and bake on the lowest rack for 15 to 20 minutes, until the loaves are golden and crusty. Bake for 5 to 10 minutes more, until a skewer inserted in the thickest part comes out with just a few crumbs on the tip (or until the center registers 208° to 210°F on an instant-read thermometer) to be sure the centers are done. Then place the pan on the floor of the oven for 2 to 4 minutes to brown the bottoms of the loaves; lift them up to check. Let stand for 10 minutes on the pan. Transfer the loaves to a wire rack, and let stand until cooled.

SERVING AND STORING: Slices best when completely cooled. Serve sliced horizontally for sandwich bread or grilling or vertically for snacking. Keeps, draped with a tea towel, at cool room temperature for 2 to 3 days. It may be frozen, airtight, for up to 2 months, but should be crisped in a pre-heated 400°F oven before serving.

neapolitan-style
pizza dough

KS QUOTIENT— Super-Easy: A minimum of ingredients, mixed all at once. Easy hand-shaping.

This is a simple, easy to handle, and virtually foolproof pizza dough calling for the most basic and economical supplies—yeast, salt, olive oil, and all-purpose flour. Some recipes call for a high-gluten flour, but I like regular flour better. The flat, thin layer doesn't need the extra gluten for support and the dough is more tender and much easier to stretch and shape without it. Because relatively little gluten development is necessary, the dough also requires less "micro-kneading" time than usual. After 4 to 12 hours on the countertop, it is ready to use, refrigerate, or freeze until needed.

The recipe makes enough dough for two 11- to 12-inch pizzas. If desired, freeze one or both dough portions for up to a month. Use *each* dough portion for one traditional tomato sauce and mozzarella pizza on the next page, or for another pizza of your own choosing. For your convenience, I've also provided my pizza sauce recipe, although you can, of course, substitute any tomato-based sauce desired. **Yield: 1 11-12 ounce pizza**

3 cups (15 ounces) unbleached all-purpose white flour, plus more as needed

Generous 1¼ teaspoons table salt

½ teaspoon instant, fast-rising, or bread machine yeast

Scant 1½ cups ice water, plus more if needed

1 tablespoon olive oil, plus more for brushing over dough and pans

FIRST RISE: In a large bowl, thoroughly stir together the flour, salt, and yeast. Vigorously stir in the water, scraping down the sides, just until thoroughly blended. Stir in the olive oil until evenly incorporated. If the mixture is too dry to mix, add in just enough water to facilitate mixing, as the dough should be firm. If the dough is soft, stir in enough more flour to firm it. Brush the top with olive oil. Cover the bowl with plastic wrap. If desired, for best flavor or for convenience, you can refrigerate the dough for 3 to 10 hours. Then let rise at cool room temperature for 4 to 12 hours.

SECOND RISE: Stir the dough to deflate it. Divide it in half using oiled kitchen shears. The dough portions can be used immediately; or refrigerated for up to 12 hours and then used; or frozen, wrapped airtight, for up to 1 month. Use each half to prepare one pizza, following the recipe on the next page or another recipe of your choosing.

tomato sauce and
mozzarella pizza

KS QUOTIENT— Super-Easy: Quick;
simple hand-shaping required.

½ recipe Neapolitan-Style Pizza
Dough (page 115), ready for the
second rise

⅓ recipe Herbed Cooked Tomato
Pizza Sauce (page 118), or ¾ cup
homemade or store-bought tomato-
based pizza sauce, at room
temperature

¼ cup coarsely sliced (pitted) black
Kalamata, Niçoise, or other flavorful
brined black olives, optional

4 to 6 ounces fresh mozzarella
cheese, thinly sliced

Traditionalists insist that only a little cooked tomato sauce and soft, fresh mozzarella should top the classic version called Pizza Margherita. Since I really like to add some black olives, too, I'll just say that my version is an almost but not quite authentic Pizza Margherita. If you feel you'll miss the meatiness of typical American pies, I won't tell if you replace the olives with thinly sliced pepperoni or hard sausage as well. Just don't overload on extras or your pizza won't crisp as it should. Also, if at all possible, use fresh mozzarella; it will instantly raise the quality of your pie to gourmet.

Note that the recipe is designed so you can ready your pizza on a 12-inch pizza pan or a sheet of baking parchment. The dough, along with its pan or parchment, is then slipped onto a preheated baking sheet set on the lowest rack of the oven. This crisps the crust and eliminates any chance of sogginess, yet obviates the need for a pizza stone or baking tiles. (It's fine to use them if you have them, of course.) Once the dough is puffed and partly baked, add the toppings, then slip the pie back into the oven for its final turn. The result will assure your reputation as a first-rate pizza maker. **Yield: One 11½- to 12-inch pizza**

SECOND RISE: Place the dough portion on a 12-inch lightly oiled pizza pan or a large sheet of nonstick spray–coated baking parchment. Drizzle lightly with olive oil, then press and stretch the dough into an 11½- to 12-inch round with oiled fingertips; if it is resistant and springs back, let it rest for a few minutes before continuing. The shape doesn't have to be perfect, but be sure to push the dough outward to slightly build up and thicken the edges (which would burn if too thin). Set aside to rise, tented with nonstick spray–coated foil, for 25 to 45 minutes, depending on whether you prefer a thin, slightly dense crust, or a lighter, medium-thick one.

BAKING PRELIMINARIES: 20 minutes before baking time, place a rack in the lowest slot of the oven; preheat to 500°F. Place a rimless baking sheet (or place a rimmed sheet upside down) on the lowest rack.

BAKING: Place the pizza pan with the dough (or the dough on the parchment) on the preheated baking sheet. Bake for 7 to 10 minutes, or until the dough begins to firm and puff up. Remove from the oven and spread the sauce to within ⅓ inch of the edge all around. Add the olives, if using, and the mozzarella slices evenly over the top. Return to the oven and bake until the top is bubbly and the edge is puffy and nicely browned, about 10 minutes longer. Transfer the pan to a wire rack and cool for 5 minutes before serving.

SERVING AND STORING: Serve hot; cut into wedges with kitchen shears or a pizza wheel. Reheat, wrapped in foil, in a 350°F oven for 5 to 10 minutes or under a microwave-safe plastic cover on medium power for a minute or so. Store airtight and refrigerated for 2 to 3 days, or frozen, airtight, for up to a week. Thaw before reheating.

herbed
cooked tomato
pizza sauce

1 tablespoon good-quality olive oil

½ teaspoon finely minced fresh garlic, or 1 tablespoon finely chopped onion

1 can (28 ounces) fine-quality crushed tomatoes, preferably imported Italian

2 teaspoons *each* dried oregano and dried thyme leaves

½ teaspoon good-quality balsamic vinegar, optional

⅛ to ¼ teaspoon *each* salt and freshly ground black pepper, or to taste

The simplest Italian pizza sauces feature fresh, full-flavored, uncooked tomatoes, but when genuine, garden-ripened tomatoes can't be had, a homemade cooked sauce made from good-quality canned tomatoes is the best alternative. It is so much better than bought, yet is easy and inexpensive and for convenience can be readied far ahead.

This recipe makes enough for three 11- to 12-inch pizzas, so I like to divide it into three ready-to-use, freezable portions. Let frozen portions of sauce thaw overnight in the refrigerator or on the countertop for 2 to 4 hours. For the crispest crust, be sure the sauce is at room temperature before topping the dough with it.

Yield: Enough to top three 11- to 12-inch pizzas

Combine the oil and garlic or onion in a heavy, medium saucepan over medium-high heat and cook, stirring, for 1 minute for garlic or 2 minutes for onion. Add the tomatoes, oregano, and thyme. Adjust the heat so the mixture boils gently and cook, stirring frequently to prevent sticking, until the sauce is cooked down and thickened, 10 to 15 minutes. Stir in the balsamic vinegar, if using, and salt and pepper. Use immediately, or refrigerate for later use.

STORAGE: Keeps in the refrigerator for up to 4 days and in the freezer for up to 2 months.

crispy roasted garlic
and parmesan
pot bread

KS QUOTIENT— Easy: Few ingredients, added all at once. No shaping required.

Infused with fresh, roasted garlic and punched up with a little Parmesan, this is a whole different animal from the typical commercial loaf peppered with garlic salt. The flavor of the roasted herb is much more subtle, earthy, and appetizing. And the cheese gives the bread a beautiful golden hue, crisp crust, and characteristic Parmesan aroma. Be sure that both the garlic and cheese are fresh and of good quality, as they are what makes (or breaks) this bread. Even if you love garlic, curb the impulse to add extra; too much of it can inhibit the yeast growth.

If you're a fan of pesto, you can add a couple tablespoons to the dough for a handsome, basil-flecked bread; see the variation at the end. Homemade pesto is best, but a high-quality commercial pesto will suffice.

The bread is lovely cut into thick slices and served with a bowl of minestrone, spaghetti, or any other Mediterranean-style dish or meal. The slices are also good grilled or toasted and used for crostini. Top with an eggplant or olive spread for a memorable munchie even vegetarians can enjoy.

Yield: 1 large loaf, 12 to 14 portions or slices

1 large head (knob) garlic

1 tablespoon good-quality olive oil, plus more for brushing dough

¼ cup freshly grated Parmesan cheese, plus 2 tablespoons for garnish

4 cups (20 ounces) unbleached all-purpose white flour or white bread flour, plus more as needed

Scant 2 teaspoons table salt

1¼ teaspoons instant, fast-rising, or bread machine yeast

2 cups plus 2 tablespoons ice water, plus more if needed

PRELIMINARIES: Peel off and discard the papery outer skin from the garlic but do not separate or pull off the cloves. Cut across the pointed tops of the cloves to expose the flesh inside; discard the cut-off portion. Put 1 tablespoon of olive oil in a small ovenproof custard cup or small bowl. Dip the cut side of the garlic into the oil to coat the cloves, then turn the head cutside up and set in the cup. Cover the cup with foil. Bake in a preheated 350°F oven for 35 to 45 minutes, or until the garlic is very soft and fragrant. Let cool, then squeeze or scrape out the garlic from the cloves into a medium bowl. Add ¼ cup of Parmesan and thoroughly mash with a fork until the mixture forms a paste. The paste may be made several days ahead and refrigerated; let warm up slightly and stir before using.

FIRST RISE: In a large bowl, thoroughly stir together the flour, salt, and yeast. Vigorously stir the water and the garlic mixture into the bowl, scraping down the sides and mixing until the ingredients are thoroughly blended. If the mixture is too dry to incorporate all the flour, a bit at a time, stir in just enough more water to blend the ingredients; don't over-moisten, as the dough should be very stiff. If necessary, stir in enough more flour to stiffen it. Brush or spray the top with olive oil. Cover the bowl with plastic wrap. If desired, for best flavor or for convenience, you can refrigerate the dough for 3 to 10 hours. Then let rise at cool room temperature for 12 to 18 hours. If convenient, vigorously stir the dough once partway through the rise.

SECOND RISE: Using an oiled rubber spatula, lift and fold the dough in towards the center, working all the way around, avoiding deflating as much as possible. Brush or spray with olive oil. Re-cover with nonstick spray–coated plastic wrap.

LET RISE USING ANY OF THESE METHODS: For a 1½- to 2½-hour regular rise, let stand at warm room temperature; for a 1- to 2-hour accelerated rise, let stand in a turned-off microwave along with 1 cup of boiling-hot water; or for an extended rise, refrigerate for 4 to 24 hours, then set out at room temperature. Continue the rise until the dough doubles from the deflated size, removing the plastic if the dough nears it.

BAKING PRELIMINARIES: 20 minutes before baking time, put a rack in the lower third of the oven; preheat to 450°F. Oil the inside of a 3- to 4-quart (or slightly larger) Dutch oven or heavy metal pot. Heat it in the oven until it just starts to smoke, then remove it (use oven mitts). Taking care not to deflate the dough, loosen it from the bowl sides with an oiled rubber spatula and gently invert it into the pot. Don't worry if it's lopsided and ragged-looking; it will even out during baking. Spritz or brush the top with water, then sprinkle over 2 tablespoons of Parmesan. Immediately top with the lid. Shake the pot back and forth to center and even out the dough.

BAKING: Reduce the heat to 425°F. Bake on the lower rack for 45 to 50 minutes. If the loaf is golden brown, continue baking, covered, for 10 to 15 minutes longer, until the top is well browned and a skewer inserted in the thickest part comes out with just a few crumbs on the tip (or until the center registers 207° to 208°F on an instant-read thermometer.) If the loaf top looks pale after the initial 45 to 50 minutes, uncover and continue baking for 10 to 15 minutes until golden brown. Then bake for 5 to 10 minutes longer to ensure the center is baked through. Cool in the pot on a wire rack for 10 to 15 minutes. Run a table knife around the loaf to loosen it. Transfer it to the rack; cool thoroughly.

SERVING AND STORING: The loaf tastes good warm but will cut much better when cool. Cool completely before storing. To maintain the crisp crust, store draped with a clean tea towel or in a heavy paper bag. Or store airtight in a plastic bag or wrapped in foil: The crust will soften, but can be crisped by heating the loaf, uncovered, in a 400°F oven for a few minutes. The bread will keep at room temperature for up to 3 days, and may be frozen, airtight, for up to 2 months.

VARIATION CRISPY ROASTED GARLIC–PESTO POT BREAD—After mashing the garlic and the Parmesan into a paste, mix in 3 tablespoons homemade or commercial pesto until well blended. Proceed exactly as for the original bread.

rustic cyprus-style herbed olive bread

KS QUOTIENT— Easy: All ingredients added at once. No hand-shaping.

4¼ cups (21.25 ounces) unbleached all-purpose white flour, preferably unbleached, plus more as needed

1¾ teaspoons table salt

¾ teaspoon instant, fast-rising, or bread machine yeast

2 cups ice water, plus more if needed

3 tablespoons chopped fresh cilantro leaves

2 tablespoons chopped fresh mint leaves

2 tablespoons chopped fresh chives or finely chopped scallion tops

¼ cup good-quality olive oil, plus more for brushing dough top

1 cup thoroughly drained, chopped (pitted) Kalamata olives

About 3 tablespoons cornmeal for dusting baking pot

Herbed olive breads often feature rosemary, and sometimes oregano or thyme, but this unusual, wonderfully savory Cypriot version goes in a deliciously different direction with chopped fresh cilantro, mint, and chives. The bread surface is crackly crisp, but the olive-studded inside is tender and almost soft, due to the ample addition of olive oil. The loaf is a large, shaggy-looking round with a slightly open texture. Wedges or chunks are pretty irresistible "plain," and sumptuous dunked in olive oil.

You'll need a Dutch oven or similar heavy pot or deep, flat-bottomed casserole for baking this bread. See page 12 if you aren't sure what to use.

Yield: 1 large loaf, 14 to 15 wedges or slices

FIRST RISE: In a large bowl, thoroughly stir together the flour, salt, and yeast. In another bowl or measuring cup, vigorously whisk together the water, cilantro, mint, and chives. Stir the mixture into the bowl with the flour until the dough is just lightly mixed. Then add the olive oil, scraping down the bowl sides and mixing until thoroughly blended. The dough should be very stiff; if necessary, add in enough more flour to stiffen it. Gently stir in the olives until evenly distributed throughout. Brush the top with oil. Tightly cover the bowl with plastic wrap. If desired, for best flavor or for convenience, you can refrigerate the dough for 3 to 10 hours. Then let rise at cool room temperature for 12 to 18 hours.

SECOND RISE: Using an oiled rubber spatula, lift and fold the dough in towards the center all the way around until thoroughly loosened from the bowl; don't deflate any more than necessary. Evenly brush the inside of a 3½- to 4-quart Dutch oven or other heavy pot or large, deep, flat-bottomed ovenproof casserole with olive oil. Add the cornmeal, then tip the pot back and forth to distribute it on the sides. Invert the dough into the pot; don't worry if it's ragged-looking or lopsided. Shake the pot to center the dough. Brush the surface with olive oil. Top the pot with its lid.

LET RISE USING ANY OF THESE METHODS: For a 1½- to 2½-hour regular rise, let stand at warm room temperature; for a 1- to 1½-hour accelerated rise, let stand in a turned-off microwave along with 1 cup of boiling-hot water; or for an extended rise, refrigerate for 4 to 24 hours, then set out at room temperature. Let rise until the dough has doubled from its deflated size.

BAKING PRELIMINARIES: 20 minutes before baking time, place a rack in the lower third of the oven; preheat to 475°F.

BAKING: Reduce the oven temperature to 425°F. Bake on the lower rack, covered, for 55 to 60 minutes or until crisp and lightly browned. Brush the loaf with olive oil and continue to bake, uncovered, testing until the top is well browned and a skewer inserted in the thickest part comes out with just a few crumbs on the tip (or until the center registers 207° to 208°F on an instant-read thermometer), 12 to 15 minutes longer. Bake for 5 to 10 minutes more to ensure that the center is done. Cool in the pot on a wire rack for 15 minutes. Run a knife around the loaf and remove it to the rack; let cool completely.

SERVING AND STORING: This loaf tastes good warm, but will cut better when cool. Cool completely before storing. To maintain the crisp crust, store draped with a clean tea towel or in a heavy paper bag. Or store airtight in a plastic bag or foil: The crust will soften, but can be crisped by heating the loaf, uncovered, in a 400°F oven for a few minutes. The bread will keep at room temperature for up to 3 days, and may be frozen, airtight, for up to 2 months.

swedish
limpa bread

KS QUOTIENT — Fairly Easy: Two-stage mixing. No hand-shaping required.

3½ cups (17.5 ounces) unbleached all-purpose white flour

2 cups (10 ounces) rye flour, plus ½ cup (2.5 ounces), plus more as needed

2¾ teaspoons table salt

1¼ teaspoons caraway seeds

1¼ teaspoons anise seeds

1¼ teaspoons instant, fast-rising, or bread machine yeast

⅔ cup light or dark molasses (not blackstrap)

¼ cup corn oil, canola oil, or other flavorless vegetable oil

2 cups ice water, plus more if needed

⅓ cup good-quality instant nonfat dry milk (don't use a generic brand)

⅓ cup packed light brown sugar

3½ tablespoons unsalted butter, melted, divided

This began as a traditional recipe e-mailed to me by a reader of a story I wrote for the *Washington Post* on no-knead breads. The writer, Suzy Hubbell, wondered if I could make over a family favorite, her grandmother Anna Danielson's Swedish limpa bread, to fit the knead-free method. Several other people wanted to their recipes converted, too, which eventually led me to provide suggestions on how to go about it in a bonus chapter in the book (see page 197).

Making over this slightly sweet bread was well worth the effort. The caraway and anise seeds in combination with molasses, brown sugar, and rye flour give it a mild yet enticing flavor that even those who don't care for rye bread usually like. I find it truly addictive, especially toasted and topped with butter. **Yield: 2 medium loaves, 12 to 14 slices each**

FIRST RISE: In a very large bowl, thoroughly stir together the white flour, 2 cups of the rye flour, the salt, caraway seeds, anise seeds, and yeast. In another bowl or measuring cup, whisk the molasses and the oil into the water until well blended. Vigorously stir the mixture into the bowl with the flours, scraping down the bowl sides and mixing until the dough is well blended and smooth. If too dry to mix completely, a bit at a time, add in enough more ice water to blend the ingredients and yield a firm but not hard-to-stir dough. Brush or evenly spray the top with oil. Tightly cover the bowl with plastic wrap. If desired, for best flavor or for convenience, you can refrigerate the dough for 3 to 10 hours. Then let rise at cool room temperature for 12 to 18 hours.

SECOND RISE: In a small, deep bowl, stir together the dry milk, brown sugar, and 2 tablespoons of the butter with 1½ tablespoons hot water until well blended. Gradually stir the milk mixture, then ½ cup of the rye flour, into the dough until well blended and no streaks remain; the mixture will be hard to stir, so you may prefer to work in the flour with well-oiled fingertips (or use a dough hook and heavy-duty mixer on low). If necessary, working in the bowl, lift and turn it while dusting with and smoothing in more rye flour, as the dough should be very stiff. Cut the dough in half with well-oiled kitchen shears. Put the dough portions in two 8½ × 4½-inch well-oiled loaf pans. Lightly brush the tops with some of the remaining melted butter. Smooth and press the dough evenly into the pans, tucking it under at the ends. Brush with more butter. Cover the tops with nonstick spray–coated plastic wrap.

LET RISE USING ANY OF THESE METHODS: For a 1½- to 2½-hour regular rise, let stand at warm room temperature; for a 1- to 1½-hour accelerated rise, let stand in a turned-off microwave along with 1 cup of boiling-hot water; or, for an extended rise, refrigerate for 4 to 48 hours, then set out at room temperature. When the dough nears the plastic, remove it and continue the rise until the dough extends ½ inch above the pan rims.

BAKING PRELIMINARIES: 15 minutes before baking time, place a rack in the lower third of the oven; preheat to 350°F.

BAKING: Reduce the oven temperature to 325°F. Bake on the lower rack for 55 to 60 minutes, or until the loaves are very well browned. Cover the tops with foil and continue baking for 15 to 20 minutes longer, until a skewer inserted in the thickest part comes out with slightly moist crumbs on the tip (or until the center registers 202° to 204°F on an instant-read thermometer). Bake for about 10 minutes longer to ensure the centers are done. Brush the loaf tops evenly with the remaining melted butter. Cool in the pans on a wire rack for 10 to 15 minutes. Run a knife around the loaves to loosen, then turn out onto the racks. Let cool thoroughly.

SERVING AND STORING: Serve warm, or cool, or toasted; the bread slices best when cool. Cool thoroughly before storing in plastic or foil. Keeps at room temperature for up to 3 days. May be frozen, airtight, for up to 2 months.

scottish
oatmeal bread

KS QUOTIENT— Easy: Two-stage mixing. No hand-shaping.

2½ cups (12.5 ounces) unbleached white bread flour, plus ¾ cup (3.75 ounces), plus more as needed

Scant 1¾ teaspoons table salt

¾ teaspoon instant, fast-rising, or bread machine yeast

¾ teaspoon ground allspice

⅛ teaspoon ground nutmeg

1¼ cups plus 2 tablespoons ice water, plus more if needed

½ teaspoon finely grated orange zest

2 tablespoons unsalted butter, at room temperature, plus more for greasing pan and loaf top

¾ cup old-fashioned rolled oats, plus 4 tablespoons for garnish

⅔ cup boiling water

6 tablespoons packed light or dark brown sugar

⅔ cup dried currants, rinsed under hot water, then thoroughly drained and patted dry

The Scots are known for eating a lot of oats, in the form of breakfast porridge, or oatmeal; as a component of various baked goods; and in their beloved haggis, which, since it involves assorted peculiar animal parts, I prefer not to dwell on here. Sometimes, Scottish recipes call for incorporating leftover oatmeal, which not only saves time and avoids waste, but in the case of yeast bread, results in an exceptional loaf. The consistency and taste are different from bread made just by tossing some uncooked rolled oats in with the flour: the texture is much moister and smoother than normal and the flavor and aroma slightly sweeter and more "oaty." (For this recipe I assume that you don't have leftover oatmeal sitting around, so it calls for preparing the right amount of partially cooked and sweetened oatmeal.)

This loaf is mild and homey, with a slightly chewy-crisp crust. Like many old-fashioned British breads, it calls for a bit of spice and dried currants. I like it for toast, or in thick, warm-from-the-oven slices spread with butter and smidge of jam and accompanied by a freshly brewed pot of tea. This is the simple, sublime way I first ate it back in the 1980s, at a bed and breakfast on a cold, damp summer afternoon in the Scottish Highlands. **Makes 1 large loaf, 13 to 14 portions or slices**

FIRST RISE: In a large bowl, thoroughly stir together 2½ cups of the flour, the salt, yeast, allspice, and nutmeg. Vigorously stir the ice water and orange zest into the flour mixture, scraping down the sides just until the ingredients are thoroughly blended. If too dry to mix, a bit at a time, stir in just enough more ice water to blend the ingredients, but don't over-moisten, as the dough should be fairly stiff. Stir in more flour to stiffen it if necessary. Brush the top with softened butter. Cover the bowl with plastic wrap. If desired, for best flavor or for convenience, you can refrigerate the dough for 3 to 10 hours. Then let rise at cool room temperature for 12 to 18 hours.

SECOND RISE: In a medium bowl, gradually stir the oats into the boiling water until well blended. Let stand for 5 minutes to partially cook. Stir in the butter and sugar until the sugar dissolves and let cool thoroughly. Vigorously stir the cooled oatmeal mixture into the dough until thoroughly incorporated. Add in ¾ cup of the flour and the currants until evenly distributed throughout, then, as needed, enough more flour to yield a very stiff dough, scraping down the bowl thoroughly. Using an oiled rubber spatula and working all the way around the bowl, fold the dough in towards the center.

Generously butter a 9 × 5-inch loaf pan. Add 2 tablespoons of oats to the pan; tip it back and forth to evenly distribute them. Invert the dough into the pan. Smooth out the top and press the dough evenly into the pan. Brush the loaf top with melted butter. Sprinkle the remaining 2 tablespoon oats over the top, pressing down to imbed them. Using an oiled serrated knife or kitchen shears, cut a 6-inch-long, ½-inch-deep slash down the loaf center. Cover the pan with nonstick spray–coated plastic wrap.

LET RISE USING EITHER OF THESE METHODS: For a 1¾- to 2½-hour regular rise, let stand at warm room temperature; for a 1- to 2-hour accelerated rise, let stand in a turned-off microwave along with 1 cup of boiling-hot water. Continue the rise until the dough nears the plastic. Remove it and continue until the dough extends just to the pan rim (it will rise a lot in the oven).

BAKING PRELIMINARIES: 20 minutes before baking time, put a rack in the lower third of the oven; preheat to 375°F.

BAKING: Bake on the lower rack for 65 to 75 minutes, until the top is nicely browned and a skewer inserted in the thickest part comes out with moist crumbs on the tip (or until the center registers 204° to 206°F on an instant-read thermometer). (As necessary to prevent over browning, cover the top with foil.) Then bake for 5 to 10 minutes longer to ensure the center is baked through. Cool in the pan on a wire rack for 10 to 15 minutes. Remove the loaf to the rack; cool thoroughly.

SERVING AND STORING: This tastes good warm, but will cut much better when cool. Cool completely before storing. The bread will keep at cool room temperature for 3 to 4 days, and may be frozen, airtight, for up to 2 months.

TIP: The extended rise option normally offered in *Kneadlessly Simple* recipes can't be used for this bread. Once the oatmeal is added to the dough, the same chemical processes that make the finished loaf exceptionally moisture retentive and sweet-tasting also begin to break down the wheat gluten needed for good loaf structure. Since the gluten breakdown continues even during refrigeration, it's best to use an accelerated or regular second rise so the dough doesn't stand too long. The high moisture retention means that this loaf needs a slightly longer than normal baking time, too.

healthful, whole-grain, multigrain, and gluten-free breads

THIS CHAPTER CELEBRATES A WIDE VARIETY OF GRAINS AND seeds, all of which can enhance the flavor, texture, visual interest, and nutritional value of bread. For the fine flavor that is the hallmark of good homemade bread, always be sure seeds, whole grains, and whole-grain flours are impeccably fresh. The high fat content of nuts and of the germ portion of grains makes them stale rapidly, so use what you buy promptly, or refrigerate or freeze (wrapped airtight) to preserve good flavor.

Whole-grain breads are well suited to the *Kneadlessly Simple* method. Bits of grain and seeds added during the long first rise have plenty of time to soften, plus the extended soaking encourages chemical processes that make them more digestible. The bubbling action of the "micro-kneading" is also advantageous because it gently jiggles rather than manhandles the dough. Regular kneading causes the coarse grain particles to cut some of the gluten strands, which reduces their ability to trap gas and puff the bread.

Nevertheless, because whole grains contain bits of bran and germ, which are heavier than the starchy parts of kernels, breads calling for large proportions of whole grains often rise more slowly and come out more compact than those made entirely with all white wheat flour. White bread flour has extra gluten that can help lift the extra weight, so it is often called for in these recipes instead of all-purpose white flour. To further lighten the whole-grain load, some recipes call for a slightly higher proportion of yeast than most of the recipes in the book.

cracked wheat

KS QUOTIENT—Easy: All
ingredients added before the first rise.
Hand-shaping required.

This big (2½ pounds), handsome, hearty, seed-studded boule boasts a wonderful, chewy-crispy crust and springy, surprisingly light crumb. The cracked wheat, wheat germ, and combination of flax, sesame, and poppy seeds boost the fiber and nutrients, as well as lend texture and a delectable earthy flavor. The light-colored, or "golden," variety of flax seeds have a particularly rich, nutty taste and aroma that contributes to the aura of the whole-grain goodness, but brown flax seeds will do perfectly well, too.

Like the other "pot" breads in this book, this one is baked in a heavy lidded Dutch oven or similar container. (See page 32 for more details on suitable pots.) When the lid is finally removed, it's always fun to see that the spiral pattern cut into the loaf top has opened up and exposed the interior, which dramatically contrasts the areas with seeds.

Use this hearty, all-purpose loaf for toast or sandwiches, or cut it into generous portions and serve warm with a hearty soup or stew.

Yield: 1 large loaf, 12 to 14 portions or slices

3 tablespoons cracked wheat (or chopped wheat berries; see tip)

2½ tablespoons flax seeds, preferably golden

⅔ cup boiling water

2½ cups (12.5 ounces) whole wheat flour, plus more as needed

2 cups (10 ounces) unbleached white bread flour

2 tablespoons wheat germ

2 tablespoons poppy seeds

2 tablespoons sesame seeds

Generous 2¼ teaspoons table salt

1¼ teaspoons instant, fast-rising, or bread machine yeast

2½ tablespoons clover honey or other mild honey

2¼ cups ice water, plus more if needed

Corn oil, canola oil, or other flavorless vegetable oil for coating dough top and pot

2 tablespoons liquid egg substitute or egg white for glaze

1½ tablespoons each flax seeds, poppy seeds, and sesame seeds mixed together for garnish

FIRST RISE: Combine the cracked wheat and flax seeds with the boiling water and let stand until cooled thoroughly. In a large bowl, thoroughly stir together the whole wheat and bread flours, wheat germ, poppy seeds, sesame seeds, salt, and yeast. In another bowl or measuring cup, thoroughly whisk the honey into the ice water. Vigorously stir the mixture and the cracked wheat–flax mixture into the bowl with the flours, scraping down the bowl sides completely and mixing just until the dough is thoroughly blended. If the ingredients are too dry to mix together, gradually add in just enough more ice water to form a fairly stiff dough. (The seeds will absorb moisture, stiffening the dough further during the rise.) If the dough is soft, add more whole wheat flour until it is firmed up but not stiff. Brush or spray the top with oil. Tightly cover the bowl with plastic wrap. If desired, for best flavor or for convenience, refrigerate for 3 to 10 hours. Then let rise at cool room temperature for 12 to 18 hours; if convenient, vigorously stir once partway through the rise.

SECOND RISE: Thoroughly stir the dough. Using a well-oiled rubber spatula, fold the dough in towards the center, working your way around the bowl. Oil a 3½- to 4-quart Dutch oven or similar ovenproof pot. Sprinkle 2 tablespoons of whole wheat flour into the pot, then tip back and forth to coat the bottom and sides. Invert the dough into the pot.

Sprinkle 2 to 3 tablespoons more whole wheat flour over the dough. Pat and smooth it into the dough surface with your fingertips. Then smooth and tuck the sides of the loaf underneath all the way around so it forms a smooth, round, high dome, about 7 inches in diameter. Brush away any excess flour, then brush the loaf all over with the liquid egg substitute. Immediately sprinkle the mixed seed garnish over the loaf (it will be heavily coated). Using well-oiled kitchen shears or a serrated knife, cut a ⅛-inch-deep spiral slash in the loaf top. Cover with the lid.

LET RISE USING ANY OF THESE METHODS: For a 2- to 4-hour regular rise, let stand at warm room temperature; for a 1½- to 2½-hour accelerated rise, let stand in a turned-off microwave along with 1 cup of boiling-hot water; or, for an extended rise, refrigerate for 4 to 24 hours, then let stand at room temperature. Continue the rise until the dough doubles from its original size.

BAKING PRELIMINARIES: 20 minutes before baking time, put a rack in the lower third of the oven; preheat to 475°F.

BAKING: Reduce the heat to 425°F. Bake, covered, on the lower rack for 55 to 60 minutes, until the top is lightly browned and firm. Bake, uncovered, for 10 to 15 minutes longer, until well browned, occasionally testing with a skewer inserted in the thickest part (or until the center registers 205° to 207°F on an instant-read thermometer). Then bake for 5 to 10 minutes more to be sure the center is done. Cool the loaf in the pot on a wire rack for at least 15 minutes before serving. Remove the loaf to the rack; cool thoroughly.

TIP: If you happen to have wheat berries, which are, in fact, just uncooked whole wheat kernels, you can turn them into cracked wheat using a food processor, coffee grinder, or blender. It will take 2 or 3 minutes in a processor but only 30 to 60 seconds in a coffee grinder or blender to chop the wheat berries to the cracked wheat stage.

SERVING AND STORING: Cut the loaf into portions; it tastes good warm but cuts much better when cool. Cool completely before storing. To maintain the crisp crust, store in a large bowl draped with a clean tea towel or in a heavy paper bag. Or, to prevent drying, store airtight in a plastic bag or foil: The crust will soften, but can be crisped by heating the loaf, uncovered, in a 400°F oven for a few minutes. The bread will keep at room temperature for up to 3 days, and may be frozen, airtight, for up to 2 months.

100 percent whole wheat–honey bread

1 cup plus 2 tablespoons boiling water

$1/3$ cup clover honey or other mild honey

$3^1/2$ cups (17.5 ounces) whole wheat flour or white whole wheat flour, divided, plus more as needed

$1^1/2$ teaspoons table salt

$1^1/4$ teaspoons instant, fast-rising, or bread machine yeast

$3/4$ cup plus 2 tablespoons ice water, plus more if needed

$2^1/2$ tablespoons corn oil, canola oil, or other flavorless vegetable oil, plus more for coating dough top and pan

Creating a 100 percent whole wheat bread would seem a simple task, but producing one that has good texture and tastes mellow instead of slightly bitter can be a challenge. The traditional tack of adding honey to balance the bitter edge of whole wheat flour works to a point, but another little known method introduced in *Peter Reinhart's Whole Grain Breads* also helps a lot. Based on brewers' techniques for making grain mash, this innovative technique involves partially cooking part of the whole wheat flour by pouring over some boiling water, then keeping the mixture barely hot by occasionally reheating it.

Yes, this requires an extra step or two, but it greatly improves the taste and texture of the finished loaf. The hot water instantly tames the harshness and creates a mixture reminiscent of very sweet, smooth cream of wheat. (The change is caused by enzymes that convert starches into sugars and cause molecules to gelatinize and hold water.) When added to the rest of the dough, the mush begins to act on the whole amount, lending the loaf an exceptionally mellow taste and moist, creamy texture.

The only catch is that the same chemical processes that sweeten and moisten also break down the gluten. So, for a loaf that holds its shape and has good structure, incorporate the mash just before the second rise, and bake the dough as soon as it is raised. Don't try to use the extended rise option, as this will result in a sunken (though very tasty!) loaf.

Wholesome yet truly good-tasting, this bread is excellent for sandwiches, toasting, and eating as is. For a loaf with a slightly lighter color, use white whole wheat flour, a recently introduced product made from a milder, lighter-colored—but still healthful—variety of wheat.

Yield: 1 large loaf, 12 to 14 slices

FIRST RISE: In a 2-quart microwave-safe bowl, make a mash by vigorously stirring the boiling water and honey into 1 cup (5 ounces) of the whole wheat flour until well blended and smooth. Cover with microwave-safe plastic and place in the microwave oven. Set a cup of boiling-hot water in the oven to help keep it warm. After 15 minutes, reheat the mash and hot water by microwaving on high power for 1 minute. Thirty minutes later, again reheat by microwaving on high power for 1 minute. Then let the mash stand, covered, in the microwave, until completely cooled. Set aside at room temperature for up to 18 hours.

In a large bowl, thoroughly stir together 2 cups (10 ounces) of the flour, the salt, and the yeast. In another bowl or measuring cup, whisk together the ice water and oil, then stir the mixture into the bowl with the flour until smooth and well blended. If the mixture is dry, add just enough more water to facilitate blending and produce a firm but not stiff dough. Brush or spray the top with oil. Tightly cover the bowl with plastic wrap. If desired, for best flavor or for convenience, refrigerate for 3 to 10 hours. Then let rise at cool room temperature for 12 to 18 hours.

SECOND RISE: Thoroughly stir the cooled mash mixture, then ½ cup (2.5 ounces) of the flour, into the dough, vigorously mixing until very thoroughly blended; if desired, use a dough hook and heavy-duty mixer on low, as this is tiring to do by hand. If necessary, using flour-dusted fingertips or the mixer, sprinkle over and work in enough more flour to yield a very stiff dough. Coat a 9 × 5-inch loaf pan with nonstick spray, then add 1 tablespoon flour, tipping the pan back and forth to evenly coat the interior.

Using a well-oiled rubber spatula, fold the dough in towards the center, working your way around the bowl. Invert the dough into the pan. Brush or spray the dough with oil. Smooth out the top and evenly press the dough into the pan with oiled fingertips; for best appearance, tuck the dough evenly underneath at the ends. Evenly dust the loaf with ½ tablespoon whole wheat flour; smooth it evenly over the loaf top. Cover the pan with nonstick spray–coated plastic wrap.

LET THE DOUGH RISE USING EITHER OF THESE METHODS: For a 2- to 4-hour regular rise, let stand at warm room temperature; for a 1½- to 2½-hour accelerated rise, let stand in a turned-off microwave along with 1 cup of boiling-hot water. Remove the plastic when the dough nears it, then continue the rise until dough extends ¾ inch above the pan rim.

BAKING PRELIMINARIES: 15 minutes before baking time, put a rack in the lower third of the oven; preheat to 375°F.

BAKING: Bake on the lower rack for 50 to 55 minutes, or until the loaf is well browned and firm on top; if the top begins to over-brown, tent with foil. Bake for about 10 minutes longer, until a skewer inserted in the thickest part comes out with just a few particles clinging to the end (or until the center registers 206° to 208°F on an instant-read thermometer). Then bake for 5 to 10 minutes more to ensure the center is done. Cool in the pan on a wire rack for 10 minutes. Turn the loaf onto the rack; cool thoroughly.

SERVING AND STORING: The loaf slices best when cool. Cool completely before storing airtight in plastic or foil. The bread will keep at room temperature for 3 days, and may be frozen, airtight, for up to 2 months.

four grain–honey bread

KS QUOTIENT— Easy: All ingredients added before the first rise. No hand-shaping.

This recipe is a perfect place to start if you're trying to woo white bread fans away from cottony loaves and down the whole-grain path. Even before it's out of the oven, the handsome, homespun look and gentle fragrance of this bread attract a waiting crowd. And, owing to a mild, soothing flavor combo of cornmeal, oats, brown rice, wheat flour, and honey, it delivers on its promise. This is a fine bread for toasting, making sandwiches, and, as my family can attest, devouring straight from the oven.

Yield: 1 large loaf

2 cups (10 ounces) unbleached white bread flour, plus more as needed

1 cup (5 ounces) whole wheat flour

½ cup white or yellow cornmeal, preferably stone-ground, plus more for garnish

⅓ cup rolled oats, plus more for garnish

⅓ cup cooked and cooled brown rice

Generous 1½ teaspoons salt

¾ teaspoon instant, fast-rising, or bread machine yeast

½ cup clover honey or other mild honey

1¼ cups ice water, plus more if needed

Corn oil or other flavorless vegetable oil for coating dough top and baking pan

FIRST RISE: In a large bowl, thoroughly stir together the bread flour, whole wheat flour, cornmeal, oats, brown rice, salt, and yeast. In another bowl or measuring cup, thoroughly whisk the honey into the ice water. Vigorously stir the mixture into the bowl with the flours, scraping down the bowl sides and mixing just until the dough is thoroughly blended. If the ingredients are too dry to mix together, gradually add in just enough more ice water to facilitate mixing; don't over-moisten, as the dough should be stiff. If necessary, mix in more bread flour to stiffen it. Brush or spray the top with oil. Tightly cover the bowl with plastic wrap. If desired, for best flavor or for convenience, refrigerate for 3 to 10 hours. Then let rise at cool room temperature for 12 to 18 hours; if convenient, stir once during the rise.

SECOND RISE: Vigorously stir the dough. Using a well-oiled rubber spatula, fold the dough in towards the center, all the way around the bowl. Dust an oiled 9 × 5-inch loaf pan with 1 tablespoon each cornmeal and rolled oats, tipping it back and forth to coat the pan sides. Turn out the dough into the pan. Brush or spray the top with oil. Smooth out the top and press the dough into the pan with oiled fingertips or a rubber spatula. Sprinkle ½ tablespoon each cornmeal and rolled oats over the top. Press down to imbed. Cut four or five 3-inch-long, ¼-inch-deep evenly spaced slashes diagonally across the loaf top. Cover the pan with nonstick spray–coated plastic wrap.

LET RISE USING ANY OF THESE METHODS: For a 2- to 4-hour regular rise, let stand at warm room temperature; for a 1½- to 2½-hour accelerated rise, let stand in a turned-off microwave oven along with 1 cup of boiling-hot water. Or, for an extended rise, refrigerate for 4 to 24 hours, then let stand at room temperature. Remove the plastic when the dough nears it, then continue the rise until the dough extends ½ inch above the pan rim.

BAKING PRELIMINARIES: 15 minutes before baking time, put a rack in the lower third of the oven; preheat to 350°F.

BAKING: Bake on the lower rack for 50 to 60 minutes, or until the loaf is well browned and firm on top; cover with foil if necessary to prevent over-browning. Continue baking for 10 to 15 minutes longer, testing until a skewer inserted in the thickest part comes out with just a few particles on the end (or until the center registers 207° to 209°F on an instant-read thermometer). Bake for 5 to 10 minutes more to ensure the center is done. Cool in the pan on a wire rack for 10 minutes. Turn the loaf onto the rack; cool thoroughly.

SERVING AND STORING: Cool thoroughly before slicing or storing in a plastic bag or foil. The bread will keep at room temperature for 2 to 3 days, and may be frozen, airtight, for up to 2 months.

rustic rye
pot bread

Made without molasses, brown sugar, cocoa powder, coffee, or any of the other ingredients often used to deepen rye bread color and gussy up its flavor, this hearty, but not heavy, loaf has an entirely different character from some of its darker-hued cousins. Here the distinctive, earthy flavor of the grain takes center stage, and, since the dough is not sweet, the pleasing slight bitterness of the rye comes through.

As is true in most deli or Jewish rye recipes, the rye taste in this version is heightened (just slightly) with a sour component, though not the usual hard-to-come-by yeast starter. Instead, the recipe calls for a longer-than-normal first rise to boost the acid (a by-product of fermentation), and then after the first rise, the pH is lowered even further with some vinegar or dill pickle juice. A combination of caraway, fennel, and dill seeds lends the best flavor to the bread, but just caraway seeds will do in a pinch.

Though this bread is baked in a pot, the method is a little different from most pot breads in the book. Instead of simply being turned out into or shaped in the baking container, it is set on parchment, which is then used as a sling to slip the dough in and out of the baking pot. Particularly if the pot has a smallish diameter (less than 10 inches), the parchment will crinkle and fold up around the loaf edges, giving it an interesting uneven ruffled shape. It almost looks as if it were baked in a classic fluted brioche pan that crumpled from the heat! While this rough-hewn appearance wouldn't suit many loaves, it seems appropriate for this homespun, craggy bread. **Yield: 1 large loaf, 12 to 14 portions or slices**

2 cups (10 ounces) rye flour, preferably dark, plus more for garnish

2 cups (10 ounces) unbleached white bread flour, plus more as needed

1½ tablespoons granulated sugar

2 teaspoons table salt

1 tablespoon assorted seeds, preferably 1 teaspoon each caraway, fennel, and dill seeds mixed together (or substitute 1 tablespoon caraway seeds), divided

¾ teaspoon instant, fast-rising, or bread machine yeast

2¼ cups ice water, plus more if needed

2 tablespoons apple cider vinegar or dill pickle juice

Corn oil, canola oil, or other flavorless vegetable oil or oil spray for coating dough

FIRST RISE: In a large bowl, thoroughly stir together the rye flour, white flour, sugar, salt, 2 teaspoons of the seeds, and the yeast. In another bowl or measuring cup, stir together the water and vinegar, then vigorously stir into the bowl with the flour, scraping down the sides until the ingredients are thoroughly blended. If the mixture is dry, add in just enough more ice water to facilitate mixing; don't over-moisten, as the dough should be stiff. If necessary, stir in enough more white flour to stiffen it. Brush or spray the top with oil. Cover the bowl with plastic wrap. If desired, for best flavor or for convenience, refrigerate for 3 to 10 hours. Then let rise at cool room temperature for 16 to 20 hours.

SECOND RISE: Vigorously stir the dough, adding more rye flour until very stiff, if necessary. Thoroughly scrape down the bowl sides. Using a well-oiled rubber spatula, fold the dough in towards the center, working all the way around the bowl. Set out a 15-inch square of baking parchment. Spray it with nonstick spray, then very generously dust it with rye flour. Invert the dough into the center of the parchment. Generously dust the dough with more rye flour. Smooth out and round the surface and firmly tuck the dough edges underneath all around to form an evenly shaped, domed loaf; it will be sticky, so flour your hands, and sprinkle more flour over the top as needed. Using the parchment as a sling, transfer the loaf to a deep bowl just slightly smaller in diameter than the baking pot to be used. Tent the bowl with nonstick spray–coated foil.

LET RISE USING ANY OF THESE METHODS: For a 1½- to 2½-hour regular rise, let stand at warm room temperature; for a 1- to 2-hour accelerated rise, let stand in a turned-off microwave along with 1 cup of boiling-hot water; or for an extended rise, refrigerate for 4 to 24 hours, then set out at room temperature. Continue the rise until the dough doubles from the deflated size.

BAKING PRELIMINARIES: 20 minutes before baking time, put a rack in the lower third of the oven; preheat to 450°F. Heat a 3½- to 4-quart heavy metal pot or Dutch oven (preferably with 10-inch maximum diameter) or a deep 4-quart heavy ovenproof saucepan in the oven until sizzling hot (check with a few drops of water), then remove it (use oven mitts). Sprinkle or spray the dough top generously with water. Sprinkle over the remaining seeds, patting down to embed slightly. Using well-oiled kitchen shears or a serrated knife, cut a ½-inch-deep, 3-inch diameter circular slash in the dough center. Using the parchment as a sling, carefully lift the dough into the pot; take care not to touch the hot pot. Immediately top the pot with its lid.

BAKING: Reduce the heat to 425°F. Bake on the lower rack for 45 minutes. Remove the lid. Using the parchment, lift the loaf from the pot and place on a baking sheet. Pull the parchment away from the loaf sides so they are exposed. (If the top is well browned, cover it with foil.) Bake for 15 to 25 minutes longer, until a skewer inserted in the thickest part comes out with just a few crumbs on the tip (or until the center registers 210° to 212°F on an instant-read thermometer). Then bake for 5 minutes longer to ensure the center is baked through. Cool in the pan on a wire rack for 10 to 15 minutes. Remove the loaf to the rack; cool thoroughly.

SERVING AND STORING: Cool before slicing and storing. The flavor improves after several hours of storage. To maintain the crisp crust, store in a large bowl draped with a clean tea towel or in a heavy paper bag. Or store airtight in a plastic bag or foil: The crust will soften, but can be crisped by heating the loaf, uncovered, in a 400°F oven for a few minutes. The bread will keep at room temperature for 3 days, and may be frozen, airtight, for up to 2 months.

raisin
pumpernickel

3 cups (15 ounces) medium or dark rye flour, divided, plus ½ cup (2.5 ounces), or as needed

1½ cups dark raisins, rinsed under hot water and drained

1¼ cups plus 1 to 3 tablespoons boiling water

2 cups (10 ounces) unbleached white bread flour

2 tablespoons unsweetened cocoa powder, sifted after measuring

2¼ teaspoons table salt

1¼ teaspoons instant, fast-rising, or bread machine yeast, divided

3 tablespoons light or dark molasses (not blackstrap)

2 tablespoon corn oil, canola oil, or other flavorless vegetable oil

1¾ cups ice water, plus more if needed

2 tablespoons apple cider vinegar

1 large egg white beaten with 1 teaspoon water for glaze, or 2 to 3 tablespoons liquid egg substitute for glaze

The mixing method for this bread is a little different than for most recipes in the book, but reminiscent of the one used for the 100 Percent Whole Wheat–Honey Bread (page 134). The raisins and some of the rye flour are hydrated with boiling water, then set aside at the same time the rest of the dough is separately set aside to rise. The boiling water plumps the raisins and activates enzymes in the rye flour, which give it a sweet, rich taste and cause it to absorb an unusually large amount of water. Once this mixture, or mash, is incorporated into the rest of the dough, the enzymes continue to work, producing a pumpernickel that is particularly mellow and moist.

Yield: 2 medium loaves, 12 to 14 portions or slices

FIRST RISE: In a medium bowl, stir 1 cup (5 ounces) of the rye flour and the raisins with the boiling water to form a thin sour cream consistency; add a little more water or rye flour as necessary. Cover and set aside at room temperature for 20 to 24 hours. In a large bowl, thoroughly stir together 2 cups (10 ounces) of the rye flour, the bread flour, cocoa, salt, and yeast. In another bowl or measuring cup, thoroughly whisk the molasses and oil into the ice water. Vigorously stir it into the bowl with the flours, scraping down the bowl sides and mixing until the dough is thoroughly blended. If too dry to mix, gradually mix in just enough more ice water to facilitate mixing; don't over-moisten, as the dough should be firm. If necessary, add in enough more rye flour to firm it. Brush or spray the top with oil. Tightly cover the bowl with plastic wrap. If desired, for best flavor or for convenience, refrigerate for 3 to 10 hours. Then let rise at cool room temperature for 20 to 24 hours; if convenient, vigorously stir once partway through the rise.

SECOND RISE: Stir the vinegar into the raisin mixture. Vigorously and thoroughly stir the raisin mixture, then ½ cup of the rye flour, into the dough until very well blended. If necessary, thoroughly stir in (or work in with flour-dusted fingertips) enough more rye flour to yield a very stiff dough.

Generously dust 2 well-oiled 8½ × 4½-inch loaf pans with rye flour. Divide the dough in half using oiled kitchen shears or a serrated knife. Turn each half into a pan. Brush or spray the tops with oil. Using well-oiled fingertips, pat and smooth the dough out into the pans. Then smooth and firmly tuck the ends underneath to form evenly shaped loaves. Brush the loaf tops evenly with egg white (or liquid egg substitute). Cover the pans with nonstick spray–coated plastic wrap.

LET RISE USING ANY OF THESE METHODS: For a 1½- to 2½-hour regular rise, let stand at warm room temperature; for a 1- to 2-hour accelerated rise, let stand in a turned-off microwave along with 1 cup of boiling-hot water; or for an extended rise, refrigerate for 4 to 24 hours, then set out at room temperature. Continue the rise until the dough almost reaches the plastic. Remove it and continue until the loaves extend ¼ inch above the rims.

BAKING PRELIMINARIES: 20 minutes before baking time, put a rack in the lower third of the oven; preheat to 400ºF.

BAKING: Bake the loaves on the lower rack for 25 to 35 minutes, or until the tops are nicely browned. Tent the tops with foil and continue baking for 20 to 30 minutes longer, until a skewer inserted in the thickest part comes out with just a few particles clinging to the bottom portion (or until the center registers 208º to 210ºF on an instant-read thermometer). Then bake for 5 to 10 minutes more to be sure the centers are done. Cool the loaves in the pans for 10 minutes. Then turn them out onto a wire rack and cool at least 1 hour before serving.

SERVING AND STORING: Serve cut into thin slices. The bread will keep at room temperature for 3 to 4 days, and may be frozen, airtight, for up to 2 months.

super seeded
almond butter
health bread

KS QUOTIENT— Fairly Easy: Lots of ingredients, but easily mixed. No hand-shaping.

4½ cups (22.5 ounces) unbleached white bread flour, plus more as needed

½ cup roasted, salted sunflower seeds

⅓ cup old-fashioned or quick-cooking (not instant) rolled oats

⅓ cup cooked (cooled) brown rice

¼ cup white or yellow cornmeal, preferably stone-ground

¼ cup millet seeds, plus 1 tablespoon for garnish

¼ cup sesame seeds, plus 1 tablespoon for garnish

2 tablespoons flax seeds, preferably golden

2½ teaspoons table salt

1¼ teaspoons instant, fast-rising, or bread machine yeast

2¼ cups ice water, plus more if needed

(continued on page 145)

Loaded with four kinds of seeds, four kinds of grain, almond butter, and honey, this high-fiber, protein-rich bread is one of the few in the book that may warrant a trip to the health food store. Not only are the seeds called for usually sold in bulk, which is most economical, but they are usually in demand and turn over rapidly there, which means they are likely to be very fresh.

The recipe also calls for unsalted toasted almond butter, which looks a bit like peanut butter, but is made with ground almonds. It boosts the protein and provides fat that helps keep the loaves moist and soft, while also lending a subtle nutty taste. Most health food stores (and some supermarkets) carry both raw and roasted almond butters, some salted, some not; choose unsalted butter that's made from roasted almonds for the most distinct flavor. (It usually has a darker color, but check the label to be sure.)

The two generous loaves are slightly sweet and moist from honey, compact, nubby from the seeds, and full-bodied enough that a slice or two makes a filling snack or substantial addition to a light meal.

Yield: 2 large loaves

FIRST RISE: In a very large bowl, thoroughly stir together the bread flour, sunflower seeds, oats, rice, cornmeal, ¼ cup each millet and sesame seeds, flax seeds, salt, and yeast until blended. In another bowl, stir together the water, honey, and almond butter until very well blended. Vigorously stir the mixture into the bowl with the flour, scraping down the sides and mixing just until very well blended. If the mixture is too dry to blend, add in just enough more ice water to facilitate mixing; don't overmoisten, as the dough should be fairly stiff. Brush or spray the top with oil. Tightly cover the bowl with plastic wrap. If desired, for best flavor or for convenience, refrigerate for 3 to 10 hours. Then let rise at cool room temperature for 12 to 18 hours.

SECOND RISE: Vigorously stir the dough, incorporating more flour to yield a hard-to-stir consistency if necessary. Cut the dough in half with well-oiled kitchen shears or a serrated knife, placing each portion in an oiled 9 × 5-inch loaf pan. Brush or spray the loaf tops with oil. Using an oiled rubber spatula or your fingertips, smooth out the tops and press the dough evenly into the pans. Generously and evenly brush each top with Cornstarch Glaze (or liquid egg substitute); immediately sprinkle ½ tablespoon of the sesame, then millet seeds, over each loaf. Using oiled kitchen shears or a serrated knife, cut a ½-inch-deep slash lengthwise down the loaf centers. Cover the pans with nonstick spray–coated plastic wrap.

LET RISE USING ANY OF THESE METHODS: For a 1½- to 2½-hour regular rise, let stand at warm room temperature; for a 1- to 2-hour accelerated rise, let stand in a turned-off microwave along with 1 cup of boiling-hot water; or for an extended rise, refrigerate for 4 to 48 hours, then set out at room temperature. Continue the rise until the dough extends ½ inch above the pan rims.

BAKING PRELIMINARIES: 15 minutes before baking time, place a rack in the lower third of the oven; preheat to 375°F.

BAKING: Reduce the temperature to 350°F. Bake on the lower rack for 45 to 50 minutes, until the loaves are well browned and firm on top. Cover the tops with foil and continue baking for 15 to 25 minutes, occasionally testing with a skewer inserted in the thickest part until it comes out with just slightly moist particles clinging to the bottom (or the center registers 208° to 210°F on an instant-read thermometer). Bake for 5 to 10 minutes more to ensure the centers are baked through. Let cool on wire racks for 15 minutes. Remove the loaves to cooling racks; let cool completely.

SERVING AND STORING: The loaves slice best when cool, but the bread is good served warm, at room temperature, or toasted. Cool completely before storing. Store airtight in plastic or foil. Store at room temperature for 2 to 3 days; freeze, airtight, for up to 2 months, then thaw, unwrapped, at room temperature.

⅔ cup clover honey or other mild honey

½ cup unsweetened, unsalted toasted almond butter, stirred well before measuring if separated

Corn oil, canola oil, or other flavorless oil for coating dough tops

2 tablespoons Cornstarch Glaze (page 189), or 2 tablespoons liquid egg substitute for finishing loaf tops

crunchy-munchy
pumpkin, sunflower, and flax seed boule

KS QUOTIENT— Fairly Easy: All ingredients added before the first rise. Easy hand-shaping required.

1½ cups (7.5 ounces) whole wheat flour, plus more as needed

1½ cups (7.5 ounces) unbleached white bread flour

¼ cup flax seeds, preferably golden

1¼ teaspoons table salt

1 teaspoon instant, fast-rising, or bread machine yeast

3 tablespoons clover honey or other mild honey

1½ tablespoons corn oil, canola oil, or other flavorless vegetable oil, plus more for coating dough top and pan

1⅓ cups plus 1 tablespoon ice water, plus more if needed

⅓ cup roasted, salted pumpkin seeds, plus 2 tablespoons for garnish

⅓ cup roasted, salted sunflower seeds, plus 2 tablespoons for garnish

(continued on page 147)

I often find the seeds in breads a distraction, but in this case they make the loaf. The generous quantity of roasted pumpkin, sunflower, and flax seeds lends a delicious and very distinctive nuttiness—not to mention crunchy texture, eye appeal, and protein. The bread is baked in a covered pot for most of its time in the oven, which crisps the crust and the seeds on it, but also prevents them from burning.

Be sure to use very fresh, appealing-tasting seeds for this recipe. If you can only find raw, unsalted sunflower and pumpkin seeds, toss them with ¼ teaspoon corn oil or canola oil and ⅛ teaspoon of salt and roast at 325°F, stirring occasionally, until lightly toasted, 7 to 9 minutes.

Yield: 1 large loaf, 12 to 14 slices

FIRST RISE: In a large bowl, thoroughly stir together the whole wheat flour, bread flour, flax seeds, salt, and yeast. In another bowl or measuring cup, thoroughly whisk the honey and oil into the water. Vigorously stir the mixture into the bowl with the flours, scraping down the sides and mixing just until the dough is thoroughly blended. If the ingredients are too dry to mix together, gradually add in just enough more ice water to facilitate mixing, as the dough should be slightly stiff. If necessary, stir in enough more whole wheat flour to stiffen it. Brush or spray the top with oil. Tightly cover the bowl with plastic wrap. If desired, for best flavor or for convenience, refrigerate for 3 to 10 hours. Then let rise at cool room temperature for 12 to 18 hours.

SECOND RISE: Working in the bowl and turning the dough as you work, sprinkle about half the pumpkin and sunflower seeds over the surface. With lightly oiled hands, work in the seeds and fold the dough over to fully incorporate them. Continue working in the remaining seeds, folding over the dough until all the seeds are incorporated and fairly evenly distributed throughout. Sprinkle the dough with a little whole wheat flour. Press and smooth it into the dough, shaping it into a ball as you work.

Oil a 3½- to 4-quart Dutch oven or similar round, ovenproof pot. Transfer the ball to the pot. Dusting the dough with more flour as needed to prevent stickiness, tuck the edges under firmly all the way around, forming a smooth, high-domed round loaf about 6½ inches in diameter. Brush off excess flour, then brush all over with Cornstarch Glaze (or egg white wash), then immediately sprinkle the surface with the remaining pumpkin and sunflower seeds for garnish. Using well-oiled kitchen shears or a serrated knife, cut a 2½-inch diameter, ½-inch-deep circle in the top. Cover the pot with its lid.

LET RISE USING ANY OF THESE METHODS: For a 2- to 4-hour regular rise, let stand at warm room temperature; for a 1½- to 2½-hour accelerated rise, let stand in a turned-off microwave with 1 cup of boiling-hot water; or for an extended rise, refrigerate for 4 to 24 hours, then let stand at room temperature. Continue the rise until the dough doubles from its deflated size.

BAKING PRELIMINARIES: 15 minutes before baking time, put a rack in the lower third of the oven; preheat to 450°F. Generously brush or spray the loaf with water.

BAKING: Lower the heat to 425°F. Bake on the lower rack, covered, for 55 to 60 minutes, or until the loaf is lightly browned. Uncover, and continue baking for 10 to 15 minutes more, until a skewer inserted in the thickest part comes out with just a few particles on the end (or the center registers 208° to 210°F on an instant-read thermometer). Then bake for 5 minutes longer to ensure the center is done. Cool in the pot on a wire rack for 10 minutes. Turn the loaf onto the rack; cool thoroughly.

SERVING AND STORING: Tastes good warm but will cut much better when cool. Cool completely before storing. To maintain the crisp crust, store draped with a clean tea towel or in a heavy paper bag. Or to prevent the loaf from drying out, store airtight in a plastic bag or wrapped in foil: The crust will soften, but can be crisped by heating the loaf, uncovered, in a 400°F oven for a few minutes. The bread will keep at room temperature for 3 days, and may be frozen, airtight, for up to 2 months.

½ to 1 teaspoon sea salt or other coarse crystal salt, optional

Cornstarch Glaze (page 189), or 1 egg white, beaten, or 2 tablespoons liquid egg substitute

hearty multigrain
boule with
molasses

2 cups (10 ounces) unbleached all-purpose white flour or unbleached white bread flour

1⅓ cups (6.66 ounces) whole wheat flour, plus more as needed

1 cup (5 ounces) medium or dark rye flour

1 cup 100 percent bran cereal, finely crushed (in a small baggie) after measuring

½ cup old-fashioned rolled oats

¼ cup wheat germ

2¼ teaspoons table salt

1¼ teaspoons instant, fast-rising, or bread machine yeast

½ cup light or dark molasses (not blackstrap)

2 tablespoon corn oil, canola oil, or other flavorless vegetable oil, plus extra for coating dough top and pie plate

2⅓ cups ice water, plus more if needed

I love this bread. (Others partial to the pungent appeal of molasses invariably like it, too.) I created it years ago in desperation, after the Alexandria, Virginia, bakery that had satisfied my hankering whenever I was willing to make the trip from my Maryland home to buy it suddenly went out of business. Guided by the ingredient label on a loaf I found buried in the freezer, I was eventually able to approximate the compact, but not dense, texture and hearty, addictive flavor.

The ample amount of molasses, in concert with the whole wheat, wheat germ and bran, rye, and small amount of oats, gives the large loaf a robust yet sweet taste and aroma vaguely reminiscent of good, "bran-y" bran muffins or perhaps dark Boston brown bread. The crumb is medium-fine and the crust springy. Smoothed with a little butter or a mild cheese, served warm or at room temperature, this bread is heaven. I also like it with seafood salad. **Yield: 1 very large round loaf, 14 to 16 slices**

FIRST RISE: In a large bowl, thoroughly stir together the white flour, whole wheat flour, rye flour, bran cereal, oats, wheat germ, salt, and yeast. In another bowl, thoroughly whisk the molasses and oil into the water. Thoroughly stir the mixture into the bowl with the flours, scraping down the sides and mixing just until well blended. If too dry to mix together, add just enough more water to facilitate mixing; don't over-moisten, as the dough should be stiff. If necessary, stir in enough more whole wheat flour to stiffen it. Brush or spray the top with oil. Tightly cover the bowl with plastic wrap. If desired, for best flavor or for convenience, refrigerate for 3 to 10 hours. Then set aside at cool room temperature for 12 to 18 hours. Stir once partway through the rise, if convenient.

SECOND RISE: Vigorously stir the dough, adding more whole wheat flour if needed to yield a very stiff consistency; then scrape down the sides. Using a well-oiled rubber spatula, fold the dough in towards the center, working all the way around the bowl. Oil a 9- to 9½-inch deep-sided pie plate or similar round 2- to 3-inch-deep pan. Sprinkle 2 tablespoons whole wheat flour in the plate, then tip back and forth to spread the flour on the bottom and sides. Invert the dough out into the plate. Sprinkle with more whole wheat flour. Pat and press it into the dough with your fingertips, shaping the dough into a ball as you work. Then press and firmly tuck the sides of the loaf underneath all the way around so it forms a smooth, round, high-domed loaf, about 6 inches in diameter; add more flour as needed to reduce stickiness. Evenly garnish with 1 more tablespoon whole wheat flour. Using well-oiled kitchen shears or a serrated knife, cut a ½-inch-deep, 3-inch square in the center top. Tent the top with nonstick spray–coated foil.

LET RISE USING ANY OF THESE METHODS: For a 1½- to 3-hour regular rise, let stand at warm room temperature; for a 1- to 2-hour accelerated rise, let stand in a turned-off microwave along with 1 cup of boiling-hot water; or for an extended rise, refrigerate for 4 to 48 hours, then set out at room temperature. Continue the rise until the dough doubles from its deflated size, removing the plastic wrap as the dough nears it.

BAKING PRELIMINARIES: 15 minutes before baking time, place a rack in the lower third of the oven; preheat to 375°F. Place a broiler pan on the oven bottom.

BAKING: Add a cup of ice water to the broiler pan, being careful of spattering and steam. Bake on the lower rack for 40 to 50 minutes until the top is nicely browned, then cover with foil as needed to prevent over-browning. Bake for 15 to 20 minutes longer, until a skewer inserted in the thickest part comes out with just a few moist particles clinging to the bottom portion (or until the center registers 208° to 210°F on an instant-read thermometer). Then bake for 5 to 10 minutes more to ensure the center is done. Let cool in the pan on a wire rack for 15 minutes. Slide the loaf onto the rack; cool thoroughly before storing.

SERVING AND STORING: Serve warm, or cool, or toasted; the bread slices best when cool. Cool thoroughly before storing in plastic or foil. Keeps at room temperature for up to 3 days. May be frozen, airtight, for up to 2 months.

brown and
wild rice
crunch bread

1¼ cups (6.25 ounces) whole wheat flour, plus more as needed

1¼ cups (6.25 ounces) unbleached white bread flour

½ cup uncooked, unseasoned long-grain brown rice and wild rice blend (or just brown rice), ground fairly fine after measuring

1 tablespoon granulated sugar

Generous 1 teaspoon table salt

¾ teaspoon instant, fast-rising, or bread machine yeast

1 tablespoon corn oil, canola oil, or other flavorless vegetable oil, plus more for coating dough top and pan

1⅓ cups ice water, plus more if needed

Breads featuring either raw brown rice or wild rice are rare, but as part of a personal campaign to incorporate more whole grains into my family's diet, I decided to grind up and add the last of a box of unseasoned brown and wild rice pilaf blend into a wheat bread recipe. The experiment was a huge success: The resulting loaf had such a lovely, distinctive, sweet grain flavor and appealing crunch that it won over even the tasters normally hostile to the slightest hint of whole grain.

I've since tried this recipe with just brown rice, and the loaf comes out a tad lighter and less crunchy, but tasting more or less the same, so the wild rice can be considered non-essential. The nutritional profile of wild rice, which is in fact a seed, not a grain, does dovetail nicely with that of the brown rice, though.

Note that because the brown rice is used uncooked, it must be ground into a flour for this recipe. Either a blender or (clean) coffee or spice grinder will work; a food processor blade isn't thin enough for the job. The mixture should end up mostly powdery, but for a little crunch, leave some particles the size of corn grits. (Larger bits will be too hard on the teeth.) Due to its popcorn-like aroma and flavor, brown basmati rice is especially appealing in this bread, but any variety of long-grain brown rice will do.

I like to serve this loaf warm and sliced thick with soups and stews. Once cooled and cut thinner, it's good for toast and sandwiches.

Yield: 1 medium loaf, 12 to 14 slices

FIRST RISE: In a large bowl, thoroughly stir together the whole wheat and bread flour, ground rice, sugar, salt, and yeast. In another bowl, whisk the oil into the water. Vigorously stir the mixture into the bowl with the flours, scraping down the sides and mixing until well blended and smooth. If the ingredients are too dry to mix together, gradually add in just enough more ice water to facilitate mixing; don't over-moisten, as the dough should be stiff. If necessary, add in more whole wheat flour to stiffen it. Brush or spray the top with oil. Tightly cover the bowl with plastic wrap. If desired, for best flavor or for convenience, refrigerate for 3 to 10 hours. Then let rise at cool room temperature for 18 to 24 hours.

SECOND RISE: Vigorously stir the dough, adding more whole wheat flour if needed to stiffen it, then carefully scrape down the sides. Using a well-oiled rubber spatula, fold the dough in towards the center, working all the way around the bowl. Invert the dough into a generously oiled 8½ × 4½-inch loaf pan. Brush or spray the dough top with oil. Smooth and press out the dough with well-oiled fingertips so it evenly fills the pan and is smooth on top. Using a well-oiled serrated knife, make 5 or 6 evenly spaced ¼-inch-deep crosswise slashes along the loaf top. Cover the pan with nonstick spray–coated plastic wrap.

LET RISE USING ANY OF THESE METHODS: For a 2- to 3-hour regular rise, let stand at warm room temperature; for a 1½- to 2½-hour accelerated rise, let stand in a turned-off microwave along with 1 cup of boiling water; or for an extended rise, refrigerate for 4 to 24 hours, then set out at room temperature. Continue the rise until the dough nears the plastic, then remove it and let the dough rise until 1 inch above the pan rim.

BAKING PRELIMINARIES: 15 minutes before baking time, put a rack in the lower third of the oven; preheat to 400°F.

BAKING: Bake on the lower rack for 35 to 45 minutes, or until the top is well browned. Continue baking for 15 to 20 minutes more, covering to prevent over-browning, until a skewer inserted in the thickest part comes out with just a few particles clinging to the bottom portion (or until the center registers 206° to 208°F on an instant-read thermometer). Then bake for 5 to 10 minutes more to be sure the center is done. Cool the pan on a wire rack for 10 minutes. Then turn out the loaf onto the rack and cool for at least 15 minutes before serving.

SERVING AND STORING: The loaf slices best when cool, but the bread is good served warm or at room temperature. Cool completely before storing airtight in plastic or foil. Keeps at room temperature for 3 days, and may be frozen, airtight, for up to 2 months.

gluten-free
light sandwich
bread

1²/₃ cups white rice flour, divided, plus more as needed

²/₃ cup old-fashioned or quick-cooking (not instant) gluten-free rolled oats

¹/₂ cup cornstarch

¹/₃ cup tapioca flour

¹/₃ cup flax seed meal or golden flax seed meal

Generous 1¹/₄ teaspoons table salt

1 teaspoon instant, fast-rising, or bread machine yeast

1¹/₃ cups ice water, plus more if needed

¹/₃ cup corn oil or canola oil, plus more for coating pan

3 tablespoons clover honey or other mild honey

1 large egg, at room temperature

¹/₄ cup plain low-fat or regular yogurt, drained of excess liquid

2¹/₂ teaspoons baking powder

Gluten, a rubbery protein abundant in wheat doughs, is normally the component that both holds yeast breads together and raises them by trapping the gas produced during fermentation. Which means that turning out yeasted baked goods without gluten is always challenging and that the results rarely stand up (so to speak) to breads made the usual wheat way.

Still, for the legions of gluten allergy sufferers with a desperate, abiding craving for bread, ersatz loaves are an acceptable alternative to never eating a sandwich, or toast, or a simple buttered slice again. According to several of my gluten-free friends who have tried many of the available commercial gluten-free products, they are better than nothing, but, often, just barely. Fresh, homemade, gluten-free breads, on the other hand, occasionally taste enough like the real thing to get them highly excited.

I am pleased to say that the following all-purpose yeasted sandwich bread recipe is one that did. Upon taking her first bite, a gluten-free friend declared this the best bread she'd eaten since forsaking gluten three years ago—so good, she said, it almost made her cry! She then carefully wrapped up her gift, took it home, and froze it so she could stretch out the pleasure over the next several weeks. She also insisted that I share this recipe with her immediately.

Admittedly, this bread isn't as springy and the taste isn't as wheaty as the usual wheat-based loaf, but a combination of carefully-chosen gluten-free flours and meals creates a light tan bread with a mild, pleasant multigrain taste and enough cohesiveness that this loaf works just fine for sandwiches. It is good for toast and eating as is, too. (For heartier, darker, seeded bread, see the variation at the end of the recipe.)

Yeast might not seem to serve a purpose in gluten-free doughs, but it does: First, it contributes the same sweet, earthy flavors and aromas that have always made people love yeast bread. Plus, there are a number of gluten substitutes (found in the gluten-free baking sections of health food stores) like tapioca starch, flax seed meal, and xanthan gum that help make the dough cohesive enough to trap at least some of the gas produced during fermentation. Baking powder provides the rest of the leavening.

Yield: 1 large loaf, 13 to 14 slices

FIRST RISE: In a large bowl, thoroughly stir together 1⅓ cups of the rice flour, the oats, cornstarch, tapioca flour, flax seed meal, salt, and yeast. In another bowl or measuring cup, thoroughly whisk together the water, oil, and honey, then stir them into the bowl with the flour and oats, scraping down the bowl sides and mixing until well blended. If the mixture is too stiff to blend together, stir in enough more water to facilitate mixing and yield a barely firm dough. (It will stiffen as it stands.) Tightly cover the bowl with plastic wrap. If desired, for best flavor or for convenience, refrigerate for 3 to 10 hours. Then let stand at cool room temperature for 12 to 18 hours. It's all right if the dough doesn't rise a lot.

SECOND RISE: Whisk the egg, then set aside 1 tablespoon to brush on the loaf top. Stir the yogurt, baking powder, and ⅓ cup of the rice flour into the remaining egg. Vigorously stir the mixture into the dough until well blended. If it is soft, stir in enough more white rice flour to yield a fairly stiff dough. Turn it out into a very well-greased 9 × 5-inch loaf pan. Evenly brush the top with oil. Smooth the surface with an oiled rubber spatula or fingertips. Brush the reserved egg over the surface. Using a well-oiled serrated knife or kitchen shears, make a ½-inch-deep cut lengthwise down the loaf. Cover the pan with nonstick spray–coated plastic wrap.

LET RISE USING EITHER OF THESE METHODS: For a 2½- to 4-hour regular rise, let stand at warm room temperature; for a 1½- to 3-hour accelerated rise, let stand in a turned-off microwave along with 1 cup of boiling-hot water. When the dough nears the plastic wrap, remove it and continue the rise until the dough extends ⅛ inch above the pan rim.

BAKING PRELIMINARIES: 15 minutes before baking time, place a rack in the lower third of the oven; preheat to 375°F.

BAKING: Bake on the lower rack for 55 to 60 minutes, until the top is nicely browned; if necessary, cover with foil to prevent over-browning. Continue baking for 10 to 15 minutes, until a skewer inserted in the thickest part comes out with only a few crumbs clinging to the bottom (or until the center registers 206° to 208°F on an instant-read thermometer). Then bake for another 5 to 10 minutes to ensure that the center is done. Cool in the pan on a wire rack for 15 minutes. Remove the loaf to the rack; cool thoroughly.

SERVING AND STORING: The loaf slices best when cool, but the bread is good served warm or at room temperature. Cool completely before storing airtight in plastic or foil. The bread will keep at room temperature for 3 days, and may be frozen, airtight, for up to 2 months.

VARIATION   HEARTY SEEDED GLUTEN-FREE BREAD—Proceed exactly as for Gluten-Free Light Sandwich Bread except: Substitute ¼ cup molasses for the honey. Substitute ½ cup cornmeal or ½ cup brown rice flour for the rolled oats. Stir together 1 tablespoon each millet, poppy seeds, sesame seeds, and flax seeds. Stir all but 1 tablespoon of the mixture into the dough before the first rise. Sprinkle the remaining 1 tablespoon over the loaf after brushing the loaf top with the egg before starting the second rise.

gluten-free faux rye bread

To put it kindly, some gluten-free breads have an "unusual" flavor and consistency. But this moist, springy loaf seems so normal and appealing that many tasters won't even realize it's gluten-free. It goes well with cheeses and smoked meats and is excellent for both sandwiches and toast. Though completely "ryeless," it has a pleasant sour rye taste, owing to the caraway seeds, molasses, and yogurt. The yeast also lends flavor and some lift. Baking powder leavens some, too.

This loaf is fairly simple to make once the various gluten-free ingredients are on hand. All are readily obtainable in the gluten-free sections of health food stores as well as in some large supermarkets.

Yield: 1 large loaf, 12 to 14 slices

FIRST RISE: In a large bowl, thoroughly stir together 1 cup of the rice flour, the brown rice flour, cornstarch, tapioca flour, flax seed meal, 1½ tablespoons of the caraway seeds, the xanthan gum, salt, and yeast. In another bowl or measuring cup, whisk together the water, oil, and molasses, then vigorously stir into the bowl with the flours, scraping down the bowl sides and mixing until well blended. If the dough is too stiff to blend together, stir in just enough water to facilitate mixing, but don't over-moisten, as it should be fairly firm. If necessary, add more rice flour to firm it. Tightly cover the bowl with plastic wrap. If desired, for best flavor or for convenience, refrigerate for 3 to 10 hours. Then let stand at cool room temperature for 12 to 18 hours. It's all right if this dough doesn't rise much.

SECOND RISE: In a small deep bowl, whisk the egg until smooth. Set aside 1 tablespoon for glazing the dough top. Stir the yogurt, baking powder, and ⅔ cup of white rice flour into the remaining egg. Vigorously stir the mixture into the dough until very well blended. If it is soft, stir in enough more white rice flour to yield a fairly stiff dough, scraping down the bowl.

1⅔ cups white rice flour, divided, plus more as needed

¾ cup brown rice flour

⅓ cup cornstarch

⅓ cup tapioca flour

⅓ cup flax seed meal or golden flax seed meal

2 tablespoons caraway seeds, divided

2 teaspoons xanthan gum

1¼ teaspoons table salt

1 teaspoon instant, fast-rising, or bread machine yeast

1½ cups ice water

⅓ cup corn oil or canola oil, plus more for coating pan

⅓ cup molasses

1 large egg, at room temperature

⅓ cup plain low-fat or regular yogurt, drained of excess liquid

2½ teaspoons baking powder

Turn the dough out into a well-greased 9 × 5-inch loaf pan. Brush the top with oil, then smooth out the surface with an oiled rubber spatula. Evenly brush on the reserved egg. Sprinkle with the remaining caraway seeds. Using well-oiled kitchen shears, make a 1/2-inch-deep slash lengthwise down the loaf. Cover the pan with nonstick spray–coated plastic wrap.

LET RISE USING EITHER OF THESE METHODS: For a 2 1/2- to 4-hour regular rise, let stand at warm room temperature; for a 1 1/2- to 3-hour accelerated rise, let stand in a turned-off microwave along with 1 cup of boiling-hot water. When the dough nears the plastic wrap, remove it and continue until the dough reaches the pan rim.

BAKING PRELIMINARIES: 15 minutes before baking time, place a rack in the lower third of the oven; preheat to 375ºF.

BAKING: Bake on the lower rack for 55 to 60 minutes, or until the top is nicely browned; cover with foil if needed to prevent over-browning. Continue baking for 15 to 20 minutes longer or until a skewer inserted in the thickest part comes out with only a few crumbs clinging to the bottom (or until the center registers 206º to 208ºF on an instant-read thermometer). Then bake for 5 to 10 minutes longer to ensure the center is baked through. Cool in the pan on a wire rack for 15 minutes. Turn the loaf out onto the rack; cool thoroughly.

SERVING AND STORING: The loaf slices best when cool, but the bread is good served warm or at room temperature. Cool completely before storing airtight in plastic or foil. The bread will keep at room temperature for 3 days, and may be frozen, airtight, for up to 2 months.

VARIATION SWEDISH-STYLE GLUTEN-FREE FAUX RYE BREAD—Proceed exactly as directed for Gluten-Free Faux Rye Bread, except reduce the caraway seeds added to the dough to 1 teaspoon and add in 1 teaspoon anise seeds and 1 teaspoon finely grated orange zest. Garnish the loaf top with 1/2 teaspoon each caraway seeds and anise seeds.

VARIATION GLUTEN-FREE FAUX DARK RYE BREAD WITH RAISINS—Proceed exactly as directed for Gluten-Free Faux Rye Bread, except add 1 tablespoon unsweetened cocoa powder (sifted after measuring) to the flour mixture. Add 1 tablespoon packed dark brown sugar and 1 cup dark, seedless raisins (rinsed and well drained) with the water-molasses mixture.

sweet breads and gift breads

WHEN MOST PEOPLE THINK OF YEAST BREADS, PEASANT rounds and sandwich loaves come to mind first, but enticing coffeecakes and festive sweet breads can be made with yeast, too. In fact, some of the most traditional holiday cakes—panettone and Mardi Gras King's cake—are actually rich yeasted breads.

Besides being aerated with yeast, the cakes and coffeecakes here differ from chemically leavened cakes in that the doughs tend to be less sweet. Yeast organisms don't grow well in the presence of a lot of sugar because as the sugar dissolves, it draws up water the yeast organisms need. More than about 2 tablespoons of sugar per cup of flour can cause yeast dehydration, even though the dough may still look very moist. So, don't be tempted to just toss in extra sugar, and follow the directions for incorporating it carefully.

It is possible to increase the level of sweetness by adding honey to a dough, or by tucking a sweet filling inside it. Another easy approach is to top the finished bread or cake with a sweet icing or glaze.

In addition to a nice selection of coffeecakes and yeasted cakes, check out the gift bread recipes at the end of the chapter. These feature easy, ready-to-use bread mixes that are attractively layered in clear jars. The recipients of these gift kits simply add water and oil and stir to create a delectable loaf of homemade bread.

mardi gras
king's cake

KS QUOTIENT— Fairly Easy: Two-stage mixing. Some hand-shaping required.

Shaped like a large, oval doughnut and gaudily decorated with alternating sections of Carnival colors (purple, green, and yellow), the yeast bread known as King's Cake is one of New Orleans' many popular Mardi Gras traditions. The "cake" is an indulgence traditionally enjoyed on the Twelfth Night (the eve of Epiphany, which begins the twelfth day after Christmas) and up until Ash Wednesday, the beginning of Lent. The name references the custom of tucking a coin, miniature china doll, nut meat, or other small tidbit in the cake before baking and declaring whoever happens upon it the king of the next Mardi Gras ball. The King's Cake, sometimes also called Twelfth Night cake, actually dates to the Carnival celebrations of medieval Europe, where the notion of serendipitously becoming nobility was even more entertaining than it is today.

Both home and commercial bakers now prepare the *Gateau du Roi*, and many are shipped around the country for those wishing to participate in Mardi Gras from afar. Good-quality versions feature a light, not too sweet brioche, often flavored with citrus zest and spice. Some bakers go all out with the toppings, adding not only the traditional bands of icing or colored sugars, but bits of candied cherries or bright nonpareils for a jewel-studded look. (My grandchildren are always in favor of the heavy décor.) Since this is a Carnival-time treat, it's really impossible to be too fanciful or go too far over the top! Incidentally, both the loaf shaping and decorating are much easier than you might think.

Yield: 12 to 15, 2- to 2½-inch servings

2½ cups (12.5 ounces) unbleached all-purpose white flour, plus 1 cup (5 ounces), plus more as needed

7 tablespoons granulated sugar, divided

1¼ teaspoons table salt

1 teaspoon instant, fast-rising, or bread machine yeast

1⅓ cups ice water, plus more if needed

Corn oil or canola oil, for coating dough top

2 large eggs plus 1 large egg yolk, at room temperature

⅓ cup good-quality instant nonfat dry milk (don't use a generic brand)

⅓ cup unsalted butter, melted and cooled just slightly

Grated zest (yellow part of the skin) of 1 large lemon

¾ teaspoon ground nutmeg

(continued on page 160)

FIRST RISE: In a large bowl, thoroughly stir together 2½ cups of the flour, 3 tablespoons of the sugar, the salt, and yeast. Vigorously stir in the water, scraping down the bowl sides and mixing until the dough is thoroughly blended. If the mixture is too dry to blend together, stir in just enough

1 pecan half (or other small edible gift to insert in the cake)

1 tablespoon whole or reduced-fat milk

2 cups confectioners' sugar, sifted after measuring

2 tablespoons lemon juice

1 to 2 tablespoons water, as needed

¼ cup each purchased yellow, green, and purple decorating sugar (or prepare your own using the sidebar recipe)

Candied cherries, candy dots, or nonpareils, optional

more ice water to facilitate mixing, but don't over-moisten, as it should be firm. If the mixture is soft, stir in enough more flour to make it firm, but not hard to stir. Evenly brush or spray the top lightly with oil. Tightly cover the bowl with plastic wrap. If desired, for best flavor or for convenience, refrigerate for 3 to 10 hours. Then let rise at cool room temperature for 12 to 18 hours.

SECOND RISE: In a medium bowl, thoroughly whisk the eggs and yolk together. Remove 2 tablespoons and set aside in a small cup, covered, for garnish. Lightly whisk the remaining 4 tablespoons sugar, dry milk, butter, lemon zest, and nutmeg into the egg mixture. Vigorously stir the egg mixture into the dough until thoroughly and evenly incorporated. (If preferred, use a dough hook and heavy stand mixer on low speed.) Stir or beat in the remaining 1 cup of flour until completely smooth; this will take several minutes. The dough should be stiff; if necessary, add in enough more flour to yield a hard-to-stir dough, then scrape down the bowl sides carefully.

Line a large baking sheet with baking parchment. Coat the parchment with nonstick spray, then dust with flour. Turn out the dough onto the center of the parchment, then dust with more flour and shape into a round. Push the pecan half (or other tidbit) down into the dough, carefully covering it up; it will be discovered by a lucky eater. With a well-oiled spatula or fingertips, form a hole in the center of the dough and work it outward until the dough forms a 15 × 12 × 3-inch oval doughnut with a 4-inch-wide center opening. Use the spatula or fingertips to work the inner circle of the dough to create a smooth, attractive edge and dust the dough with flour as needed to reduce stickiness. Brush or spray the top with oil and tent with nonstick spray–coated foil.

LET RISE USING ANY OF THESE METHODS: For a 1½- to 2½-hour regular rise, let stand at warm room temperature; for a 1- to 2-hour accelerated rise, let stand in a turned-off microwave along with 1 cup of boiling-hot water; or for an extended rise, refrigerate for 4 to 24 hours, then set out at room temperature. Continue the rise until the dough nearly doubles from the deflated size. Carefully remove the foil.

BAKING PRELIMINARIES: 20 minutes before baking time, put a rack in the lower third of the oven; preheat to 375°F. Whisk the reserved egg mixture together with the milk. Brush the dough surface evenly with the egg wash, wiping up any drips.

BAKING: Bake on the lower rack for 25 to 30 minutes, or until the top is nicely browned. Cover with foil and continue baking for 15 to 20 minutes, or until a skewer inserted in the thickest part comes out with just a few particles on the end (or until the center registers 206° to 207°F on an instant-read thermometer). Let cool in the pan on a wire rack.

Meanwhile, prepare the icing: In a small bowl, stir together the powdered sugar, lemon juice, and 1½ tablespoons water until smooth and well blended. Gradually add more water or more sifted powdered sugar to obtain a pourable but not runny consistency. Working in sections, pour the icing over the cool cake top, quickly spreading it over the surface and then sprinkling with colored sugar; work quickly so the icing doesn't dry before the sugar is added. Add the sugars in alternating yellow, purple, and green bands (using each color four or five times conveniently divides the cake into 12 or 15 servings). If desired, add small nonpareils by sprinkling over the top; add cherries or candy dots by lightly dipping them in the icing and then pressing into place on the cake.

SERVING AND STORING: Serve warm or at room temperature. Cool completely before storing airtight in a cake keeper or plastic container. Keeps at room temperature for up to 3 days, and may be frozen, airtight, for up to 2 months.

TO MAKE COLORED SUGARS:
For each color, put ¼ cup granulated sugar in a small resealable plastic bag; add two drops of liquid food color, seal, and squeeze until thoroughly blended. For purple, combine a drop of red and blue first, then mix with the sugar. Let the sugars stand to dry out slightly before using if they seem wet.

panettone

KS QUOTIENT— Fairly Easy: Two
stage mixing. No hand-shaping
required.

2¼ cups (11.25 ounces)
unbleached all-purpose white
flour, plus ¾ cup (3.75 ounces),
plus more as needed

1¼ teaspoons table salt

1 teaspoon instant, fast-rising, or
bread machine yeast

1 cup plus 2 tablespoons ice water,
plus more if needed

Corn oil or canola oil for dough top
and baking dish

½ cup granulated sugar

⅓ cup good-quality instant nonfat
dry milk (do not use a generic
brand)

7 tablespoons unsalted butter,
melted and cooled just slightly

2 large eggs, at room temperature

1 tablespoon finely grated orange
zest (orange part of the skin)

(continued on page 163)

Panettone is a much-loved holiday bread throughout Italy and Sicily. According to legend, "Toni's bread" originated in Milan around 1490, when a young man created it to impress his sweetheart's father, a baker. (Some stories say that Toni was the name of the baker, some say it was the name of the suitor.) Since the bread is enriched with eggs and butter and studded with candied and dried fruits, it was once a luxury of the wealthy, but it is now enjoyed in even modest homes at Christmastime.

Modern recipes often call for *Fiori di Sicilia* (Flowers of Sicily), a potent, deliciously complex extract boasting notes of citrus, vanilla, and almond. Until recently it was hard to find in the United States, but now gourmet shops occasionally carry it, and it can also be ordered from the King Arthur Flour Company (www.bakerscatalog.com). If necessary, a combination of almond, vanilla, and orange extracts can be successfully substituted, as indicated below.

Panettone loaves are traditionally baked in a fairly tall cylindrical pan, but if you don't have one, a soufflé dish makes a satisfactory substitute. While it is not customary to add an icing, I like the festive look and zing of the Powdered Sugar–Lemon Drizzle over the top.   **Yield: 1 large round loaf**

FIRST RISE: In a large bowl, thoroughly stir together 2¼ cups of the flour, the salt, and yeast. Vigorously stir in the water, scraping down the bowl sides and mixing until the dough is thoroughly blended. If the mixture is too dry to blend together, stir in just enough more water to facilitate mixing; don't over-moisten. If the mixture is soft, stir in enough more flour to make it firm, but not hard to stir. Evenly brush or spray the top lightly with vegetable oil. Tightly cover the bowl with plastic wrap. If desired, for best flavor or for convenience, refrigerate for 3 to 10 hours. Then let rise at cool room temperature for 12 to 18 hours.

SECOND RISE: In a medium bowl, lightly whisk together the sugar, dry milk, and butter, then thoroughly whisk in the eggs, orange zest, and extract(s) until well blended. Stir in the raisins and candied orange. Vigorously stir the mixture into the dough until fully and evenly incorporated; this will take several minutes. (If desired, mix using a dough hook and heavy-duty stand mixer on low.) Stir in the ¾ cup flour until completely smooth. The dough should not be batter-like; if necessary, vigorously stir in enough more flour to yield a firm dough, thoroughly scraping down the bowl. Turn out the dough into a well-oiled 8-cup soufflé dish. Spray with nonstick cooking spray and cover with nonstick spray–coated plastic wrap.

LET RISE USING ANY OF THESE METHODS: For a 1½- to 2½-hour regular rise, let stand at warm room temperature; for a 1- to 2-hour accelerated rise, let stand in a turned-off microwave along with 1 cup of boiling-hot water; or for an extended rise, refrigerate for 4 to 48 hours, then set out at room temperature. Continue the rise until the dough nears the plastic. Remove it and continue until the dough reaches ½ inch above the pan rim.

BAKING PRELIMINARIES: 15 minutes before baking time, place a rack in the lower third of the oven; preheat to 375°F.

BAKING: Bake on the lower rack for 25 to 30 minutes or until the top is nicely browned. Cover with foil and continue baking for 15 to 20 minutes, or until a skewer inserted in the thickest part comes out with only a few particles at the bottom (or the center registers 205° to 207°F on an instant-read thermometer). Then bake for another 5 to 10 minutes to ensure the loaf is baked through. Cool in the pan on a wire rack for 15 minutes. Run a knife around the sides to loosen the loaf, then transfer it to the rack and let cool at least to barely warm before cutting.

If desired, decoratively top the cooled panettone with the Powdered Sugar–Lemon Drizzle, allowing it to drip attractively down the sides. Let the cake stand for a few minutes until it sets.

SERVING AND STORING: The loaf slices best when cool. It is good at room temperature or toasted. Cool completely before storing airtight in plastic or in a cake keeper. The bread will keep at room temperature for 2 to 3 days, and may be frozen, airtight, for up to 2 months.

Generous ½ teaspoon *Fiori di Sicilia* (Flowers of Sicily) extract (if unavailable, substitute ½ teaspoon almond extract, 1 teaspoon vanilla extract, and 1 teaspoon orange or lemon extract)

⅓ cup plump dark raisins

⅓ cup plump golden raisins

¼ cup diced candied orange peel

Powdered Sugar–Lemon Drizzle (see page 191), optional

all-purpose enriched sweet dough

2⅓ cups (11.66 ounces) unbleached all-purpose white flour, plus ⅔ cup (3.33 ounces) plus more as needed

5 to 7 tablespoons granulated sugar, to taste, divided

1¼ teaspoons table salt

1 teaspoon instant, fast-rising, or bread machine yeast

1¼ cups ice water, plus more if needed

Flavorless vegetable oil for brushing

⅓ cup good-quality instant nonfat dry milk (do not use a generic brand)

6 tablespoons unsalted butter, melted and cooled just slightly

2 large eggs, at room temperature, beaten

This is a versatile, slightly sweet dough suitable for making coffeecakes, various enriched loaves, and dessert breads. For a very easy yet festive loaf, simply stir in ¾ cup of diced mixed candied fruit and 1 teaspoon anise seeds into this dough before the second rise. (Follow the baking instructions for Cornish Saffron Bread, page 168.) Then top the loaf with the Powdered Sugar–Lemon Drizzle (page 191).

This dough is used in the Streusel Coffeecake, Cornish Saffron Bread, Spiced Cranberry Bundt-Style Coffeecake with Orange Glaze, Holiday Cranberry-Apple Coffee Ring, and Apple–Cream Cheese Pinwheel Pastries recipes.

Since the dough can be put to different purposes, you can adjust the amount of sugar slightly to suit your taste. However, for proper gluten development and yeast growth, be sure to add the sugar in two stages, as directed, and don't add more than the maximum called for.

Yield: Enough dough for 1 generous loaf or coffeecake or batch of pastries

FIRST RISE: In a large bowl, thoroughly stir together 2⅓ cups of the flour, 2 tablespoons of the sugar, the salt, and yeast. Vigorously stir in the water, scraping down the bowl and mixing until the dough is thoroughly blended. If the mixture is too dry to incorporate the flour, a bit at a time, mix in just enough more water to blend the ingredients. If the mixture is soft, stir in enough more flour to make it firm, but not hard to stir. Evenly brush the top lightly with vegetable oil. Tightly cover the bowl with plastic wrap. If desired, for best flavor or for convenience, refrigerate for 3 to 4 hours. Then let rise at cool room temperature for 12 to 18 hours.

SECOND RISE: In a medium bowl, stir together the remaining 3 to 5 tablespoons of sugar, the milk powder, and butter, then mix in the eggs until well blended. Gradually add the egg mixture, then ⅔ cup flour, to the dough, mixing until evenly incorporated; this will take several minutes so it's best to use a dough hook and heavy-duty mixer on low, if possible. If necessary, add in enough more flour to yield a hard-to-stir dough, scraping down the bowl sides carefully. Proceed with the dough as directed in the individual recipes.

simple streusel
coffeecake

1 batch Make-Ahead Streusel, prepared as directed (page 196) (if just made, it should be refrigerated until firmed up slightly; if made ahead, it should be set out until warmed up just slightly but still firm)

1 batch All-Purpose Enriched Sweet Dough, prepared as directed (page 164) (adding the eggs, butter, etc., and maximum amount of sugar called for, then proceeding with preparing the coffeecake as follows)

This coffeecake truly is simplicity itself, yet it has a lovely buttery taste and texture that will ensure your reputation as a talented baker. The outside is wonderfully crisp-tender and strewn with a crunchy, nut-accented sugar-cinnamon streusel. The inside is moist, soft, and studded with more little nuggets of streusel. It is great warm from the oven, especially for breakfast, brunch, or a coffee klatch. The coffeecake can be baked and served in a flat 9 × 15-inch baking pan, or, for a fancier presentation, baked in an angel food pan, then lifted off and plated attractively.

The recipe is super-convenient because the streusel can be made well in advance and used to jazz up a coffeecake as needed. Better yet, the coffeecake can be completely assembled and refrigerated for up to 36 hours. By planning ahead, you can remove it from the refrigerator to warm up and rise (allow for a 4½- to 5-hour regular rise, or a 3- to 3½-hour accelerated rise) and time the baking to have a fresh, warm coffeecake coming from the oven just when you need it.

Don't forget that this recipe starts with a batch of All-Purpose Enriched Sweet Dough. All the first- and second-stage ingredients should be already incorporated into the dough when the following preparations begin.

Yield: 1 large coffeecake, 12 to 15 portions or slices

SECOND RISE: Stir a generous half of the streusel into the batch of dough. For a shaped, round coffeecake, turn out the dough into a well-oiled or nonstick spray–coated 8- to 12-quart angel food pan. For a rectangular coffeecake, turn out the dough in a well-oiled 9 × 13-inch flat baking dish. Spread the dough out evenly using an oiled rubber spatula. Sprinkle the remaining streusel evenly over the dough. Cover the pan or baking dish with nonstick spray–coated plastic wrap.

LET RISE USING ANY OF THESE METHODS: For a 2- to 3-hour regular rise, let stand at warm room temperature; for a 1½- to 2½-hour accelerated rise, let stand in a turned-off microwave along with 1 cup of boiling-hot water; or for an extended rise, refrigerate for 4 to 36 hours, then set out at room temperature. If the dough nears the plastic wrap, remove it and continue the rise until the dough has doubled from its deflated size.

BAKING PRELIMINARIES: 15 minutes before baking time, place a rack in the lower third of the oven; preheat to 350°F.

BAKING: Bake on the lower rack for 30 to 40 minutes for the rectangular coffeecake or 40 to 50 minutes for the ring-shaped coffeecake, until the top is nicely browned and a skewer inserted in the thickest part comes out with only a few particles at the bottom end (or the center registers 205° to 207°F on an instant-read thermometer). If necessary, cover with foil for the last 15 to 20 minutes to prevent over-browning. Then bake for another 5 to 10 minutes to ensure the center is done. Cool in the pan on a wire rack for 15 minutes. If baked in an angel food pan, run a knife around the center tube and sides to loosen the loaf, then lift it up and onto the rack.

SERVING AND STORING: Serve the rectangular cake from its pan; serve the round version on a cake plate. The coffeecake slices best when cool, but is delicious warm. Cool completely before storing airtight in plastic or foil; or store the round coffeecake in a cake keeper. Keeps at room temperature for up to 3 days, and may be frozen, airtight, for up to 2 months.

cornish
saffron bread

1 tablespoon granulated sugar

⅛ to ¼ teaspoon saffron threads, to taste

2 teaspoons finely grated lemon zest

1 recipe All-Purpose Enriched Sweet Dough (page 164), ready for the second rise

1 cup golden raisins, rinsed under hot water, drained well, and patted dry

About ⅓ cup (1.66 ounces) unbleached all-purpose white flour, or as needed

This is my reworking of an old English bread that has been popular in various similar forms since the 1700s. An 1810 recipe featured in Elizabeth David's classic work, *English Bread and Yeast Cookery*, was titled "To Make the Famous Saffron Cake." It is not a cake as we use the term today, but rather, a highly aromatic, slightly sweet bread. The saffron gives the loaf a beautiful golden yellow color, and here and there small flecks of it, as well as golden raisins, brighten the soft crumb even more. Some versions of this bread call for other spices as well, but saffron has such a heady, complex aroma and taste I think it's better solo. On the other hand, I do think lemon zest is a worthy addition because it actually intensifies the taste of the spice and adds a subtle, enticing zing.

It's fine to bake this in a loaf pan, but since saffron is rare and pricey, I like to show the bread off by using a Bundt, kugelhopf, or other decorative tube pan. Note that due to the open area provided by the tube, the loaf will be done a little sooner.

Remember to have a batch of All-Purpose Enriched Sweet Dough with the eggs, butter, and milk powder incorporated as indicated in the original directions and ready for its final rise when beginning this recipe.

Yield: 1 large loaf, 12 to 14 portions or slices

SECOND RISE: Grind the sugar and saffron together using a mortar and pestle (or using a coffee mill dedicated to grinding spices) until the saffron is mostly powdery, but has some fine bits remaining. (Alternatively, mash the mixture with the back of a spoon, or grind in a food processor until the saffron is fairly fine but not completely powdery.) Vigorously stir the saffron mixture and lemon zest into the dough until thoroughly and evenly incorporated. Fold in the raisins and enough flour to yield a stiff, but still stirrable, dough.

Turn out the dough into a well-oiled 9 × 5-inch or similar large loaf pan or in an 8- to 10-cup Bundt-style pan. Evenly brush or spray the top lightly with oil. Spread the dough out and pat down evenly using an oiled rubber spatula. Cover the pan with nonstick spray–coated plastic wrap.

LET RISE USING ANY OF THESE METHODS: For a 1½- to 3-hour regular rise, let stand at warm room temperature; for a 1- to 2½-hour accelerated rise, let stand in a turned-off microwave along with 1 cup of boiling-hot water; or for an extended rise, refrigerate for 4 to 48 hours, then set out at room temperature. If the dough nears the plastic wrap, remove it and continue the rise until the dough extends ⅛ inch above the rim if using a loaf pan or 8-cup tube pan, and ¾ inch below the rim if using a 10-cup Bundt-style pan.

BAKING PRELIMINARIES: 15 minutes before baking time, place a rack in the lower third of the oven; preheat to 350°F.

BAKING: Bake on the lower rack for 30 to 40 minutes, until the top is nicely browned. Cover with foil and bake for 10 to 20 minutes longer or until a skewer inserted in the thickest part comes out with only a few particles at the end (or the thickest part registers 205° to 207°F on an instant-read thermometer). Then bake for another 5 to 10 minutes to ensure the center is baked through. Cool in the pan on a wire rack for 15 minutes. Remove the loaf to the rack; cool thoroughly.

SERVING AND STORING: The loaf slices best when cool. It is good at room temperature or toasted. Cool completely before storing airtight in plastic; or store the round loaf in a cake keeper if desired. The bread will keep at room temperature for up to 3 days, and may be frozen, airtight, for up to 2 months.

spiced cranberry
bundt-style coffeecake

1½ cups dried sweetened cranberries, soaked in hot water for 10 minutes, then well drained

1 tablespoon grated orange zest

½ cup chopped walnuts or pecans, optional

1 batch All-Purpose Enriched Sweet Dough (page 164), ready for the second rise

¼ cup (1.25 ounces) unbleached all-purpose white flour

1 teaspoon ground cardamom

1 teaspoon ground coriander

Powdered Sugar–Lemon Drizzle (page 191)

Cardamom, coriander, and orange zest give this festive bread a wonderful and distinctive aroma and flavor. The cranberries, of course, contribute color, but since they are fully plumped, they also add succulence. I like the loaf best topped with a little powdered sugar drizzle, but a simple dusting of powdered sugar will work fine if time is short. This makes a spectacular holiday breakfast, brunch, or coffee-klatch treat. By choosing the extended rise option, you can do most of the preparation up to 2 days ahead, then bake the coffeecake on the day it will be served.

Have ready one batch of All-Purpose Enriched Sweet Dough prepared using the maximum or nearly the maximum amount of sugar called for in the recipe. Be sure that the eggs, butter, and milk powder are already incorporated and the dough is ready for the second rise before proceeding with the instructions given here.

Yield: 1 large round coffeecake, 12 to 14 portions or slices

SECOND RISE: Vigorously stir the cranberries and orange zest (and nuts, if using) into the dough until thoroughly incorporated. In a small bowl, stir together the flour, cardamom, and coriander until well blended, then stir into the dough until thoroughly incorporated. Stir in more flour if needed to yield a fairly stiff dough. Turn it out into a well-oiled or nonstick spray–coated 8- to 10-cup Bundt pan (or similar decorative tube pan) or angel food pan. Brush or spray the top with oil. Spread the dough and smooth out using an oiled rubber spatula. Tent the pan with nonstick spray–coated foil.

LET RISE USING ANY OF THESE METHODS: For a 2- to 3-hour regular rise, let stand at warm room temperature; for a 1½- to 2½-hour accelerated rise, let stand in a turned-off microwave along with 1 cup of boiling-hot water; or for an extended rise, refrigerate for 4 to 48 hours, then set out at room temperature. If the dough nears the foil, remove it and continue the rise until the dough has doubled from its deflated size.

BAKING PRELIMINARIES: 15 minutes before baking time, place a rack in the lower third of the oven; preheat to 350°F.

BAKING: Bake on the lower rack for 45 to 55 minutes, until the top is nicely browned; cover with foil partway through, if needed, to prevent over-browning. Continue baking for 5 to 10 minutes more, or until a skewer inserted in the thickest part comes out with only a few particles on the end (or the thickest part registers 205° to 207°F on an instant-read thermometer). Then bake for another 5 minutes to ensure the bottom of the loaf is done. Cool in the pan on a wire rack for 15 minutes. Run a knife around the center tube and sides to loosen the coffeecake, then invert it onto the rack. Let cool, then brush off any crumbs from the surface. Transfer to a serving plate. Sift powdered sugar over the top just before serving, or top the cooled coffeecake with the Powdered Sugar–Lemon Drizzle, allowing it drip attractively down the sides. Let the coffeecake stand for a few minutes until the icing sets.

SERVING AND STORING: The coffeecake slices best when cool, but is good warm, at room temperature, or toasted. Cool completely before storing airtight in a plastic container or cake keeper. Keeps at room temperature for 2 to 3 days, and may be frozen, airtight, for up to 2 months.

TIP: A Bundt pan, angel food pan, or a kugelhopf mold with a dull finish is the best choice for baking this bread. A shiny aluminum surface hinders browning.

holiday cranberry-apple coffee ring

Generous ¾ cup light brown sugar, packed

2 tablespoons cornstarch

¼ teaspoon ground cinnamon

1¾ cups fresh (or frozen) thawed cranberries, coarsely chopped

1 cup peeled and chopped (¼-inch) Granny Smith or similar tart apples

½ teaspoon freshly grated orange zest

⅔ cup dark or golden raisins or a combination

1 recipe All-Purpose Enriched Sweet Dough (page 164), ready for the second rise

Unbleached all-purpose white flour for dusting

1 large egg beaten with 1 teaspoon water for wash

Transparent Powdered Sugar Glaze (page 190) or Powdered Sugar-Lemon Drizzle (page 191), optional

This eye-catching and delectable coffeecake is one of my favorites. Pinwheel swirls of crimson-colored filling stand out against the light-colored dough and an icing drizzle accents the top. The cranberry-apple-raisin medley adds a sweet-tart taste and helps keep the ring moist and succulent. This is perfect for a holiday breakfast, brunch, or buffet. The filling may be made up to 4 or 5 days ahead and refrigerated if desired. Bring it back to room temperature before using.

Don't forget that the eggs, butter, and milk powder need to be added to the All-Purpose Enriched Sweet Dough called for before it is ready for the second rise and can be used here. **Yield: 1 large coffee ring, 12 to 14 servings**

READY THE FILLING: In a medium heavy saucepan, thoroughly stir together the sugar, cornstarch, and cinnamon. Stir in the cranberries, apples, and orange zest. Cook, stirring, over low heat until the fruits begin to release their juice. Raise the heat slightly and cook, stirring, until the mixture thickens and the apples soften a bit, about 5 minutes. Stir in the raisins. Set aside until cooled.

SECOND RISE: Dust the batch of All-Purpose Enriched Sweet Dough all over with flour, turning to coat it evenly. Let it rest for 10 minutes. Coat an 18-inch-long sheet of baking parchment (or wax paper) with nonstick spray and generously dust with flour. Turn out the dough onto the center of the parchment. Dusting the dough with flour to prevent stickiness as needed, pat and press it into a rough 9-inch-long rectangle with flour-dusted fingertips. Dust with more flour, then press or roll out the dough into a 10 × 16-inch evenly thick rectangle. Evenly spread the room temperature fruit filling over the dough to within ¼ inch of the edge all around.

Tightly roll up the dough from a 16-inch-wide side to form a long pinwheel log; use flour-dusted hands and lift up the parchment to assist the rolling and pinch the seam tightly closed as you work. Roll the log onto a parchment-lined baking sheet, placing seam-side down. Stretch the log out from the center until evenly thick along the length. Bring the ends together to form a ring, pressing and smoothing and pulling away from the center so the ring is evenly thick and smooth and the center opening is at least 3 inches in diameter. If an ovenproof custard cup or small ramekin is available, coat the outside with nonstick spray, then set it in the center of the ring so it will stay open during baking. Using well-oiled kitchen shears, make 1½-inch-deep cuts into the ring sides at about 2-inch intervals so the filling is exposed, then turn the cut portions on a slight diagonal so the pinwheel design shows. Brush the ring evenly with the egg wash. Tent it with nonstick spray–coated foil.

LET RISE USING ANY OF THESE METHODS: For a 1½- to 2½-hour regular rise, let stand at warm room temperature; or for an extended rise, refrigerate for 4 to 48 hours, then set out at room temperature. Continue the rise until the ring has doubled from the deflated size.

BAKING PRELIMINARIES: 15 minutes before baking time, place a rack in the lower third of the oven; preheat to 375°F.

BAKING: Bake on the lower rack for 40 to 50 minutes, until the top is well browned; cover the top with foil partway through as necessary to prevent over-browning. Carefully loosen, then remove the cup from the ring center. Bake for 5 to 10 minutes more, until a skewer inserted in the thickest part comes out with only a few particles on the end (or until the thickest part registers 204° to 205°F on an instant-read thermometer) to ensure the ring is done. Let the pan cool on a wire rack until the ring has cooled for 15 minutes. Brush the ring with Transparent Powdered Sugar Glaze, or drizzle with the Powdered Sugar–Lemon Drizzle. Then slide the ring onto a serving platter and serve.

SERVING AND STORING: Cool thoroughly before storing. Store airtight in a cake keeper or plastic container. The coffee ring will keep at room temperature for 2 to 3 days, and may be frozen, airtight, for up to 2 months.

apple–cream cheese
pinwheel pastries

KS QUOTIENT— Fairly Simple: Very decorative looking. Hand-shaping required.

1 batch All-Purpose Enriched Sweet Dough (page 164), ready for the second rise

Unbleached all-purpose white flour as needed

Apple Filling

$2/3$ cup granulated sugar

3 tablespoons unbleached all-purpose white flour

$1\frac{1}{4}$ teaspoons ground cinnamon

1 tablespoon cold unsalted butter, cut into bits

$2\frac{3}{4}$ cups peeled and diced ($\frac{1}{4}$-inch pieces) Granny Smith, Winesap, or other tart cooking apples

Cream Cheese Filling

One 8-ounce package cream cheese, at room temperature

$3\frac{1}{2}$ tablespoons granulated sugar

1 large egg yolk, at room temperature

$\frac{1}{2}$ teaspoon vanilla extract

(continued on page 175)

These are reminiscent of cream cheese–apple Danish pastries, but the dough is easier to prepare. The fresh spiced apple and cream cheese fillings contribute greatly to the fine flavor, yet come together quickly. And, if desired, they can be readied well ahead.

It's easiest to bake the pastries on parchment set on two large baking sheets, but feel free to substitute whatever flat baking sheets or pans you have. Or bake the pastries in batches: Hold some on parchment on a tray in the refrigerator, then slip the completed first batch off onto a wire rack, and reuse the pan for a second batch. (Let the pan cool before reusing it.)

Before beginning the pastries, make sure that the eggs, butter, and milk powder are incorporated into the All-Purpose Enriched Sweet Dough as directed on page 164, so it is completely ready for the second rise.

Yield: Sixteen 4½-inch pastries

SECOND RISE: Thoroughly stir the dough, adding more flour if necessary to yield a very stiff consistency. Dust the dough all over with flour, then work it into the surface with flour-dusted fingertips. Let the dough rest, covered with plastic wrap, for 10 to 15 minutes. Line several very large baking sheets with baking parchment.

PREPARE THE APPLE FILLING: In a heavy medium saucepan, thoroughly stir together the sugar, flour, and cinnamon. Stir in the butter and apples. Cook, stirring, over low heat until the apples begin to release their juice, about 5 minutes. Raise the heat slightly and cook, stirring, until the mixture thickens and the apples soften a bit, about 5 minutes longer. Set aside until cool. (May be made up to 4 days ahead. Cover and refrigerate; bring back to room temperature before using.)

PREPARE THE CREAM CHEESE FILLING: In a small deep bowl, vigorously stir or beat together the cream cheese, sugar, egg yolk, vanilla, and lemon zest until completely smooth and well blended. Cover tightly. (May be made up to 2 days ahead. Cover and refrigerate; bring back to room temperature before using.)

Coat an 18-inch-long sheet of baking parchment with nonstick spray, then generously dust it with flour. Turn out the dough onto the center of the parchment. Evenly dust the dough with flour, then pat it into a rectangle with flour-dusted fingertips. Dusting with more flour as needed to prevent sticking, stretch and press out the dough into an 7 × 16-inch evenly thick rectangle; lift it several times and dust the parchment to ensure against sticking. Spread the surface evenly with the cooled apple filling to within ¼ inch of the edge all around.

Tightly roll up the dough from a 16-inch side to form a long pinwheel log; use flour-dusted hands, dust with more flour as needed, and lift up the parchment to assist the rolling as you work. Pinch the seam tightly closed all along the log length to prevent it from unrolling and leaking, then turn seam-side down. Stretch the log out from the center until evenly thick along its length and about 18 inches long. Using well-oiled kitchen shears or a large, sharp, oiled serrated knife, cut off and discard the uneven ends. Cut the log in half, then cut each half into 8 equal slices; they will be somewhat soft. Using an oiled wide-bladed spatula, transfer the slices to the parchment-lined baking sheets, spacing about 3 inches apart. Pat each slice down to flatten, then press down in the center to form a deep, 1¼-inch diameter well in each. Divide the cream cheese filling among the pastry wells. Tent the pans with nonstick spray–coated foil.

LET RISE USING EITHER OF THESE METHODS: For a 1½- to 2½-hour regular rise, let stand at warm room temperature; or for an extended rise, refrigerate for 4 to 48 hours, then set out at room temperature. Continue the rise until the pastries have doubled in size and are about 3½ inches in diameter.

BAKING PRELIMINARIES: 15 minutes before baking time, place a rack in the lower third of the oven; preheat to 350°F.

BAKING: Bake on the lower rack for 15 to 20 minutes, or until the pastries are well browned. Then cover the pans with foil to prevent further brown-

¼ teaspoon finely grated lemon zest ,or ⅛ teaspoon almond extract or vanilla extract

Powdered Sugar–Lemon Drizzle (page 191) for garnish

ing and bake for 5 to 7 minutes more (or until the center registers 204º to 205ºF on an instant-read thermometer) to ensure the centers are done. Cool the pastries on a wire rack set over a baking sheet for at least 5 minutes. Then garnish by drizzling the Powdered Sugar–Lemon Drizzle back and forth over the pastry tops. Let cool slightly, then serve.

SERVING AND STORING: Cool thoroughly before storing so the drizzle can set. Store airtight in a single layer in a plastic container. The pastries will keep at room temperature for 2 to 3 days, and may be frozen, airtight, for up to 2 months. Reheat, tented with foil, in a 350ºF preheated oven before serving.

yeasted banana
bundt-style
coffee ring

Banana quick breads are always popular, and now that a rather simple yeasted, chocolate chip–studded version can be made without kneading, I hope it will catch on, too. The combination of banana and chocolate is spectacular, and, since the ring is shaped as it bakes in a Bundt or other decorative tube pan, it also looks terrific.

For a milder, sweeter flavor, accent the coffeecake with the Glossy Chocolate Drizzle (page 192); for a significant bittersweet presence suited to serious chocolate fans, cover the entire top with Chocolate Ganache Glaze (page 193). **Yield: 1 large Bundt-style loaf**

FIRST RISE: In a large bowl, thoroughly stir together the flour, salt, and yeast. Place the bananas in a medium bowl, then whisk in the honey, oil, and orange zest. Then whisk in the water until well blended. Vigorously stir the mixture into the bowl with the flour, scraping down the bowl sides and mixing until the dough is well blended; it will be rubbery. Vigorously stir in the butter. If the dough is not stiff, add enough more flour to make it hard to stir. Lightly brush the top with butter. Cover the bowl with plastic wrap. If desired, for best flavor or for convenience, refrigerate for 3 to 10 hours. Let rise at cool room temperature for 12 to 18 hours.

SECOND RISE: Vigorously stir the dough; add enough more flour to make it very stiff. Then gradually fold in the chocolate morsels and nuts (if using) until evenly distributed throughout. Turn out the dough into a 10- to 12-cup well-oiled Bundt pan or similar tube pan. Evenly brush the dough top with melted butter. Using a greased rubber spatula or fingertips, press down and smooth out to even the surface all over. Tent the pan with nonstick spray–coated foil.

3½ cups (17.5 ounces) unbleached white bread flour, plus more as needed

1 teaspoon table salt

¾ teaspoon instant, fast-rising, or bread machine yeast

1⅓ cups thoroughly mashed overripe banana (about 3 bananas)

6½ tablespoons clover honey or other mild honey

2 tablespoons corn oil or canola oil, plus extra for coating dough top and baking pan

1½ teaspoons finely grated orange zest

¾ cup plus 2 tablespoons ice water, plus more if needed

2 tablespoons unsalted butter, melted and cooled slightly, plus more for brushing dough top

1½ cups (9 ounces) semisweet chocolate morsels

(continued on page 178)

¾ cup chopped walnuts, plus 1 tablespoon more for garnish, optional

Glossy Chocolate Drizzle (page 192) or Chocolate Ganache Glaze (page 193), optional

LET RISE USING ANY OF THESE METHODS: For a 1½- to 2½-hour regular rise, let stand at warm room temperature; for a 1- to 1½-hour accelerated rise, let stand in a turned-off microwave along with 1 cup of boiling-hot water; or for an extended rise, refrigerate for 4 to 48 hours, then set out at room temperature. When the dough nears the foil, remove it and continue the rise until the dough doubles in bulk.

BAKING PRELIMINARIES: 15 minutes before baking time, place a rack in the lower third of the oven; preheat to 375ºF.

BAKING: Bake on the lower rack for 25 to 30 minutes or until the top is nicely browned. Cover with foil and continue baking for 15 to 20 minutes, or until a skewer inserted in the thickest part comes out with only a few particles at the bottom end (or the center registers 208º to 210ºF on an instant-read thermometer). Then, bake for another 5 to 10 minutes to ensure the interior is baked through. Cool in the pan on a wire rack for 15 minutes. Run a knife around the coffeecake to loosen, then remove it to the rack and let cool.

If garnishing with the Glossy Chocolate Drizzle or Chocolate Ganache Glaze, drizzle or spread over the coffeecake after it has cooled completely. If desired, sprinkle with a tablespoon of chopped walnuts; add before the glaze or drizzle has time to set.

SERVING AND STORING: Serve at room temperature. Cool completely before storing airtight in a cake keeper or plastic container. The coffee ring keeps at room temperature for 2 to 3 days, and may be frozen, airtight, for up to 2 months.

cherry and chocolate coffee ring with kirsch

Attractively yet effortlessly shaped in a Bundt, kugelhopf, or angel cake pan or large ovenproof ring mold, this delectable sweet bread makes a festive holiday brunch, teatime, or coffee-klatch treat. I took my cue from the inspired German custom of pairing cherries with kirsch (a heady cherry brandy) and chocolate. It's all right to skip the kirsch if you don't have it on hand or prefer to avoid spirits, but it does highlight the cherry flavor and lends a heavenly fragrance. The aroma that fills the kitchen during baking is almost enough reason to make this bread.

Garnish this coffeecake with Transparent Powdered Sugar Glaze (page 190) or Glossy Chocolate Drizzle (page 192), or both.

Yield: 1 large loaf, 12 to 14 portions or slices

FIRST RISE: In a large bowl, thoroughly stir together 2¼ cups of the flour, the salt, and yeast. Vigorously stir in the water and kirsch (or orange juice), scraping down the bowl sides and mixing until the dough is thoroughly mixed. If necessary to facilitate mixing, stir in enough more water to yield a firm, but not hard-to-stir, dough. Evenly fold in the cherries. Brush or spray the top lightly with vegetable oil. Tightly cover the bowl with plastic wrap. If desired, for best flavor or for convenience, refrigerate the dough for 3 to 8 hours. Then let the dough rise at cool room temperature for 12 to 18 hours.

SECOND RISE: Stir together the sugar and butter, then stir in the egg until smooth. Vigorously stir the mixture and the chocolate into the dough until evenly distributed. (If preferred, use a dough hook and heavy-duty stand mixer on low.) Add in ⅔ cup of the flour, then, if necessary, enough more to yield a very firm dough, scraping down the sides carefully. Turn out the dough out into a well-oiled or nonstick spray–coated Bundt pan, angel food pan, or other 10- to 12-cup tube pan. Smooth and even out the

KS QUOTIENT— Fairly Easy: Two-stage mixing. Sophisticated look, yet requires no hand-shaping.

2¼ cups (11.25 ounces) unbleached all-purpose white flour, plus ⅔ cup (3.33 ounces), plus more as needed

¾ teaspoon table salt

1 teaspoon instant, fast-rising, or bread machine yeast

1 cup ice water

3½ tablespoons kirsch (clear cherry brandy), or orange juice if preferred

1¼ cups dried sweetened cherries (avoid dried-out, hard ones), rinsed under hot water and drained well

Flavorless vegetable oil for brushing

6½ tablespoons granulated sugar

5 tablespoons unsalted butter, melted and cooled slightly

1 large egg, at room temperature

1 cup (6 ounces) chopped (chocolate mini-morsel size) bittersweet or semisweet chocolate

Transparent Powdered Sugar Glaze (page 190) for brushing over top, or Glossy Chocolate Drizzle (page 192) for drizzling over top, or both surface with a well-oiled rubber spatula. Cover the bowl with nonstick spray–coated plastic wrap.

LET RISE USING ANY OF THESE METHODS: For a 2- to 3-hour regular rise, let stand at warm room temperature; for a 1½- to 2½-hour accelerated rise, let stand in a turned-off microwave along with 1 cup of boiling-hot water; or for an extended rise, refrigerate for 4 to 48 hours, then set out at room temperature. If the dough nears the plastic wrap, remove it and continue the rise until the dough has increased about a quarter over its deflated size. (Don't worry if the dough doesn't expand much during the rise; it will rise a lot in the oven.)

BAKING PRELIMINARIES: 15 minutes before baking time, place a rack in the lower third of the oven; preheat to 375°F.

BAKING: Bake on the lower rack for 30 to 35 minutes, until the top is nicely browned. Cover the top with foil and continue baking for 20 to 25 minutes, until a skewer inserted in the thickest part comes out with only a few particles at the bottom end (or an instant-read thermometer inserted in the thickest part registers 205° to 207°F). Then bake for another 5 to 10 minutes to ensure the interior is baked through. Cool on a wire rack for 15 minutes. Run a knife around the center tube and sides to loosen the loaf, then invert it onto the rack. Add the transparent glaze while the coffeecake is still warm and the chocolate drizzle when cooled.

SERVING AND STORING: Slices best when cool, but is good slightly warm or at room temperature. Cool completely before storing airtight in plastic or foil. Keeps at room temperature for 2 days, and may be frozen, airtight, for up to 2 months.

TIP: Any 10- to 12-cup ovenproof pan with a center tube will do, so long as the surface is not too reflective. Most metal surfaces work fine, but those that are as shiny as aluminum foil will prevent the bread from browning well.

chocolate–chocolate chip
bread kit

MIX RECIPE

KS QUOTIENT — Easy: Easy mix, readied with few ingredients. Makes a great gift.

This appealing bread mix looks like the layered sand art creations of the 1970s and is reminiscent of the bars-in-jars cookie mixes found in some gourmet shops. It makes a great gift from the kitchen, especially for bread fans who also love chocolate. **Yield: 1 quart of mix, yielding 1 large loaf**

2½ cups (12.5 ounces) unbleached white bread flour or all-purpose white flour, divided

¼ cup granulated sugar, plus 1 tablespoon for garnish

3½ tablespoons unsweetened cocoa powder

1 teaspoon table salt

1½ cups (about 9 ounces) semisweet chocolate morsels, divided

1 packet instant, fast-rising, or bread machine yeast

Set out a completely dry clear glass or transparent plastic 1-quart or 1-liter jar, along with its lid. Set out a square of heavy-duty aluminum foil to use as a funnel. (Or use a funnel, if you have one.)

Place 2¼ cups (11.25 ounces) of the flour on the foil, then use it as a funnel to add the flour to the jar. Rap the jar on the counter to even the layer. In a food processor, combine the remaining ¼ cup flour (1.25 ounces), ¼ cup of the sugar, the cocoa powder, salt, and ½ cup chocolate morsels. Process until the chocolate morsels are ground to a powder, about 2 minutes. Turn out onto the foil and add to the jar. Rap the jar to even the layer. Add the remaining 1 cup chocolate morsels to the jar in an even layer. Put the remaining 1 tablespoon sugar in a small plastic bag and close tightly. Push the bag of sugar and the yeast packet into the neck of the jar. If it will be shipped, stuff any empty space in the top with crumpled wax paper. Attach a sheet or card with the instructions for making the bread to the jar.

STORAGE: The unopened mix will keep for up to 1½ months unrefrigerated, 3 months refrigerated.

Don't forget to give the following recipe along with your gift:

CHOCOLATE-CHOCOLATE CHIP BREAD RECIPE (USING MIX)

Just mix together this kit following the easy instructions. The reward is a moist, chewy-crusty loaf studded with chocolate chips and bursting with chocolate flavor.   **Yield: 1 large loaf, 12 to 14 slices**

1 small bag granulated sugar (from the kit)

1 teaspoon yeast (measure it out from the kit packet)

1 jar Chocolate–Chocolate Chip Mix

Scant 1¼ cups ice water (add ice cubes to cold water and stir for 30 seconds before measuring), plus more if needed

3 tablespoons corn oil, canola oil, or safflower oil, plus more for coating pan and dough top

FIRST RISE: Remove the bag of garnishing sugar and the yeast packet from the jar; set aside. Turn out the jar of dry mix into a large bowl. Measure out and thoroughly stir in 1 teaspoon yeast. In a medium bowl, measure out a scant 1¼ cups ice cold water and whisk the oil into it. Vigorously stir the water mixture into the dry ingredients, scrape down the bowl sides, and continue stirring until thoroughly blended and smooth. If the mixture is too dry to incorporate all the flour, a bit at a time, stir in just enough more ice water to blend the ingredients; don't over-moisten, as the dough should be very stiff. Brush the top with a little oil. Tightly cover the bowl with plastic wrap. If desired, for best flavor or for convenience, refrigerate the dough for 3 to 8 hours. Then let rise at cool room temperature (about 70°F) for 12 to 18 hours.

SECOND RISE: Turn out the dough into a well-oiled 9 × 5-inch loaf pan. Brush the top lightly with oil, then smooth and press out evenly in the pan with an oiled rubber spatula (or fingertips). Cut a ½-inch-deep slash down the dough center using oiled kitchen shears or a serrated knife. Cover with nonstick spray–coated plastic wrap.

LET RISE USING EITHER OF THESE METHODS: For a 2½- to 4-hour regular rise, let stand at warm (74° to 75°F) room temperature; for a 1½- to 2½-hour accelerated rise, let stand in a turned-off microwave along with 1 cup of boiling-hot water. Let rise until the dough doubles from its deflated size or nears the pan rim, then remove the plastic and continue until the dough extends just above the rim. Sprinkle over the sugar from the plastic bag.

BAKING PRELIMINARIES: 15 minutes before baking time, place a rack in the lower third of the oven; preheat to 350°F.

BAKING: Bake on the lower rack for 50 to 60 minutes, or until the top is puffed and well browned and a skewer inserted in the thickest part comes out with only a few moist particles at the end. Then bake for 10 to 15 minutes more to ensure that the center is done. If the top browns too rapidly, cover it with foil. Cool in the pan on a wire rack for 10 minutes. Remove the loaf to the rack and cool completely.

SERVING AND STORING: The loaf slices best when cool, but the bread is good served warm or at room temperature. Cool completely before storing. To maintain the crisp crust, store draped with a clean kitchen towel; or to prevent the loaf from drying out, store airtight in plastic or foil. Store at room temperature for 2 to 3 days; freeze, airtight, for up to 2 months, then thaw, unwrapped, at room temperature. When thawed, re-crisp the crust in a 375°F oven for a few minutes.

going with the grain bread kit

KS QUOTIENT — Easy: Easy mix, few ingredients. Makes a great gift. No hand-shaping required.

3 cups (15 ounces) unbleached white bread flour

¼ cup (1.25 ounces) whole wheat flour

¼ cup brown rice flour

2 tablespoons rolled oats or quick-cooking (not instant) oats

2½ tablespoons granulated sugar

1½ teaspoons table salt

1½ tablespoons *each* sesame seeds, poppy seeds, and flax seed, mixed together

2 tablespoons cornmeal, preferably yellow

1 packet instant, fast-rising, or bread machine yeast

This recipe enables you to prepare an appealing jar of bread mix to give a friend, relative, or anyone on your gift list. (I like to make up an extra jar, so I can easily treat myself once in a while.) Even a novice baker can turn out this crusty, attractive loaf without muss or fuss and no ingredients other than water and a little vegetable oil. The big, rustic, versatile loaf has a mild yet addictive grain flavor and a light, springy, slightly holey crumb. It smells and tastes like an artisan bread, yet requires no artisan skills.

The flavor comes from the subtle blending of four grains, including some brown rice flour, and three seeds, including flax seed. These ingredients are not likely to be on hand in your cupboard, but are usually stocked in the gluten-free baking sections of health food stores, as well as in some large supermarkets.

Alternatively, prepare your own brown rice flour by grinding uncooked brown rice to a powder using a blender or clean coffee mill. (Measure out the ¼ cup after the flour is ground.) Regular long-grain brown rice will do, but if you can find it, brown basmati rice delivers the sweetest flavor. In a pinch, omit the flax seed from the recipe and add an extra 2 teaspoons each of the sesame and poppy seeds. The bread flavor will not be quite as irresistible, but will still be very good. **Yield: 1 quart of mix, yielding 1 large loaf**

Set out a completely dry clear glass or transparent plastic 1-quart or 1-liter jar, along with its lid. Set out a square of heavy-duty aluminum foil to use as a funnel. (Or use a funnel, if you have one.)

Place the white flour on the foil, then use the foil as a funnel to add the flour to the jar. Rap the jar on the counter to even and compact the layer. Thoroughly stir together the whole wheat flour, brown rice flour, oats, sugar, salt, and all but 1½ tablespoons of the seed mixture on the foil. Add to the jar; rap it again to even the layer. Put the remaining seeds and the cornmeal in a small plastic bag; close tightly. Push the bag and the yeast packet into the neck of the jar. If it will be shipped, push crumpled wax paper into any extra space at the top. Attach a sheet or card with the instructions for making the bread to the jar.

STORAGE: The unopened mix will keep for up to 1½ months unrefrigerated, 3 months refrigerated.

Don't forget to give the following recipe along with your gift:

GOING WITH THE GRAIN BREAD RECIPE (USING MIX)

Along with ice water and vegetable oil, this kit makes a crusty-topped artisan-style loaf with a slight crunch and light, enticing flavor and aroma of grain. Great for eating warm or cooled, slathered with butter, for toasting, and for making sandwiches.

Yield: 1 large loaf, 12 to 14 slices

1 teaspoon yeast (measured out from enclosed packet)

Cornmeal-seed mixture for garnish (from the enclosed bag)

1 jar Going with the Grain Mix

Scant 2 cups ice water (add ice cubes to cold water and stir for 30 seconds before measuring), plus more if needed

About 1½ tablespoons corn oil, canola oil, or other flavorless oil for coating pan and dough top

FIRST RISE: Remove the yeast packet and cornmeal-seed package (used for garnish) from the jar. In a large bowl, thoroughly stir together the jar of mix and 1 teaspoon of the yeast. Vigorously stir the ice water into the dry mix, scraping down the bowl sides and stirring until completely blended. If the dough is too dry to mix, gradually stir in just enough more ice water to blend the mixture; the dough should be stiff. Brush the top with a little oil. Tightly cover the bowl with plastic wrap. If desired, for best flavor or for convenience, refrigerate for 3 to 10 hours. Then let rise at cool room temperature (about 70°F) for 12 to 18 hours.

SECOND RISE: Generously oil a 9 by 5-inch loaf pan. Sprinkle half the cornmeal-seed mixture into the pan. Stir the dough briefly. With an oiled rubber spatula, scrape the dough in towards the center, working all the way around the bowl. Invert the dough into the pan. Brush the top lightly with oil, then smooth out and press into the pan with oiled fingertips. Brush the top generously with water, and immediately sprinkle the remaining cornmeal-seed mixture over the top. Cut a ½-inch-deep slash down the dough center using oiled kitchen shears or serrated knife. Cover the pan with nonstick spray–coated plastic wrap.

LET RISE USING EITHER OF THESE METHODS: For a 2- to 4-hour regular rise, let stand at warm (74º to 75ºF) room temperature; or, for a 45-minute to 2-hour accelerated rise, let stand in a turned-off microwave along with 1 cup of boiling-hot water. When the dough nears the plastic, remove it and continue the rise until the dough extends ½ inch above the pan rim.

BAKING PRELIMINARIES: 15 minutes before baking time, put a rack in the lower third of the oven; preheat to 450ºF. Set the broiler pan on the oven floor.

BAKING: Reduce the heat to 425ºF. Add a cup of water to the broiler pan, being careful of splattering and steam; don't refill if it boils dry. Bake on the lower rack for 35 to 45 minutes, or until the loaf is nicely browned. Cover the top with foil and continue baking for 20 to 25 minutes, until a skewer inserted in the thickest part comes out with just slightly moist particles clinging to the bottom portion (or until the center registers 204º to 207ºF on an instant-read thermometer). Bake for 5 minutes more to ensure the center is fully done. Remove the loaf to the rack and cool completely.

SERVING AND STORING: The loaf slices best when cool, but is good served warm or at room temperature. Cool completely before storing. To maintain the crisp crust, store wrapped in a clean kitchen towel. Or store airtight in a plastic bag or wrapped in foil; this will prevent the loaf from drying out, but will cause the crust to soften. Store at room temperature for 3 days; freeze, airtight, for up to 2 months, then thaw, unwrapped, at room temperature. When thawed, re-crisp in a 375ºF oven for a few minutes, if desired.

toppings, sauces, glazes, drizzles, and finishing touches

HERE ARE THE EXTRAS AND ADDITIONS TO THE BREADS IN *Kneadlessly Simple*—the sauces, glazes, drizzles, and other toppings used throughout the book. They can add a little something extra—even give breads a professional look—yet are quick and easy to make.

cornstarch glaze

KS QUOTIENT—Super-Easy: Minimal ingredients, easy preparation. Can be made ahead.

A light coating of cornstarch glaze is a simple way to give a crust a shiny, lacquered look. While still wet, the glaze also provides a tacky surface great for capturing and holding seeds or other garnishes sprinkled over the top. It is a good substitute for an egg glaze when breads will be eaten by vegans or those allergic to egg products, or when you're out of eggs.

Yield: Enough to glaze 2 or 3 loaves

2 teaspoons cornstarch

Scant $\frac{2}{3}$ cup cold water, divided

1 pinch salt

In a small saucepan, whisk together the cornstarch and about half the water until the cornstarch is smooth. Stir in the remaining water and the salt. Bring the mixture to a boil over medium heat, whisking constantly. Reduce the heat until the mixture simmers gently and continue cooking, whisking occasionally, until it thickens slightly and becomes translucent, about 2 minutes. Let cool to room temperature before using; the glaze will thicken as it stands. Use immediately, brushing it lightly but evenly over the loaf top using a pastry brush (or dabbing it on with a paper towel). Or cover and refrigerate for up to 1 week. Let warm to room temperature, then, if necessary, thin with a little warm water before using.

transparent powdered sugar glaze

½ cup powdered sugar, sifted after measuring if lumpy

3 tablespoons kirsch, Calvados, peach schnapps, apricot brandy, or orange juice

1 tablespoon water

⅛ teaspoon almond extract, or ¼ teaspoon vanilla extract, or 4 to 5 drops *Fiori di Sicilia* (Flowers of Sicily) extract, or ¼ teaspoon finely grated lemon zest

This thin glaze is a nice, subtle finishing touch, adding a light sheen, seductive flavor, and hint of sweetness. It gradually disappears into the dough, infusing the interior with flavor and moistness. Taking a cue from pastry chefs, I sometimes top this glaze with the Powdered Sugar–Lemon Drizzle; the two go together very well. The basic recipe can be tailored to enhance different breads by changing the particular brandy or other type of spirits used. As a general rule, kirsch pairs particularly well with cherry and cranberry; Calvados with apple; and orange juice with citrus and spice breads.

Yield: Enough to lightly glaze1 large loaf

In a small saucepan, whisk together the sugar and spirits (or juice) until smooth. Stir in the water. Bring the mixture just to a full boil over medium heat. Remove from the heat. Stir in the extract (or zest). Immediately brush the glaze evenly over slightly warm bread or coffeecake using a pastry brush (or dab on with a damp paper towel).

powdered sugar–lemon drizzle

For a touch of sweetness and a quick, light icing that sets up and stays firm, use this recipe. The bit of lemon juice keeps it from being too sweet. The recipe makes enough for attractively drizzling back and forth, but can be doubled if you wish to completely cover the top and sides of a large coffeecake.

Yield: Enough to accent 1 large coffeecake, loaf, or recipe of buns or pastries

KS QUOTIENT — Super-Easy: Few ingredients. Easy preparation.

1 cup powdered sugar, sifted after measuring if lumpy, plus more if needed

1½ teaspoons fresh lemon juice

2 teaspoons water, plus more if needed

3 to 4 drops vanilla, almond, or lemon extract

In a small bowl, stir together the powdered sugar, lemon juice, water, and extract until blended and smooth. The glaze should be fluid enough to drizzle, so adjust the consistency by adding a little more powdered sugar or water if necessary. Immediately drizzle the glaze over the cooled loaf top. For a Bundt-style coffeecake or other tall loaf, let the icing drip attractively down the sides. The glaze will set up firm in about an hour.

glossy chocolate drizzle

KS QUOTIENT— Easy: Modest list of
ingredients. Easy preparation.

½ cup powdered sugar, plus more if
needed

1½ tablespoons good-quality
unsweetened cocoa powder

3 tablespoons hot water or fresh hot
coffee

1 tablespoon light corn syrup

1 ounce (about 3 ½ tablespoons)
finely chopped unsweetened
chocolate or ultra-bittersweet
chocolate

As its name suggests, this glaze has a beautiful sheen and looks wonderfully appetizing. Drizzle over any coffeecake or sweet bread that can benefit from a pleasantly chocolaty accent.

Yield: Enough to accent 1 large coffeecake

Sift the powdered sugar and cocoa powder into a small, heavy saucepan. Stir in the water and corn syrup and bring to a boil over medium heat, stirring constantly. Boil for 1 minute; immediately remove from the heat. Place the chocolate in a small, deep bowl and pour the cocoa mixture over it; don't stir. Let the mixture stand for 3 to 4 minutes, until the heat melts the chocolate. Stir until completely smooth, then let cool to warm; it will gradually thicken and develop a drizzling consistency as it stands.

If it stiffens too much, thoroughly stir in a little warm water. Drizzle the warm mixture decoratively over the coffeecake or bread. Then let stand until completely cooled. The glaze will set up glossy and will firm up in about an hour.

chocolate
ganache glaze

KS QUOTIENT— Easy: Easy preparation. Adds a gourmet touch.

Use this glaze when you want a big, bold chocolate presence, not just a decorative squiggle here and there. Be sure to choose a good-quality chocolate with a flavor and degree of sweetness you like, as it will predominate and no sugar is added. (Sugar sometimes makes the consistency gritty. To add a touch of sweetness, incorporate a little honey.) Don't use an ultra-bittersweet chocolate or one with a cacao percentage over 70 percent; these can be difficult to blend in and may stiffen too much when cool. Don't substitute chocolate morsels either, or the glaze may not stiffen enough or have a bold chocolate flavor.

Yield: Enough to fully glaze 1 large coffeecake

1 cup (6 ounces) coarsely chopped top-quality semisweet or bittersweet chocolate (not ultra-bittersweet or any chocolate with over 70 percent cacao)

¼ cup heavy (whipping) cream

2 teaspoons light corn syrup

⅛ teaspoon vanilla extract

1 tablespoon clover honey or other mild honey, optional

In a small, deep bowl, microwave the chocolate on 50 percent power for 1 minute. Stir well, then microwave for 1 minute longer on 50 percent power. Microwave the cream in another bowl or measuring cup on high power for about 1 minute, or until it comes to a boil and just begins to bubble up the sides. Immediately pour it over the chocolate, but do not stir. Let the mixture stand for 3 minutes so the chocolate can further melt from the heat.

Vigorously stir until the chocolate and cream blend together and are completely smooth. Stir in the corn syrup and vanilla until evenly incorporated. Set the glaze aside until cooled and thickened to spreading consistency, usually 15 to 20 minutes; if it thickens too much to spread easily, thin it with a teaspoon or two of warm water. Spread over the top and sides of a bread or coffeecake with a long-bladed spatula or spreader. The glaze will firm up as it stands.

caramel
sticky bun sauce

⅓ cup granulated sugar

⅓ cup packed light brown sugar

⅓ cup dark corn syrup

½ cup heavy (whipping) cream

⅛ teaspoon salt

½ teaspoon vanilla extract

Easy, but amazing, the combination of brown and granulated sugar, dark corn syrup, and heavy cream makes a very gooey, rich-tasting caramel sauce for sticky buns. And for convenience, it can be made well ahead and refrigerated until needed. **Yield: Enough for 12 large sticky buns**

In a heavy 2-quart saucepan or pot, thoroughly stir together the granulated and brown sugars, corn syrup, cream, and salt. Bring to a boil over medium-high heat, stirring constantly. Adjust the heat so the mixture boils briskly. Carefully wipe any sugar from the pan sides using a pastry brush dipped in warm water (or use a damp paper towel). Briskly boil, gently stirring and scraping the pan bottom, for 3 minutes. Immediately remove the pan from the heat. Gently stir in the vanilla just until evenly incorporated. Set aside until cool and slightly thickened before using. Or, cover and refrigerate for up to 1 week. Bring back to room temperature before using; thin with a teaspoon of warm water if very thick.

maple-butter
sticky bun sauce

KS QUOTIENT — Easy: Few
ingredients; simple preparation.

This is a pleasant change of pace from caramel-flavored sticky bun sauce, particularly for those who love the taste of maple syrup. Note that syrup labeled "medium amber" or "dark amber" will have a more intense maple taste than the "fancy" or lighter-colored and is a better choice in this recipe. **Yield: Enough for 12 large sticky buns**

⅓ cup granulated sugar

¼ cup light corn syrup

¼ cup (½ stick) unsalted butter, softened

⅛ teaspoon salt

⅔ cup pure maple syrup, preferably medium or dark amber

½ teaspoon vanilla extract

In a heavy 2-quart saucepan or pot, thoroughly stir together the sugar, corn syrup, butter, and salt, stirring and heating over low heat until the butter melts. Bring to a boil over medium-high heat, stirring constantly with a long-handled wooden spoon. Carefully wipe any sugar from the pan sides using a pastry brush dipped in warm water or a damp paper towel. Adjust the heat so the mixture boils briskly. Briskly boil, occasionally gently stirring and scraping the pan bottom, for 2 minutes. Gently stir in the maple syrup and boil for 1 minute longer. Immediately remove the pan from the heat. Gently stir in the vanilla just until evenly incorporated. Cool to warm before using. Set aside at room temperature for up to several hours; re-warm just slightly before using if the sauce stiffens during standing.

make-ahead
streusel

KS QUOTIENT — Easy: Modest list of ingredients. Easy preparation; may be made ahead.

1 cup packed light brown sugar

¾ cup unbleached all-purpose white flour

2 teaspoons ground cinnamon

¼ teaspoon salt

½ cup (1 stick) unsalted butter, melted

⅔ cup chopped walnuts or pecans

This is a simple, cinnamon-and-butter streusel mixture that can be stashed in the refrigerator and tossed together with a dough to create a great coffeecake almost instantly (see the Simple Streusel Coffeecake recipe, page 166).   **Yield: Enough for 1 large coffeecake**

In a medium bowl, thoroughly stir together the brown sugar, flour, cinnamon, and salt, breaking up any lumps of sugar as you work. Stir in the butter until evenly incorporated and the mixture forms small clumps. Stir in the nuts. Refrigerate until firmed up, about an hour. Just before using, break up any large clumps with fingertips or a pastry cutter. Use as directed in the coffeecake recipe. If not using immediately, refrigerate, airtight, for up to 3 weeks. Let warm up slightly before using.

kneadlessly simple
recipe makeover guide

HOW TO CONVERT TRADITIONAL
YEAST RECIPES TO THE KS METHOD

MANY PEOPLE HAVE ASKED ME IF IT'S POS-sible to take their old-fashioned convention-ally proofed and kneaded yeast recipes and turn them into *Kneadlessly Simple* breads. The answer is absolutely! Even first attempts usually yield breads that are quite good, and, if you take what you've learned from the first try and make the necessary adjustments, second efforts often produce bread comparable to or even better than the original. And with a lot less work!

Revamping does involve a little bread science, so it's best to read the section on the chemistry behind the *Kneadlessly Simple* method starting on page 3 before jumping in.

The *Kneadlessly Simple* method aims to accomplish two major goals:

- To eliminate the traditional risk and work of yeast proofing and kneading; and

- To streamline all the other traditional bread-making steps (without sacrificing quality) as much as possible.

To get a feel for how to proceed with a makeover, start by making a few recipes in the book. Choose at least one that's similar to the revamping candidate. For example, if your bread is an old-fashioned white loaf, prepare or at least carefully examine a simple white bread recipe in the book (see page 29). If your recipe is a butter-and-egg laden coffeecake, check out a coffeecake that's along the same lines (see page 166). While the list of basic ingredients in the two recipes will usually be similar, you'll likely see that the order of incorporation and method of handling are very different.

Using the *Kneadlessly Simple* version as a guide, jot down your recipe's ingredients in the revised order. Next, compare the amount of water and yeast in the two. As a rule, *Kneadlessly Simple* recipes will require less yeast because it has more time to become very active. But they need more water, or other liquid, partly so doughs can be stirred rather than kneaded, of course, but also because the moistness helps promote "micro-kneading." (See the "Yeast" and "Water" sections that follow for more on the "whys.") Always replace the warm water with ice water, and let the dough stand for a 12- to 18-hour slow first rise instead of the shorter rise originally called for. Use the same options as those given in *Kneadlessly Simple* for the second rise.

Normally, follow the lead of the appropriate *Kneadlessly Simple* recipe on the amount of yeast. Or, use this rule of thumb: Add a scant ¼ teaspoon of yeast per cup of flour in lean breads containing mostly white flour, little fat, and little sugar. Add a generous ¼ teaspoon of yeast per cup of flour in rich breads: very sweet breads; those containing lots of whole grains; and those containing cinnamon, cloves, nutmeg, cardamom, garlic, or onions (more on these ingredients under "Additions" later).

Trial and error is the best way to determine the amount of water needed for the makeover, though if there are no other liquid ingredients (including honey or molasses) in the recipe, a scant ½ cup water per 1 cup of flour is a good place to start. After mixing together the yeast and other dry ingredients following the selected *Kneadlessly Simple* recipe model, just stir in enough ice water to make a slightly stiff, but stirrable dough. Immediately note the amount required on your revised recipe. If you overdo it and the mixture looks more like pancake batter than bread dough, fix it simply by adding more flour until the mixture is just slightly stiff; the finished bread will still be perfectly good. (Too much water yields a doughy bread that will be prone to collapsing during baking.) Be sure to note how much extra flour was used. Then, next time around, either decrease the water or increase the flour, following your notes.

In taking stock of the *Kneadlessly Simple* recipes, you may wonder why some conveniently incorporate all the ingredients before the first rise, while others require a two-step approach, or why certain ingredients turn up more or less often here than in traditional recipes. Bread chemistry and food safety issues are usually the reason, as explained here:

Yeast—To shield the yeast from the shock of ice water, in *Kneadlessly Simple*, the dry granules are always stirred together with the flour before the water is added. Usually ¾ to 1 teaspoon of yeast is plenty for a recipe calling for 3 to 4 cups of flour. As already mentioned, for breads containing significant amounts of whole-grain flours, increase the amount of yeast slightly to compensate for the coarseness and weight of the whole-grain particles. Also, boost the yeast in doughs containing even ¼ teaspoon of cinnamon per cup, as cinnamon contains a chemical that inhibits yeast growth. Ground cloves, allspice, nutmeg, mustard, oregano, thyme, garlic, and onion also inhibit yeast growth, but to a lesser extent. For recipes calling for large amounts of these, to ensure vigorous yeast growth, it is best to use extra yeast and, if convenient, to hold off adding the retarding ingredients until just before the second rise, which will then proceed more slowly than normally.

Water—Revamped recipes need somewhat more water than conventional recipes during the first rise, because the slightly wetter dough facilitates more "micro-kneading." This is what I call the process in which key protein molecules bounce around during fermentation and hook up to form gluten. Revamped doughs should be moist enough that they can be mixed by vigorous stirring, but in most cases, they should seem slightly stiff, not batter-like; some soft, buttery rolls (see page 63) are an exception. During the second rise it is important to incorporate enough more flour to yield a stiff dough. While extra water facilitates plenty of the "micro-kneading" that develops gluten, during the second rise too much water "dilutes" the gluten and weakens the bread structure.

Sweeteners—For recipes with quite a bit of sugar (more than 1 tablespoon per 1 cup flour), don't add the full amount before the first rise.

Although doughs appear to be wetter after sugar is incorporated, the sugar actually draws up moisture and dehydrates the dough. This deprives the yeast organisms of vital water and retards their activity. If it's convenient, add up to 1 tablespoon sugar per cup of flour initially, then add the rest before the second rise. Note that honey and molasses don't rob the yeast of moisture, as they are already in liquid form. They can be conveniently combined with water and incorporated before the first rise, a procedure that's commonplace in this book.

Dairy Products—Highly perishable items such as eggs and milk, etc., shouldn't be added until just before the second rise, as they can't safely be left unrefrigerated for the long countertop first rise called for in *Kneadlessly Simple* recipes. So, it's usually necessary to replace the milk or buttermilk that would have been added initially in a conventional recipe with water and then compensate by adding the appropriate quantity of instant nonfat dry milk or buttermilk powder before the second rise. To adjust for the lower butterfat in nonfat dry milk, you can stir in 1 to 2 teaspoons of melted butter along with the nonfat dry milk. To ensure good flavor and smooth incorporation, be sure to use top-quality brands of *instant* dry milk and buttermilk powder.

Eggs are likewise perishable and must be added after the initial rise. They need to be beaten with a fork first. And because their water content will make the dough wetter than it should be for a second rise, some more flour will need to be incorporated to stiffen the dough.

Salt—For most recipes, salt should be added at the same time as the yeast and in the same quantities as in the original version.

Fats—Fats can't all be handled the same way or randomly substituted for one another in the *Kneadlessly Simple* method because they solidify at different temperatures. Corn oil and canola oil (often called for in *Kneadlessly Simple*) do not solidify at very cold temperatures, so they can be simply whisked together with ice water and incorporated during the first mixing. But olive oil and butter will both harden in ice water, so they must be either stirred in separately from the water or added before the second rise.

Additions—Besides the spices and herbs containing chemicals that retard yeast growth, dried fruits inhibit yeast growth by robbing the dough of water as they rehydrate. If it's convenient, add raisins and dried cherries before the first rise. But be sure they are fresh and plump and are rinsed or soaked, which partially rehydrates them, first. Note that dried fruits added during the second rise don't always have to be rinsed under water first, as they will absorb some of the excess water in the dough that is no longer needed for "micro-kneading."

It's fine to add seeds and bits of grain that need to soften at the initial mixing. Just remember that a dough that starts out fairly moist will be stiff by the time raisins, seeds, wheat berries, grits, and various other kernels of grains have absorbed the moisture they need. Flavorings including vanilla and other extracts and citrus zests may all be added during the first mixing, if desired.

Baking—A major consequence of creating wetter-than-normal doughs is that baking times will increase. Sometimes baking temperatures must be lowered slightly as well, so the outside doesn't burn before the inside is done. Because these doughs are already moist, it's harder to tell when *Kneadlessly Simple* doughs are baked through in the center. Inserting a skewer in the thickest part until it comes out with just slightly moist, but not gummy, particles attached is one way to check. Using an instant-read thermometer and baking until the center of the loaf reaches 207° to 210°F (be sure the tip doesn't touch the pan bottom) is an alternative and more foolproof approach. Since there is little danger of drying out these supersaturated doughs, if a thermometer isn't available, bake them for an extra 5 to 10 minutes after they seem done, which helps avoid the chance of under-baking. To prevent over-browning, simply cover the top with foil.

index